Max and the Americans

Max

and the Americans

KATHERINE LYON MIX

The Stephen Greene Press

BRATTLEBORO, VERMONT

This book has been produced in the United States of America: designed by R. L.
Dothard Associates, composed by American Book–Stratford Press, and printed and
bound by The Colonial Press.
It is published by the Stephen Greene Press, Brattleboro, Vermont 05301.

Mix, Katherine Lyon.

Max and the Americans.

Includes bibliographical references.
1. Beerbohm, Sir Max, 1872–1956—Friends and
associates. 2. Beerbohm, Florence Kahn, 1876–1951.
I. Title.
PR6003.E4Z75   824′.9′12 [B]   73–86033
ISBN 0–8289–0209–7

74 75 76 77 78 79 9 8 7 6 5 4 3 2 1

Contents

Prefatory Note

MAX BEERBOHM—most frequently known simply as "Max" because of the signature he attached to his cartoons—has been the subject of many articles and reviews, as well as six book-length studies and two bibliographical compilations. His letters to his friend Reginald Turner and a collection of his verse have been published. In 1972 he was the subject of a play on Broadway, and most recently a Catalogue of his caricatures has been issued. For a man in whose life, as he himself declared, little had happened, this might seem adequate recognition. However, the present writer, an American, felt that one portion of his biography had not been fully explored—his relations with the United States, its politics, its culture, and its people: especially its people, of whom his wife was one.

For help in the preparation of this work grateful acknowledgment is made to the kind persons in many libraries, to other workers in the vineyard, to the collectors of Maximiliana, and to the friends and kin of Max and Florence Beerbohm: specifically to the Library of Congress; Harvard College Library; Princeton University Library; Research Library of the University of California at Los Angeles, Honnold Library of the Claremont Colleges; Library of the University of Kansas; New York Public Library; the British Museum; at Oxford University the Bodleian Library, the Ashmolean Museum, and the Library of Merton College; Brotherton Library at Leeds University; British Theatre Museum and British Film Institute, where I have worked; and to the Human Research Center at the University of Texas, Yale University Library, William Andrews Clark Memorial Library, and Amherst College Library, which have lent me material. I have had personal conversations with Lord David Cecil, Sir Rupert Hart-Davis, Sir John Rothenstein, Alan Dent, Sir Edward Beddington-Behrens, Mrs.

Ellis Roberts, Professor Donald Wing, Robert H. Taylor, George Freedley, Johnson Briscoe, Professor John Espey, Robert Speaight, Mrs. G. L. Vogt, and Mrs. Scott Zeitlin. Assistance in other ways has been received from Miss Isabel Wilder, Mrs. Theophile Steiffel, Mrs. Mary E. Carpenter, Herbert S. Stone, William Devlin, Professor Arnold T. Schwab, Mr. and Mrs. Melville E. Stone, and Irving Drutman. Most important has been the help of Mrs. Constance Kahn Starr, a niece of Florence Kahn; Morris Kahn, Florence's brother, and Herbert Rossett, her cousin; Alexandra Bagshawe, Florence's niece, and her husband, George, and daughter Marion.

I am especially grateful to Mrs. Eva Reichmann for making the letters of Max to Florence available to me and for giving me her friendship over the years. I have found Dr. J. G. Riewald's *Sir Max Beerbohm, Man and Writer* of such help in collating the English and American editions that I feel I should thank him personally. Dr. Cora Downs was kind enough to read my manuscript, and Janet Greene has been a meticulous and inspiring editor. Financially I have appreciated grants from the Council of Learned Societies, the Kansas City Council of Higher Education, and Baker University.   K.L.M.

Drawings and Photographs

Introduction

SIR MAX BEERBOHM, English essayist, critic, and caricaturist, who died at Rapallo in 1956, was generally believed to take an unfavorable view of the United States. Such an assumption is easily credible when the characteristics of this country and the known likes and dislikes of Sir Max are compared.

First, there was the matter of size. America was a huge land of mountains, plains, and cities, traversed by long lines of railroads equipped with Pullman cars in which one could sleep at night. Max liked small, cosy hamlets which could be reached in a day's journey, comfortably wrapped in one's rug in a first-class compartment. The climate of America was as diverse as its scenery—very hot, very cold, always changing. Max liked moderation in temperature—not too hot, not too cold, monotonous but enjoyable. America was full of people, shoving, jostling, engulfing him. Max preferred to be alone, withdrawn; he did not appreciate close and continuous contact with the common man, and in America, the common man was much in evidence. Why not? The country was a democracy, and Max had neither much faith in that form of government nor in the breed that engendered it. Nor was he more inclined towards the new education that followed in the wake of democracy. Along with the general education went the big spectacular games and contests, very boring to the man who had come no closer to cricket than interviewing the famous C. B. Fry of Wadham College, Oxford, and who sometimes dipped a tentative paddle in the Cher, and who considered a stroll on Hampstead Heath robust exercise.

He was amazed and awed by the great energy and verve of the Americans; he himself frankly acknowledged a certain inertia and indolence, an unwillingness to push beyond his prescribed limits. As an individual, he was impatient of American mass production. For the dandy, whose clothes should possess "the perfect flower of outward elegance," whose morning coat should fit impeccably, whose top hat should be smooth and shining, the land of the celluloid collar and the ready-made had small appeal.

If not by birth, certainly by nature and upbringing, Max was an aristocrat. As such, he was scornful of royalty and labor alike—but in America, both were glorified. American women idolized titles and American businessmen cringed before labor. Max liked a stable, durable government, Tory in its outlook; every four years the States underwent a political upheaval—but despite this shift in power, the corruption and graft with which he thought American cities were riddled, went on just as before.

As a dramatic critic he had observed American plays and players on the London stage, noting divergencies from accepted British procedure, occasionally with approval, more often with horror. Painful, too, he found American materialism, with its corollary greed for wealth and possessions. Max asked only a sufficiency of this world's goods, enough to live pleasantly, to have books, music, good wine, sun and the sea—and such amenities should be savored slowly, at one's leisure. America's mania for speed was distasteful to the man who had never traveled by air, never owned an auto, and had ridden a bicycle with extreme reluctance.

Americans were practical folk, leaders in science, more avid for new inventions than for the promotion of culture, but when zeal for artistic betterment was felt, it often resulted in the relentless acquiring of treasures from the Old World. Max had no knowledge of science, nor did he desire any. Mechanical processes were beyond his comprehension, but Americans took to such things naturally. In the years after the Second War he blamed them for splitting the atom.

As he looked nostalgically back to the past when life had been more graceful and civilized, he realized that America had no comparable past to remember; it lived only in the present or the future. It was a land of continued change where one skyscraper was torn down to make room for another, just as hideous. Max, who liked the Georgian squares of Bayswater, hated what he considered the monstrosities of Chicago.

Yet in spite of these prejudices he was intrigued by the New World, its thinking and philosophy, its business and industry, and above all, its people. His first American friends were the transplanted artists and writers who had taken root in London; on his visit to the States in 1895 he added men of letters and of the theatre to this list, and over the years, as Americans visited England, the roster grew. Nearest and dearest to his heart was the red-haired actress from Memphis, Tennessee, whom he married in 1910.

Although Max wrote and drew in criticism of America, he was as trenchant in his examination of his own little island. Only, America was larger: it gave him more scope for irony, it stimulated his satiric impulse. As he said in the Nineties, "When I am laughing at anyone I am generally rather amusing, but when I am praising anyone I am always deadly dull." At any cost he would not be that.

He was sincere in his dislike of much he considered deplorable in the land across the Atlantic but his antipathy did not extend to all its citizens. He remembered the kindness and hospitality shown him on his visit to the States; he would always be grateful to the generous people who had made him welcome. In the 1930's he wrote to an admiring young American, "I can't stand America at any price, but Americans (of whom my Wife is one), are quite another matter; and (if Mr. Mix will allow me to say so to you) I love them."

Perhaps that is the thesis of this book.

Max and the Americans

I

Max Discovers America

IN MID-JANUARY of 1895, Max Beerbohm, aged twenty-two and an undergraduate at Merton College, Oxford, sailed from England on his first and only trip to America. He traveled as the secretary of his half-brother, Herbert Beerbohm Tree, the actor-manager, who was taking his London Haymarket Company on a tour of the States.

Although he had not yet completed the work for an Oxford degree, Max was already a budding man of letters and a coming caricaturist. In March 1893, over the signature "An American," he had published an article on Oscar Wilde in the *Anglo-American Times* which had given Oscar great pleasure. A few months later he had contributed an essay titled "The Incomparable Beauty of Modern Dress" to the *Spirit Lamp,* edited at Oxford by Lord Alfred Douglas. He had written, but not published, another piece on Wilde, "A Peep into the Past," as though looking back on him from a distant future, and hinting obliquely at his social aberrations. At the suggestion of his friend Aubrey Beardsley, art editor of the *Yellow Book,* Max's essay "A Defence of Cosmetics" had appeared in the first number of that controversial quarterly, and "A Letter to the Editor" in the second. His account in the *English Illustrated Magazine* of the renowned Oxford cricketer C. B. Fry had been praised by *The Times.* His caricatures were sometimes on display at Shrimpton's in Oxford and his witty drawings might be seen in the *Strand,* the *Pall Mall Budget* or *Pick-Me-Up.*

Max was twelve years younger than his brother Herbert. Both had the same father, but Max's mother was a sister of Herbert's mother, who had died in 1858. Julius Beerbohm, their father, was a corn merchant and sufficiently prosperous to support a family which included four children from his first marriage—Julius, Ernest, Herbert, and Constance—and Agnes, Dora, and Max from his second. Before going to Oxford, Max had attended Charterhouse. At Oxford he rather avoided dons and lectures, but he belonged to a dining club called the Myrmidons, owned a part interest in a canoe; and on weekends was often found at his brother's theatre. In London he was part of the group that gathered around John Lane at The Bodley Head, publisher of the *Yellow Book,* and attended evenings at the Cromwell Road residence of Henry Harland, its editor. He knew many young writers and artists just coming into prominence, among them Charles Conder, who painted beautiful fans, and Robert Ross, art critic and journalist, who was to prove his unselfish devotion to the dying Oscar Wilde. From a respectful distance he admired such esteemed men of letters as Edmund Gosse and Henry James, and he looked with some uncertainty on Frank Harris, the literary sensation of the decade who had just bought the *Saturday Review* and become its editor. In the social world Max was carrying on a mild flirtation with Mrs. Ada Leverson, a witty and amusing contributor to *Punch.* He often took tea with her and advised her about the decoration of her drawing room, where Oscar Wilde was frequently to be met. Just before Max left for America Mrs. Leverson had done an interview with him for the *Sketch.*

At Oxford his best friend was Reginald Turner, a fellow Myrmidon whose humor was a match for his own. He and Reggie carried on an enduring correspondence—brisk in the early years, lagging later—until Reggie's death in 1938. After Max's death, Rupert Hart-Davis edited a book of Max's letters to his friend, and Stanley Weintraub wrote a life of Turner. Another good friend of Max's was Will Rothenstein, a young artist trained in Paris, whom he first met in 1893 when Rothenstein came to Oxford to do a series of twenty-four drawings of Oxford celebrities in which he included Max as the only undergraduate. Will also belonged to the *Yellow Book* circle.

In the Nineties excursions to the States were becoming increasingly popular for writers and actors from the British Isles. Oscar Wilde had set such a precedent in 1882, when, after winning over many an audience prejudiced against him for his extremes in the Aesthetic Movement, he had made a generous profit from his transatlantic lecture tour. Max had said in his unpublished satire on Wilde, "The visit to America, that is still so fresh in the old gentleman's memory, doubtless influenced his style in no small degree." (Max's visit apparently had little effect on *his.*)

When Wilde heard that Beerbohm Tree was setting out on a tour rather similar to his own, he advised him to take two secretaries, one to answer correspondence, the other to send out locks of hair. A wag, overhearing, suggested for the latter post one of the seven Sutherland Sisters, a family noted for long, luxuriant tresses.

Tree's company had already sailed for the States when Herbert, Maud—his wife and leading lady—Lionel Brough, and Max embarked on the Cunard liner *Majestic.* When it docked in New York a fine voyage was reported, but Max did not concur. Herbert admitted they had preferred to

Shades of "Fry of Wadham": "Mr. Max Beerbohm," by himself, was exhibited at the Carfax Gallery in 1901, and accompanied an article in the February 1902 *Pall Mall Magazine* by Aymer Vallance titled "One Hundred Caricatures by Max Beerbohm."   © Eva Reichmann.

take most of their meals on deck, but Max had not preferred to take any anywhere. At quarantine the ship was met by a tug bearing reporters and members of the company who had already arrived. They found Tree on deck, while Brough, a seasoned traveler, pointed out the wonders of Brooklyn Bridge and the New York skyline, which Herbert pronounced "magnificent." Max wrote Robert Ross that he had told a reporter the Statue of Liberty was vulgar and must come down, but this remark does not seem to have found its way into print.

This Lady of the Lifted Torch made an unpleasant impression on Max. He mentioned her in several letters, saying in one to Ada Leverson, "In the harbour there is a colossal statue of Vulgarity which is illuminate at night— and is the constant pride of the city." This letter to "My dearest Mrs. Leverson," began

> I positively hate America. The voyage here was also loathsome. I had a wretched time. It is wonderful after the first few days how little one gets accustomed to the motion of these great liners. No more floating palaces for me! I am thankful to be ashore. I do not think I could have stood Lionel Brough's trifling with telescopes one day longer.

The Trees stayed at the Waldorf, New York's most luxurious hotel, which Max belittled in a letter to Reggie as

> . . . this hideous hotel where everything is worth a king's ransom. I sleep in an enormous double drawing-room which is furnished like a Pullman Car. There are lots of common coloured prints in very massive frames on the wall—no electric light or bell near the bed— nothing set to rights when one goes from one's room in the morning or when one has dressed at night. One returns and finds shirts and débris scattered all over the floor.

On their arrival the Trees were caught up in a round of lavish entertainments, and Max complained that Maud was always asking whether the So-and-so's were really people to whom she should present a letter of introduction. How many of these affairs Max attended is not certain; his name is found in some guest lists in the daily press, not in others. However, he did not join his brother and Maud on the Saturday night before their opening when they went to the theatre to see the farewell performance of Mrs. and Mrs. Kendall, another pair of English actors just concluding their visit in New York. Max had pressing business elsewhere.

Nearly two years before, at the Empire in London, he had first seen a young music-hall singer, Cissie Loftus, and had become her ardent admirer. She was the very young daughter of another singer, Marie Loftus, had been raised in a convent, and was, Max felt, far too young and innocent to be singing on a variety stage. He called her his "little saint," his "white girl," his "Mistress Mere," and all his quixotic impulses were roused by her situation. Night after night he went to the theatre to watch her imitations and listen to her songs, dreaming romantically that some day he might rescue her by marriage. He confided his passion to his friends Will Rothenstein and Reggie Turner, but not to the lady. By asking to interview her for a paper he had made her acquaintance, and she gave him her photograph, inscribed "Sincerely yours, Cissie Loftus." Then just as suddenly it was all over: disillusion set in: she was not the naïve little saint he had imagined, and he wanted only to forget it all.

Now she was performing in New York, no longer little Cissie but the bride of Justin McCarthy, the playwright, and Max took the first opportunity to test his cure. Between the acts he went backstage to see her and was relieved that no faint echo of his love returned to him. He could write Reggie quite dispassionately that "Cissie Loftus, poor little dear, is well liked here." Whatever Cissie's response to Max's visit may have been, she added an imitation of Herbert to her repertory.

On Monday night, 28 January, the Trees opened at the Abbey Theatre with two plays, *The Red Lamp* and *The Ballad-Monger,* which allowed the star to show his versatility in make-up and characterization. The house was full and applause generous. Afterwards a group of admirers came backstage, among them the rising American playwright Clyde Fitch, whose meeting with Max was the beginning of a real and lasting friendship.

During his three weeks' stay Herbert alternated his plays, using also *A Bunch of Violets, Merry Wives of Windsor, Hamlet,* and *Captain Swift.* The reviews were usually good, Maud being praised as well as her husband. The whole company was invited to a special matinée of Clyde Fitch's *The Masqueraders,* and Fitch took Max to see Edward Harrigan, the American comedian, soon to retire from the stage. More than half a century later Max told S. N. Behrman he would always remember Harrigan's walk, "at once comic and extraordinarily graceful." Mr. and Mrs. Reginald De Koven gave a musicale at which Melba sang and Max was enough impressed by his hostess to write to Ada Leverson asking if that name meant anything to her. Mrs. De Koven was a contributor to the American *Chap-Book,* a less pretentious but similar venture to the *Yellow Book.*

When Max first arrived he had written to Reggie Turner that he was going to write a slashing article on "N'York" for the *Yellow Book,* and in a letter to Mrs. Leverson he described the city as built on "piles of vulgarity."

> Only the shops are tolerable in my eyes— They have enormous windows—blazing with electric light and backgrounds of scarlet velvet and then, in the very middle of them, just one or two tiny little expensive things. The horses that draw the carriages are rather beautiful also. Nearly all the coachmen are negroes and are swathed in huge astrachan tippets.

He disliked "the abnormally hot houses and the unnaturally chilly streets"; the noise of the city gave him a headache; he shuddered at the thunder of the elevated trains and the clatter of horses' hoofs on the rough pavements.

His secretarial duties proved more arduous than he had expected, and his meticulous care in composing Herbert's letters finally caused his brother to engage more expert help, while still continuing to pay Max's salary. One example of Max's secretarial style which does not reveal any agonizing labor may be found in a letter to Herbert S. Stone, editor of the *Chap-Book,* who had apparently asked Herbert for an article:

> Dear Sir:
>
> Mr. Tree wishes me to say how sorry he is that he is acting over here too much to be able to write at present. Perhaps at some later date, he may be able to contribute.
>
> > Sincerely yours,
> >
> > Max Beerbohm

Max now had more time for his own interests. As a figure in the *avant garde* literary circles in London, he had not gone unnoticed in New York. Shortly after his arrival a well-known literary critic named James Gibbons Huneker had recorded in the *Musical Courier* the presence of this "clever young man of the Wilde-Beardsley type," who wrote "fantastically garbed prose." The January number of the *Yellow Book,* which contained Max's essay "1880," reached the newsstands while he was in New York and critics viewed it no more favorably than they had previous issues. The *New York Times* dubbed it a "yellow nuisance," calling Max's contribution "flat twaddle." The *Tribune* could not believe that this "jig-saw blue-light school will be suffered to continue," while the *Critic,* a weekly, wondered how long the public would stand the "vulgar indecencies of Mr. Beardsley's pencil or Mr. Beerbohm's pen."

The New World had its own publications to compete with the *Yellow Book,* among them the *Chap-Book,* recently moved from Boston to Chicago, *Moods* in Philadelphia, and *Vanity,* just brought into being by Eugene and Thomas Kelly in New York. How the Kellys made contact with Max or Max with them is not known, but he sold them two essays on "Dandies and Dandies," for twenty-five dollars each. The editors rushed this British celebrity into print, using part of an essay in their initial number of 7 February 1895 and frugally spreading the remainder over three later numbers. Max hastened to send copies back to London, suggesting to Mrs. Leverson that she share hers with his mother. The *New York Times,* welcoming the new publication, declared, "The Vanities it treats of are the harmless and frequently amusing occupations of the idle and elegant world." *Vanity* survived less than a year.

Max's initial hostility towards New York was beginning to weaken. He was given a card to the Players Club, where he could chat with men of the theatre. He was enjoying his friendship with Clyde Fitch and wrote Reggie Turner that the playwright admired him very much. In fact, New York was a beautiful town. When the English-Canadian novelist Gilbert Parker, who was in New York, said he loathed America and its institutions, Max reported to Ada Leverson that he had in his suave way stuck up for the Republic; and when a journalist told him that the country was corrupt to the core, he politely dissented. To Reggie he wrote, "I have had a charming time here—New York has given itself to me like a flower. Tomorrow I must throw away the petals, for we start to Chicago, which everyone says is quite a beastly place."

Herbert closed his engagement on 23 February with a grand finale which included one act from *Captain Swift,* one from *Merry Wives* and two from *Hamlet.* In his curtain speech he announced that he would return on 8 April for a week's engagement.

Max's first impression of Chicago confirmed what New Yorkers had told him. It was "one huge pillar of smoke by day and one huge pillar of electric light by night." Most of the company stayed at the Auditorium Hotel, a vast pile, which looked to Max as if it "had been built downward from Heaven by tasteless angels." He told Mrs. Leverson that connoisseurs pronounced it the ugliest building in America and he saw no reason to doubt their verdict.

Herbert added to his repertory here Ibsen's *An Enemy of the People,* about whose reception he was dubious because he knew Ibsen was not admired in the States. It was a sensational success. This play of corruption and reform seemed to have a local application in every word, Max said, and the audience loved it. On a previous night playgoers had been cold to the "inane vulgarities" of a *Bunch of Violets,* a critic in the Chicago *Tribune* saying it might as well have been called "A Dish of Prunes."

Max later admitted in a Boston interview that the corruption of Chicago had surprised him, "not in itself, you know, but because there was so much of it. Athens and Greece and those places required hundreds of years to get thoroughly corrupted, but Chicago had done it in twenty." He had an opportunity to witness the worst side of Chicago when he and Herbert and Lionel Brough were taken on a night tour of the city's low dives, an experience which sickened him.

In Chicago the Trees were entertained as lavishly as in New York, a frequent host being Joseph Leiter, whose sister had just become engaged to the future Lord Curzon. Until this announcement Londoners had believed Curzon was in love with Mrs. Pearl Craigie, who wrote under the pseudonym of John Oliver Hobbes and had been a fellow contributor with Max on the first number of the *Yellow Book*. Max caricatured Leiter when he came to London in 1898. At one Chicago dinner party Max sat next to a Shakespeare enthusiast who had a quotation from the Bard for every topic. "That couldn't happen in England," Max later told an interviewer from the *Bookbuyer:* "We think it enough honour to have bred Shakespeare. We don't need to read him."

Max was now seeing more of the girls in his brother's company—Una Cockerell, "very stupid and sweet," whom he liked but was not in love with; the sisters Hanbury; and Grace Conover, an Irish girl from New York. He hastened to assure Mrs. Leverson that though he had no lack of feminine society he could not possibly forget her, "the most charming and irresistibly delightful person on the face of the earth." The account which he wrote Reggie of Miss Conover—whom he had nicknamed "Kilseen"—was different: he was really very much in love with her, he had even suggested marriage; "but," he warned, "not a word of this to dear Mrs. Leverson."

Between social engagements—"I am being rather lionized"—and holding hands with Kilseen, he had managed to find time for his literary endeavors, finishing "Be It Cosiness" and posting it off to the *Pageant* in London. He found that many people had read him in the *Yellow Book,* and when he met the twenty-four-year-old editor of the *Chap-Book,* H. S. Stone, he promised to write for him an essay on arson: he thought Chicago fires were worth recording. Later, in "The Infamous Brigade," he wrote, "In Chicago extinction is not attempted. A fire is enjoyed; then the building is reproduced and burned down at leisure." Herbert and Max came in for added publicity when the Chicago *Tribune* reported the marriage of their elder brother Ernest to a Zulu woman in North Africa. The item referred rather pointedly to "another brother of Mr. Tree."

Another British subject making headlines in early March was Oscar Wilde, who was suing the Marquess of Queensberry (Alfred Douglas's father) for criminal libel. On Sunday, 3 March, Max wrote Ada Leverson,

I read this morning the sad news about O and A—O will not be able to remain in England I fear— I wish I were on the spot. What a lurid life Oscar does lead—so full of extraordinary incidents. What a chance for the memoir writers of the next century—the Thackerays and the Max Beerbohms of the future! I wonder if Bosey Douglas will post back from Morocco and be called as a witness. What a very bad witness he would make and what a clever witness Oscar would be. It is all very terrible.

Forgetting the plight of Oscar, Max told Mrs. Leverson he was "rather enamoured" of Chicago, adding, "altogether everything is very nice over here and I shall always have a love for America because the people are so very sympathetic . . ." Now he was about to meet other people as the company left for Philadelphia on Sunday, 10 March. On their arrival Herbert invited the cast to a champagne supper, only to be told that no wine could be served in the Quaker city on the Sabbath. Now it was Herbert's turn to denounce the land of the free and all its inhabitants, until someone suggested that the wine cellar might be "opened with a golden key." When that had been done, a festive meal was enjoyed.

In Philadelphia the company stayed at the Metropole Hotel, where the actor Nat Goodwin and his leading lady, Blanche Walsh, were also registered. Goodwin was opening in *A Gilded Fool* at the Broad Street the same night as Tree opened with *Captain Swift* at the Opera House. Herbert and Goodwin preserved an *entente cordiale* in public, whatever their private jealousies might have been, and several nights later Goodwin hurried his curtain to see Tree as Gringoire in *The Red Lamp,* a part he himself had played. The next week Goodwin gave a special matinée of Augustus Thomas's *In Missouri* for the visitors. Maud presented him with a bunch of roses, and in his speech of thanks Goodwin praised Tree for the hospitality he showed American actors in London.

At the close of the engagement, the Philadelphia *Public Ledger* declared that Mr. and Mrs. Tree had been "taken up, wined, and fêted," as though they were guests of the city. Nowhere on their tour were the reviews more flattering; the only disappointment was *An Enemy of the People,* which was considered over the heads of a majority of the audience.

Recalling his American trip in "From a Brother's Standpoint" in his memorial volume to Herbert, Max said that in Philadelphia he went to see *Trilby,* which Herbert thought he might like to buy. Actually, however, Paul Potter's dramatization of the George du Maurier novel was not playing in Philadelphia during the Trees' visit, although it was in Boston when the company opened there on 25 March. So apparently it was in Boston that

Max went to see the girl with the beautiful feet, and condemned the play as utter nonsense. (When Tree returned to New York, *Trilby* was there; he went to see it and at the end of the second act bought it for his Haymarket Company.)

Max thought Bostonians looked more like the English than Americans elsewhere, and he was pleased when he rated interviews with two leading newspapers, the Boston *Transcript* and the *Herald*. "A Chat with a Decadent" was the heading in the *Transcript,* but the title in the *Herald* was more agreeable: "A Young Man with a Style." After establishing Max's connection with Beerbohm Tree and his literary background, the *Herald* interview proceeded:

> Mr. Beerbohm is only twenty-two years of age. He is so young that, according to all literary tradition, he has no business to pretend to possess a style—that is to say, a prose style . . . But Mr. Beerbohm, though young, can write such prose as many a man would give his ears to catch the trick of—flowing and sedate.
>
> He is also a caricaturist and a decadent. . . . As a decadent, Mr. Beerbohm, though adhering to another method of art, is an amateur of the work of Mr. Aubrey Beardsley. "It is inevitable," says Mr. Beerbohm. "Is he not of my period?" For the decadents, say themselves, are exact and punctual contemporaries of the time, looking neither before nor after.

Questioned about Beardsley, his work and his health, Max said, "Beardsley is doing better work than he has done; he is discarding the Burne-Jones influence and the Japanese influence and is thinking more for himself." Asked how he liked America, Max replied:

> "I like it, I like your American language; it is so crisp, so different."

Where had he found it in the greatest perfection? And the answer—

> "In Chicago, by all means. Chicago is beautiful, it is so wicked and corrupt and vicious. I cannot understand how a city so young should be so vicious. It is splendid, Babylonish, wonderful."
>
> Mr. Beerbohm said that he had not read "If Christ Came to Chicago" and added, with as much of a twinkle as can decently consort with a London-made frock coat: "I did not care greatly for Chicago. It is a very dirty city."
>
> "And how did you like New York?"
>
> "The best of all."
>
> "And Boston?"
>
> "I have been at work; I haven't seen much of it. But it is too like

England. You would think you were in London. Why, the people talk English."

The reporter inquired about the *Yellow Book* and Max was optimistic about its future: it would continue, it was a success. The final question was "Are you writing anything here?"

"I met Kimball in Chicago—Stone & Kimball, you know—and I am writing something for the *Chap-Book*. It is going to be about arson, its value and beauty. I saw a splendid fire in Chicago, beautiful white and red flames, and pretty soon a lot of men with hats rushed in and threw water on the fire. It was an act of vandalism."

This interview appeared in the *Herald* for 30 March, a Saturday, and on the following day Max was taken to task in the same paper:

Bostonians speak English though Mr. Beerbohm possibly thought they spoke Choctaw. Another of this decadent's affectations was to decry the play of *Trilby,* and bemoan a taste that made the dramatization of du Maurier's story a success. Probably, if the unnatural twist of this amusing contributor to the *Yellow Book* had straightened out for a moment, the criticism he had made of Mr. Potter's work would have been less droll, though more truthful, more just. . . .

The reporter for the *Transcript* began with a description of Max—of medium stature, smooth-shaven, long black hair parted in the middle and sleeked back to the nape of the neck where it curled up a little, a mobile mouth, and musing eyes with a suggestion of a twinkle. As he talked he sat in a large lounging chair at the Vendome Hotel, legs crossed, arms folded on his knees, indolently puffing a cigarette and dreamily gazing out the window at a red brick wall. Asked his impression of Boston, he said, "You perceive that my opportunity for seeing much of Boston is limited," though he had seen a good deal when he got lost walking back from the theatre. He had liked New York, though it was so very cold. He repeated his surprise at the corruption of Chicago. He had also disliked the wind there; it blew from all directions. "You never knew when it would catch you. It had a way of swooping down upon you from unexpected quarters and in the most unforeseen manner. It was—well really, you know—it was embarrassing." He did not remember much about Philadelphia; it seemed a quiet place. Pressed for more details of his trip, Max had little to say, but he added:

I might give you my imaginary impressions; you remember there is quite a discussion nowadays about whether the most interesting things that a man can describe are those which he has seen or those which he has only imagined. I was going to write a little sketch called "The Dreamer," dealing with an idea connected with that subject, for the *Chap-Book*. It was to tell about a poet who lived in a great city and was a universal favorite with the people because of the many strange and wonderful things that he told them about. One day he passed through the city and wandered out into the country; and, as he went along, golden leopards now and then crossed his path, and the sun was bright and the air full of life and joy; and he came to the shore of a beautiful lake where were nymphs with breasts like silver moons who rose and moved about him. And he passed on thinking and thinking; and the day went by and the brown dusk of evening fell, and he turned back, and as he was returning, a sleek golden leopard came out of a dark wood and approached him and walked beside him and then disappeared. And again he saw the beautiful lake and the nymphs with breasts like silver moons. And he pushed on and came to the city at nightfall. And the people gathered about him and asked, "What have you seen? Tell us what you have seen in your walk." And he answered them, "I saw nothing. I saw nothing whatever."

So I might tell you a great deal that I could imagine, but I have seen nothing whatever.

On second thought Max decided not to write this for the *Chap-Book,* and presented it to the interviewer for what it was worth. A day or so later the *New York Times* reprinted this chat, but left out "The Dreamer."

In Boston the Trees were as usual hurried from one social event to another, their most memorable experience being a visit to Harvard College where Herbert was invited to address the Harvard Press Club. Sanders Theater was packed for the lecture and Maud was thrilled with young America, "so fresh, so eager, so warm in their welcome, so tumultuous in their delight." After his serious speech on the mission of the drama, Herbert initiated a reading which later became a great favorite, giving Hamlet's "To be or not to be" soliloquy in the manner of Falstaff, and Falstaff's speech on honor as Hamlet might have spoken it.

One can imagine Max on this visit to America's most famous university, his neat cataloguing of its salient features, his silent comparison of the Yard with the quadrangle at Merton, his interested appraisal of the students, and his busy mind storing up details and impressions for future use. Those well-stocked pigeonholes later did him good service.

On 1 April this note appeared in the Washington *Post:*

Mr. and Mrs. Beerbohm Tree, Mr. Max Beerbohm, maid and man, is the way the popular actor's party is registered at the Shoreham. They

Chauncey Depew's fame as an after-dinner speaker inspired this impression of the American lawyer-politician-friend of tycoons. Hitherto unpublished, it was drawn by Max presumably in 1895 during or shortly after his visit to the States, and exhibited in 1928 (Leicester Galleries). © Eva Reichmann.

arrived about four o'clock yesterday from Boston. Shortly afterward the party, minus maid and man, went out to dine with friends and did not return until a late hour.

So began a week which was to be divided between performances in Washington and Baltimore. Tree opened in Washington with *A Bunch of Violets* before a distinguished audience, with President and Mrs. Cleveland occupying a box, but the critic of the *Post* did not like the play, and the next night pronounced *Captain Swift* "a tiresome melodrama."

If the critics did not warm to the Trees, Washington society did, and they had more invitations than they could accept. At the luncheon given by Mrs. Leiter, mother of the fiancée of the Honourable George Curzon and of Joseph Leiter, who had entertained them in Chicago, Max must have looked with speculative gaze on daughter Mary who had won the future Viceroy of India away from the attractive Mrs. Craigie in London.

One evening after the theatre the Trees gave what the *Post* called "a small select spread" in their apartment at the Shoreham. Among the guests were Thomas Nelson Page, novelist and diplomat, Colonel John Hay, soon to be ambassador to England, and Rudyard Kipling, then living in Vermont with his American wife. In *Portrait of Max,* S. N. Behrman says that Max told him that he met Kipling in Baltimore when Herbert asked him to go into the audience and bring Kipling backstage. On learning of Max's identity, Kipling murmured, "You are Max Beerbohm? So young to have a style." But at the time of the "select spread" Herbert had not yet played in Baltimore, so it seems probable the meeting took place in Washington. If Kipling made the same flattering remark there, Max should have warmed to him, but no person would ever be more bitterly caricatured by Max than Kipling. On the other hand, he liked Thomas Nelson Page, was glad to see him some years later in London, and even considered writing about him, as his notebook shows.

In Washington, Herbert was approached by reporters saying that his name had been mentioned at the Oscar Wilde-Lord Queensberry libel trial; he was said to have received a letter bearing on the case; would he care to make a statement? Herbert declined, but he was fairly certain to what the story referred: during the London rehearsals of Wilde's *A Woman of No Importance,* he had been handed an incriminating letter said to be from Wilde to Lord Alfred Douglas; he had returned it to Wilde. Herbert was concerned enough by the question, however, to cable Richard Carson, Q.C., counsel for Queensberry, asking for information. The next day he was able to show reporters a cable from Justice Collins, the judge in the case, exonerating him of any connection save what was honorable and praiseworthy.

Wilde's case was now in its apogee, with his suit against Queensberry collapsing under damaging testimony; on 5 April Queensberry was acquitted and Wilde himself was arrested and charged with acts of gross indecency. Washington papers gave the story front-page coverage; Herbert and Max read the accounts with foreboding.

After four performances in Baltimore the company returned to New York and Herbert had an opportunity to discuss the situation with John Lane—publisher of Wilde's plays as well as the *Yellow Book*—who was newly arrived from London with Richard Le Gallienne, the poet. After being more than a week on board ship without newspapers, the Englishmen were anxious to learn the news—and the American press was not reassuring. Kipling, also in New York, was drawn into the discussion. Lane, convinced that Wilde and his profitable plays were lost, wondered if he could save the *Yellow Book* and Beardsley, its art editor, who had illustrated Wilde's *Salome*. The Bodley Head had figured in the trial, but Lane and the editors had carefully excluded Wilde from the daffodil covers of the *Yellow Book*. Surely that absence was fortunate. Lane and Max were particularly anxious to exonerate Beardsley, for they knew he had not been an intimate of Wilde's circle. Although Lane said later that Kipling supported Beardsley, could Kipling have said something at this time which initiated Max's prejudice?

Monday evening Herbert entertained with a party at the Waldorf. John Lane was present "in full bloom," said *Vanity,* talking hopefully of the *Yellow Book*. Chauncey Depew, politician and noted after-dinner speaker, sat on Herbert's right and Max must have noted his features carefully and later transferred them to his sketchbook, for the caricature he did of him is dated 1895. Max never drew from the life. As he once told Edmund Gosse, "no pen, no notebook, merely a mild attentive gaze."

In an interview given 12 April, Lane re-iterated his faith in Beardsley, pointing out that his sly caricatures of Wilde had done much to discredit the playwright, but a few days later he yielded to pressure from London and allowed Beardsley's dismissal.

On his return engagement in New York Herbert did not find the critics quite so friendly as they had been. He opened with *An Enemy of the People* and both he and Ibsen met harsh treatment, but his closing night was a triumph when he presented acts from *Captain Swift, The Red Lamp* and *Hamlet.* The company had a few days before sailing and most went to see Niagara Falls. Neither the Trees nor Max made this trip, however, for Herbert wanted to see *Trilby.* Years later Max apologized for avoiding the sight of this natural wonder by saying, "I was never fond of water." On 18 April 1895 the Trees and Max departed from the New World on the *Paris.*

During the return voyage Max must have had time to think over and adjust his impressions of this former British possession, to weigh his likes and his dislikes. He now had a firsthand knowledge of America: he appreciated its size; its cities were no longer merely names to him; he had seen its people, from the stockmen of Chicago to the well-dressed Manhattanites, from the politicians of Washington to the literate Bostonians. He remembered some with pleasure, others he hoped to forget. Although he tried to be modest, he was flattered by the attention he had received, but there had been criticism and disapproval, too. The lavish, open-handed hospitality, the wealth, the easy spending, and the importance placed on material possessions had impressed him. He had heard about the corruption and the sharp political practices of a democracy, and some of both he had seen. He was aware of the newness of the country in comparison with the Old World; beneath its glamour and excitement he had sensed a crudeness and uncertainty.

The weeks spent in this brother's company had given him a better understanding of the theatre, its problems, techniques and intrigues, and the insight would prove useful to him in his later career. Now it was a relief to be free from the hustle and bustle and noise; the lesser motion of the ship seemed endurable; the ministrations of his steward erased the impression of negligence left by hotel chambermaids. He anticipated being home again and introducing Kilseen Conover to his family. She had now become the most important part of his life; he was in love, not with Cissie Loftus, a white, slight figure on the stage, not with Ada Leverson, a pretty, witty woman who had a husband to be considered, but with a lively sweet young girl who loved him. Thinking of Kilseen he tried to forget the nagging problem of Oscar, who was now in prison awaiting trial.

II

Max and the Expatriates

MAX WAS BACK in London the last week of April 1895, and found the sad fate of Oscar could no longer be put aside. Max was worried about Reggie Turner; unfortunately he and Robert Ross had been with Oscar in the Cadogan Hotel at the time of his arrest. Immediately afterwards, like many of Wilde's friends, they had crossed the Channel to France. Max urged Reggie to return, to show himself on English soil, and put an end to the talk about him, but Reggie did not come. It may be taken as evidence of Max's non-involvement in the Wilde circle that he did not go into retirement, but every day attended Oscar's trial at the Old Bailey, demonstrating his sympathy for the accused, and his own detachment. On 1 May the jury disagreed, and a new trial was ordered. Oscar was released on bail and an awkward situation developed: where was he to stay? No hotel would take him; he could not go home. Then Ernest and Ada Leverson courageously invited him to stay with them. Max admired Ernest for this generosity, for he belonged to the solid business world naturally hostile to the Decadent Movement. It was different with Ada—she was an Advanced Woman. Max dined at the Leversons' one evening, finding Oscar at first silent and depressed but becoming his old talkative self as the wine went round. In the second trial, lasting from 20 to 25 May, Oscar was found guilty and sentenced to two years at hard labor.

Max had now given up the idea of taking his degree from Oxford. He settled into the top floor of the Beerbohm house in Hyde Park Gate, hoping to support himself by writing and drawing. He was still in love with Kilseen Conover and saw her frequently, taking an interest in her stage career, and inviting her to meals with the family.

In the States he had subscribed to the *Chap-Book,* and an item in the issue of 1 July caught his eye. The editor said he had read a month or so before "with lively interest in an Eastern newspaper that Mr. Beerbohm had said he was going to write an article for the Chap-Book on 'The Value of Arson.' " The editor had certain prejudices in favor of receiving such news at firsthand, but the article apparently was to be "spritely and amusing" and he should have liked to have it. "Will someone see Mr. Beerbohm, or write the article himself?"

Max took the hint and, deferring his defense of arson, wrote for the *Chap-Book* of 15 February 1896 his "De Natura Barbatulorum" with its quips at the sartorial oddities of Carlyle, Jerome K. Jerome, James McNeill Whistler, and Hall Caine. His Promethean observations came later, in the London *Daily Mail* for 5 December 1896 titled "An Infamous Brigade." He said in part:

> Americans, as yet inferior to us in the appreciation of most fair things, are more spirited than we are about fires. Many years ago, when all Chicago was afire, the Mayor, watching it from the Lake-side, exclaimed in a loud voice, "Who will say now that ours is not the finest city in all the world?" I remember, too, that some years ago, on the eve of my departure from Chicago, a certain citizen, who was entertaining me at supper, expressed his great regret that they had not been able to show me one of their fires. And indeed it must be splendid to see those twenty-three story buildings come crashing down in less time than was required to build them up.

Max added that he was going to form an Artists' Corps dedicated to hindering the efforts of firemen. When the essay was later included in *More,* a critic in the American *Bookbuyer* scored Max's utter unreasonableness in wishing to exterminate London firemen "because they go about extinguishing beautiful, artistic fires."

During 1896 Max contributed caricatures to five numbers of the *Chap-Book,* portraying Clyde Fitch, Andrew Lang, William Archer, George Bernard Shaw, and himself.

In August 1896 Max wrote Will Rothenstein that he had an idea for some kind of a skit: possible parodies of various writers on the subject of Christmas. As "Seasonable Tributes Levied by Max Beerbohm," the piece was to include Alice Meynell on "Holly," Arthur Symons on "Christmas Eve in Piccadilly," Henry James never actually mentioning Christmas, and so on. He proposed to do them for the 1896 Christmas Supplement of the *Saturday Review,* and he immediately began work on an expanded list, putting Henry James aside for further consideration. In September Herbert Stone of the *Chap-Book* wrote a friend, "We have some parodies by Max Beerbohm on George Meredith, Marie Corelli, [Ian] MacLaren, H. G. Wells, Le Gallienne et al. They are the best things we've had in years and I know you'll be amused." Thus the American mid-December *Chap-Book* and the English *Saturday Review* Christmas Supplement were both festooned with Max's first "Christmas Garland."

The authors parodied included Marie Corelli, with "The Sorrows of Millicent"; Richard Le Gallienne, with "The Blessedness of Apple-Pie Beds"; H. G. Wells, "The Defossilized Plum-Pudding"; Ian MacLaren, "Beside the Bonnie Mark"; Alice Meynell, "Holly"; George Meredith, "Victory of Aphasia Gibberish"; and the parodist himself with "A Vain Child." Beerbohm's parody of Beerbohm showed clearly his awareness of his own stylistic idiosyncrasies, even his delight in archaic or invented words, such as "two patulous Christmas trees," the "furial inrush of the tailor," and his "combed hair fungient in the breeze."

The *Chap-Book* did not prove such a dependable source of income as Max had hoped. On 26 October 1896 he wrote its London representative:

> I have not been receiving my usual "Chap-Book" just lately—not since my drawing of "Clyde Fitch" appeared— Would you send me any issues that have accrued since—I think there must be two that I have not seen. Also could I have a portion, at least, of the money owing me for the drawings as I am desperately hard up just now.

During these first few years several more importunate letters were written to Stone for payment of the "Christmas Garland" and other caricatures at fifteen dollars each.

Encouraged by the deference shown to Max on his trip to the States and by his appearance in the *Chap-Book,* in June 1896 John Lane optimistically sent 1,000 copies of *The Works of Max Beerbohm,* Max's first published volume, to Charles Scribner's Sons in New York. Within the month American readers were given an explanation of the title by Arthur Waugh's "London Letter" in the *Critic.* Max had been lunching with "a distinguished man of letters [Edmund Gosse]" and the conversation had turned on one of the current "booms" of the season—authors being asked what works had most influenced them. "When I am asked," said the man of letters jovially, "I shall reply that I owe most to the works of Max Beerbohm," whereupon Max so titled his slender red volume.

In keeping with the conceit, Lane appended a Bibliography, and a Life of the Author mentioning Max's recent visit to the States. He went, said John Lane, "with a view . . . to establish a monarchy in that land. Mr. Beerbohm does not appear to have succeeded in this project. . . ." Among the acknowledged sources of Lane's information was Miss Grace Conover. This appendix was omitted from the American edition, a small brown volume with gold and blue decorations.

In July 1896 the *Bookman* in New York listed *The Works* among books received, but gave it no further attention. In the *Critic* (18 July 1896) a reviewer commented on the "unblushing paradoxes of these essays, the calm matter-of-fact way in which they are defended," deciding that they belonged to "a type of humor better understood in this country than in Europe." But he had no doubt about the "cleverness of this little volume." A reviewer in the *Nation* differed: these essays could have been produced only by the life in London; "London essays they emphatically are . . . marked with a good deal of humor and cleverness, they are marred by a single fault—[the writer] has nothing to say." A more laudatory review in the *Bookbuyer* (July 1896) commented, "This young English author's work has become almost as suddenly famous as Stephen Crane's," though their productions were very dissimilar.

Apparently more Americans accepted the *Nation*'s verdict, for few copies of *The Works* were sold in America and legend has it that the remainder were destroyed to get rid of the incriminating evidence. However, a young artist named A. E. Gallatin bought a copy at Scribner's bookstore on Fifth Avenue, thus beginning one of the most famous Beerbohm collections in the United States.

For some months after his return from America, Max had nothing in the *Yellow Book,* but in April 1896 he returned with "Poor Romeo." Henry Harland, the editor, was an expatriated American who could listen with nods of approval to Max's strictures against American speech, weather, habits, and industrialism. Born in Norwich, Connecticut, Harland had begun his writing career as "Sydney Luska," then had abandoned this pseudonym and gone to England in 1893 to write in a new vein. His first book of short stories had won him critical approbation, and his editorship of the *Yellow Book* added to his renown. He and his wife Aline, also a writer, lived on Cromwell Road where they were at home on Thursday evenings to writers and artists. Max was usually the youngest person present, edging out Beardsley by only a few days, and justifying Ada Leverson's calling him "Baby Beerbohm," though his dandyism also won him the title of "Boy Brummell."

Not long before he left for America Max had lunched with the Harlands, a fellow guest with Elizabeth Robins, the actress, and Aubrey Beardsley. About the luncheon party he wrote to Mrs. Leverson, "We fed by the light of candles with nice thick green curtains between us and the day. Altogether —a rather pleasing meal." He was refusing an invitation from her because, "Harland wants my 1880 by then and my time will be full."

Max was often amused, as were others, by Harland's exuberance and volatility, though when he was most zestful Max and his friends tried to avoid him. He seemed less conspicuous in France and there Max often joined him and Aline in Ste. Marguerite or Dieppe. In 1897 Max wrote Robert Ross that he was leaving in a few days, "possibly for France, although the Harlands have been sighted there. I say this in order to humour your . . . delusion that everyone abuses the poor Harlands. Surely they are a fairly popular couple as couples go." From the Grand Hotel at Dieppe in 1899 Reggie Turner wrote Max that the Harlands were there and John Strange Winter had dubbed Aline "Penny-a-line Harland."

Max respected Harland as an editor, saying years afterwards that he was "an enlightened and fine one," but he sometimes objected to his arbitrary methods. "I must go on with the loathsome George [Lord George Hell] at present," he wrote Ada of his essay on George the Fourth; "Harland wired this morning, 'why no copy? Answer.' I think he might have said 'Please answer.' It would have been less rude, and I should not have felt compelled to send it at once, as I do now." He must have been pleased, however, when Harland wrote him about "the Happy Hypocrite" in the October 1896 issue, calling it "work of the highest and finest genius; far and away the best thing you have done."

John Lane, also delighted, brought out a separate edition of *The Happy Hypocrite* as Bodley Booklet Number One, printed by Will H. Bradley at the Wayside Press at Springfield, Massachusetts. This first edition (according to Gallatin's *Bibliography*) made little impression at the time, but was later printed and re-printed. The *Bookbuyer* (April 1897), said it was a "feathery little story, for tired men, well enough adapted to its purpose, albeit Mr. Beerbohm's manner is, at times, calculated in itself to tire strong men."

After the ending of the *Yellow Book* in 1897, the Harlands watched Max's career with proprietary interest and when in 1898 Max succeeded George Bernard Shaw as dramatic critic of the *Saturday Review,* they read him approvingly. Aline Harland wrote him about his review of an Anthony Hope play, saying it "cheered the hearts of the minority." They had read it to Henry James at his house in Rye and "we all agreed it was in your best Maxian . . ."

Max caricatured Harland several times; one drawing appeared in his *Caricatures of Twenty-five Gentlemen,* inspired portrayals of his contemporaries which Leonard Smithers published in 1896, but which did not come out in the States. Except for Harland no American was included.

One of Max's uncompleted efforts at this time was on himself as a best-dressed man. In the outline for this series one section was based on Max's trip overseas:

Mr. Beerbohm criticizes American dress—Are New Yorkers over-dressed? What Mr. Beerbohm thought about men's styles in Boston, Chicago, New York. Paper collars and other absurdities which he noticed at a fashionable function in Chicago . . . how he discovered a man of exquisite taste in Hoboken.

Max's first regular writing assignment began in January 1897 with Alfred Harmsworth's *Daily Mail,* for which he wrote a weekly article titled "A Commentary by Max Beerbohm"; the series ended in April of that year. Then he looked to other outlets and his essays could be read in *Tomorrow,* the *Sketch, London Life* and the *Saturday Review.*

In 1895 Frank Harris, who considered himself a naturalized American citizen, had bought the *Saturday Review* and by his editing made it one of the most significant literary weeklies of the decade. Probably born in Ireland, though on occasion he claimed Wales as his birthplace, Harris had gone to public school in England, migrated to the United States, worked as a cowpuncher in Texas, enrolled as a student at the University of Kansas, studied law, and returned to England in the 1880's. After editorial assignments on the London *Evening News* and the *Fortnightly Review,* he acquired the *Saturday Review* and drew to its masthead such distinguished men of letters as D. S. MacColl, John F. Runciman, and George Bernard Shaw. He was a stanch friend of Oscar Wilde and later wrote his biography.

Harris's rise to fame was phenomenal and he became one of the most influential entrepreneurs in the world of letters, but his reputation outside the literary field was not unblemished. His amorous adventures were often recounted at the Café Royal and his business dealings were not always trustworthy. In 1895 Max wrote to Robert Ross, "Frank Harris is going about as a howling cad, seeking whom he may blackmail." Nevertheless he was pleased when Harris accepted his reviews for the *Saturday.* However uncertain he might feel about Harris's ethics, he realized his probity as an editor. He told Reggie Turner that Harris's *Saturday* supplement was the "most *beautiful* and *distinguished* thing ever published." Max parodied him in the *Christmas Garland* under the title "Christmas and Shakespeare," for Harris had an absorbing interest in the Bard; but Max added a placating note—a most unusual procedure—saying Harris was very much a man of genius and he rated his writing about Shakespeare "higher than those of all the 'Professors.' "

If Harris's literary success was fantastic, his decline was nearly as sensational. He gave up the editorship of the *Saturday Review* and undertook a new venture, the *Candid Friend,* which did not prosper; by the turn of the century things were going badly for him. When he was in jail on a contempt of court charge, Max visited him in prison, commemorating the occasion by a cartoon of himself and Harris, seated convivially over a bottle of wine— "The Best Talker in London with one of his best listeners." Harris, who was then editing *Modern Society,* promised not to use the drawing for commercial purposes, but with characteristic treachery at once arranged to have it printed as an advertising poster for his magazine. Max was barely able to seize the plates in time to stop the publication.

At the beginning of the First World War Harris's pro-German sympathies caused him to leave France, where he was then living, and seek asylum in the States. His editorial career in New York was as unfortunate as it had been fortunate in London. At the helm of *Pearson's Magazine* he boasted he had turned it from loss to profit in six months; however, its quality sank in the process. His series of four *Contemporary Portraits,* rather unreliable accounts of eminent people he had known, or pretended to have known, was published first in America. When Max read about himself as Harris saw him, he was deeply pained. Harris died in France in 1931. Max would have thought it ironic that a man who was at one time an admired author, an enlightened editor, and a friend to aspiring writers, should be remembered only by *My Life and Loves.*

But Harris's downfall was still in the future when the *Saturday Review* of 20 November 1897 printed Max's "Papillon Rangé," a criticism of a new edition of *The Gentle Art of Making Enemies* by James McNeill Whistler. This American artist had come to London via St. Petersburg and Paris in 1863 and achieved success as a painter and a wit.

Although Max was never a friend of Whistler's as he was of other American artists like Sargent and Pennell, he acknowledged his artistic genius and deplored his liking for litigation. He told Will Rothenstein, "Whistler once made London a half-way house between New York and Paris and wrote rude things in the visitors' book."

While Max was in New York, Whistler was much in the press: Sir William Eden was currently bringing suit against Whistler for painting out the face of Sir William's wife from a commissioned portrait as protest at the meagre fee he was given by Eden, which, however, he had not returned. At the time Max viewed the case with impartial and wicked delight, but he later sympathized with Whistler because Eden was a rich man and could afford to pay.

In 1892 Max had bought Whistler's earlier edition of *The Gentle Art* and admitted that he often read it. His first reference to Whistler in print appeared in his piece on Oscar Wilde in the *Anglo-American Times* (March 1893): "We have steeled our nerves against Mr. Whistler's shrill fury at the notion of his friend, 'the amiable, irresponsible, esurient Oscar,' having pilfered from the famous '10 o'clock lecture' . . ." Max appreciated the dandy in Whistler: in "De Natura Barbatulorum," appearing in the *Chap-Book* in February 1896, he had called Whistler's silk hat a "real nocturne, his linen a symphony *en blanc majeur.*"

The second edition of *The Gentle Art of Making Enemies* was issued by

Heinemann in 1897 and contained an introduction by Joseph Pennell, who implied it had been necessary to persuade the author to consent to this new edition. In "Papillon Rangé" for the *Saturday,* Max seriously considered Whistler's idiosyncrasies, noting with great Pennell's tendency to dignify Whistler and Whistler's evident delight in being thus dignified. Whistler was certainly recognized in the field of painting, but how was it, asked Max, that "he, a great artist, could steal from the practice of his art, time and energy enough to be a wit, a fop, a flâneur, a collector, a litigant, a show-man, a creature of innumerable channels?" Because, answered Max, he "has never tried conclusions with life, has never"—and here Max yielded to his pleasure in archaic words—"has never tewed with those realistic problems" faced by others. He had not essayed actuality except in his early work. He had had plenty of time for "dalliance with Mammon." His pen had let loose "a fount of witty and angry letters to the weekly papers," though generally he was in the wrong. "Stranger to all pity," charged Max, "he has sent his barbed and envenomed shaftlets deep into the most in-offensive hearts. He was a gay, but terrible, antagonist."

From Paris Whistler hastened to reply in a letter to the editor of the *Saturday Review:*

> Your new gentleman—a simple youth of German extraction—"be-lockter Jüngling"—I take it, from his light hearted conviction that he is "in among 'em" and his free use of Limburger French . . . tewed is strange to me—Yiddish I dare say—don't let him translate it. I trust I may never know what it means . . . I congratulate you, Sir, upon your latest acquisition in all his freshness, and I would say to him, as Marshal MacMahon said to the Negro, "Continuez."

On 30 November Max confided to Reggie Turner, "I think I score off Whistler next Saturday," so a Note in the *Saturday Review* of 4 December was probably from Max:

> In our last week's issue there appeared a letter from Monsieur J. Mc-Neill Whistler criticising our contributor Mr. Max Beerbohm. The letter was in M. Whistler's best butterfly style . . . we will not imitate M. Whistler's manner; the airiness of the youthful, irresponsible beau is antiquated now; the white plume that used to stand out so bravely against the dark locks is now indistinguishable, the boyish imper-tinences of a maiden aunt; but . . . we are . . . curious to know why M. Whistler should parry thrusts that do not, he avers, go near his skin.

Later Max wrote to Will Rothenstein, "I see that Whistler has done a 'cover design' for Whibley's book—I always knew he would come to a bad and humble end." Charles Whibley was Whistler's brother-in-law. The youthful Max was reluctant to credit Whistler with talent in either colors or words, though he was impressed with Whistler's comment on Wilde's *Salome* that "Oscar has scored another brilliant—exposure." And once, after seeing some chalk sketches Whistler had done of a nude woman, he told Will Rothenstein that perhaps he was right to idolize Whistler, that perhaps he really was a genius.

Max admitted that Whistler was much loved by many people, but he "was not in the ordinary sense of the word, 'lovable.' As a rule he inspired fear rather than love." Walter Sickert, another artist friend of Max's, had been a disciple of Whistler's until the *"Saturday Review* case" when Whistler disowned him. The suit developed after Sickert had written an article criticizing Joseph Pennell's method of making his lithographs, implying it was dishonest to use paper to transfer the design to the stone instead of working directly on the slab. Pennell demanded an apology, Sickert refused, Frank Harris, the editor, upheld him, and Pennell sued them both for libel. Whistler, who sometimes used lithograph paper himself, took Sickert's charge as a personal affront and was drawn into the case. Hot words were exchanged on the witness stand, and another friendship was ended. Max did a caricature of Whistler testifying at the trial. Whistler often went to Dieppe in the summer; so, too, did other artists. In August 1899 Max wrote Reggie Turner, "Sickert is still at Dieppe and has seen Whistler, but not to speak to."

As Max grew older he became more charitable, and a year after Whistler's death in 1903 he wrote in the *Pall Mall Magazine* an article titled "Whistler's Writing," calling him a born writer: "He wrote, in his way, perfectly . . . When I dub Whistler an immortal writer, I do but mean that so long as there are a few people interested in the subtler ramifications of English prose as an art-form, so long will there be a few constantly recurring readers of *The Gentle Art.*" Even now, however, he could not forgive Whistler's controversial writing: "An urchin scribbling insults upon somebody's front door would not go further than Whistler often went. Whistler's mode of controversy reminds me, in another sense," said Max, "of the writing on the wall. They who were so foolish as to oppose him really did have their souls required of them."

About the same time, writing of W. S. Gilbert's prose in the *Saturday Review* (14 May 1904) he said, "It is possible to use the medium of prose wittily; though few people are aware of the possibility, and fewer still have the gift." Whistler had it; he could play pranks with words. (So, too, could Max.) Again, he said that Whistler's writing "achieved perfection through pains which must have been infinite for that we see at first sight no trace of them at all." Of his own credo Max said: "To seem to write with ease and delight is one of the duties which a writer owes to his readers, to his art, and to contrive that effect involves very great skill and care." One notes the similarity. Undoubtedly J. G. Riewald was right when he said that Max's style shows the influence of Whistler. Others also have recognized this debt less pleasantly by speaking of the Whistlerian affectations of Max Beerbohm.

In "No. 2 The Pines," Max remembered the clash between Whistler and Algernon Swinburne when the poet wrote a criticism of Whistler's *Ten o'Clock Lecture,* and Whistler replied with a letter to the *World,* naming "one Algernon Swinburne—outsider—Putney." Theodore Watts-Dunton, Swinburne's companion, could not forgive him for that. Long after, when Watts hyphenated his name to Watts-Dunton, Whistler sent him a card, "Theodore! What's Dunton?" but the sally was not answered. Max wished that Watts-Dunton had responded; he saw Whistler's message as "a signal waved jauntily, but in truth wistfully, across the gulf of years and estrangement."

Max could not accept one thesis of Whistler's, that only artists were capable of criticizing other artists' work. In "Enoch Soames" he said: ". . . This law (graven on the tablets brought down by Whistler from the summit of Fujiyama) imposed certain limitations. If other arts than painting were not utterly unintelligible to all but the men who practiced them, the law tottered—the Monroe Doctrine, as it were, did not hold good."

In "Hethway Speaking," a section of Max's projected *Mirror of the Past* which he never completed, he imagines Carlyle's story of Whistler painting his portrait. Whistler was "a wee young man with a mop of black ringlets and a quizzing glass—a sort of pocket D'Israeli by the look of him, but American in his talk, of which there was much." When he went to Whistler's studio he saw the portrait of Whistler's mother: "There she sat—side-face, a sad figure, all in black . . . against pale grey wall of parlour." When his own portrait was completed, Whistler showed him the result, and—"there I sat, side-face, all in black . . . against pale grey wall of parlour." Whistler awaited his comment. " 'Well, young man,' I said at last, 'ye're verra filial, verra filial indeed.' "

Max found Whistler a tempting subject for caricature and used him many times. When he caricatured Joseph Pennell, he put the cartoon of Whistler by "Spy" (Leslie Ward) on the wall behind him, and seated Pennell in the pose of Whistler's mother "thinking of the old 'un." Pennell was one of the few who managed to keep his friendship with Whistler, and became his biographer.

Joseph Pennell and his wife, Elizabeth, were Philadelphia Quakers who had come to England in the Eighties on an assignment from the *Century Magazine* and had never gone home. Joseph, an artist, was best known for his etchings, and Elizabeth for her writing; together they did travel sketches and illustrated articles. Mrs. Pennell had "evenings" at their Buckingham Street flat, attended by William Ernest Henley and his young men from the *National Observer* (the "Henley Regatta," Max called them), and the Harlands and their *Yellow Book* group. The Pennells had lent their support to that quarterly in its preliminary stages, though Mrs. Pennell did not contribute to it and her husband did so only in the first number. Both Beardsley, to whom Pennell had been helpful, and Max, whom Mrs. Pennell admired, went frequently to the Buckingham Street gatherings, and Max often saw the Quaker emigrés on his summer expeditions to France. But in a blustery review of *A Masque* at the Guildhall in the *Saturday* of 1 July 1899 he said, "I have not the pleasure of considering myself a great admirer of Mr. Joseph Pennell's prose style, nor of his method of criticism, nor of his manners." Max did not approve of Pennell's illustrations for Henry James's *Italian Hours,* calling them "very dismal and feeble pastels."

With another American artist very much at home in London, John Singer Sargent, Max had a more enduring relationship. Sargent had come to London from Paris in 1885 with his Bostonian mother and sister Emily. He had known Whistler and Henry James in Paris; indeed, Whistler had been one of the first to draw attention to Sargent's work, though characteristically he later criticized it. The two men were very different, Sargent being as kind and benevolent as Whistler was biting and quarrelsome. Max liked Sargent, who was a friend of his brother Herbert and a helpful adviser to Will Rothenstein. He was a member of the Royal Academy and the Chelsea Art Club, a dichotomy not managed by many artists.

By the mid-Nineties Sargent had become the most successful portrait painter in London; he excelled, said Max, in "depicting the restlessness of great ladies on priceless sofas." Max was amused at this popularity and used it in several caricatures. In one, "31, Tite Street," a queue of fashionable ladies is waiting outside Sargent's Chelsea residence (which had once belonged to Whistler), with messenger boys holding places for latecomers, while Sargent peers happily from a window. Max pretended to believe that Sargent's fame had been assured when King Edward in 1901 described him in royally winged words as the "great painter, Sargent."

Sargent was a social being, and, like Henry James, a great diner-out. Both portrayed the same world—James in his novels, Sargent in his paintings. Both belonged to the charmed circle of Mrs. Charles Hunter of Hill

"Mr. Sargent at Work"—described by Max on the opposite page—was exhibited at the Carfax Gallery in 1907 and included in *A Book of Caricatures* that same year. © Eva Reichmann; Patrick Baldwin Collection.

Hall near Epping, a circle Max was beginning to penetrate. Her house was said to be filled with Sargent's paintings and Henry James's books. Sargent's sketch of Henry James was reproduced in the first number of the *Yellow Book,* but Sargent, unlike James, refused to appear in a second number. A musician as well as a painter, he had many friends in the musical world and was said to improvise on the piano while giving his subjects a rest. His invitations to Max for an evening at his Tite Street house often contained the warning, "if a stiff dose of French music does not frighten you." Max often used this musical theme in the caricatures he did of Sargent. About one of these he wrote in a letter, "I have just done a rather good 'Mr. Sargent at Work'—more or less suggested by a musical party he gave some nights ago. Two fiddlers and a 'cellist in the foreground, and a duchess on a platform in the background, and he in between, dashing at a canvas, with a big and swilling brush in either hand." In his *Catalogue* of Max's caricatures, Rupert Hart-Davis lists seventeen of Sargent.

Sometimes Max wondered if he were not being too unkind in his treatment of the artist, but he wrote Frank Harris of the *Saturday Review,* "As for Sargent, he has suffered so much and so uncomplainingly at my hands that I don't think an outrage more or less can now affect him." Perhaps the subject was not so unmoved as Max thought, for when Max sent him a caricature he had done of him, Sargent said he hastened to thank him before it arrived and his disposition was "spoilt forever."

The fees Sargent received for his portraits interested Max, whose cartoons sold for considerably lower prices. He once calculated that Sargent got as much for a single portrait as he did for a collection. Perhaps it was envy that prompted Max to say, after viewing an exhibit of Sargent's landscapes at the Suffolk, "I would pay a good many hundreds of pounds if I had them, not to possess a landscape by Sargent." He did not like the lunettes Sargent did for the Boston Public Library. "Jehovah consists of two arms, two feet, the head and face hidden by a cowl," he complained, "under which there seems to be no face or body—but only an immense void." He realized it was hard in a non-anthropomorphic age not to be ridiculous in portraying Jehovah; a non-imaginative painter had to shirk this difficulty, but the effect of such shirking was unimpressive.

In 1913 Max was to have an idea for a caricature of Sargent which he did not carry out. At the time of Henry James's seventieth birthday, a committee working to arrange a suitable demonstration of esteem approached Max for a contribution to pay for a portrait of The Master to be painted by Sargent. Max was shocked to find Sargent's name on the committee; he was sure Sargent, such a proper and sensitive man, did not know his name was to appear. Then, on second thought, Max wondered why Sargent, such a devoted friend of James's, might not have offered the portrait as his gift. It occurred to him that he could do a wonderful cartoon of James arriving at Sargent's studio for his sitting and the ensuing conversation, but since the letter of solicitation had been marked "Private and Confidential," he knew this inspiration could not be realized.

Max considered Sargent's later work to be inferior, that he had become the portrayer of appearance rather than of character. He took the Henry James portrait as proof of his opinion. In his Introduction to *The Portrait Drawings of William Rothenstein* (1926) he developed this idea. Although he called Sargent the "great master," "an intellectual," and "fastidious," in all ways, he had too frequently painted inferior subjects. He had suffered too much from many commissions to paint vapidity or vulgarity, with the result that he had come to dislike portrait painting; when he was confronted by a real challenge he could not rise to it. No portrait, Max said, "could be superficially more like Henry James . . . but it will rather puzzle the students of that writer's work in future ages." John Felstiner said in *The Lies of Art* that Max called the portrait "a dead failure."

In 1911 Max made somewhat the same charge in *Zuleika Dobson* when he spoke of the "slickness" of Sargent's portrait of the Duke: "Yes, all the splendid surface of everything is there——" but not the soul.

Although Whistler, Sargent, the Pennells, and the Harlands were the Americans who interested Max most at the time of his return to London, they did not exhaust the roster of his American acquaintances. His friendship with Logan Pearsall Smith, the Philadelphia Quaker who had been at Oxford with him, was long lasting. He knew and respected the work of Harold Frederic, a journalist from Utica, New York, and a fellow contributor to the *Yellow Book*. He thought Frederic a self-assertive American, patriotically and flamboyantly ready to point out all the faults of the British, but a born story-teller. Max did not know, except by reputation, Frederic's great friend, Stephen Crane. In 1897 Max wrote Reggie Turner that he was staying with the Harmsworths in Kent, and "Stephen Crane was asked, but couldn't go." Too bad, for he and Crane could have talked of their mutual admiration for Ouida.

And then there was Henry James.

III

The Importance of Being Henry James

PRE-EMINENT AMONG American expatriates in Max's opinion was the Boston-reared Henry James, who had made his home in London since 1877, living in De Vere Gardens in the Nineties until, in 1897, he acquired Lamb House at Rye, where he spent his summers. When Max was in New York in January 1895 the *New York Times* had reported the failure of James's play *Guy Domville* at the St. James's Theatre in London, and during Max's stay in Boston a woman had written in the *Evening Transcript* of her sensation of "absolute writhing misery" when James had been led before the curtain to be met by a fusillade of booing from the gallery. Max was shocked at such treatment, but not entirely surprised at this outcome of James's desire for a success in the theatre. On his return to London he saw James occasionally at the Gosses' or the Harlands', where James had a habit of dropping in "just for the space of a moment or two, for I am mortally unwell tonight." James had been a fellow contributor with Max to the first number of the *Yellow Book,* indeed his name was the most prestigious attached to that provocative venture, though he acknowledged apologetically that he had written the piece for money and to please the devoted Harland. Max was well aware of the difference between the established reputation of Henry James and his own controversial commencing. He looked at James with awe and admiration, but a little amusement, too, and kept a respectful distance, being content to study *le Maître* from afar. He was fascinated by James as an individual as well as a writer, trying to analyze his character, probing beneath the surface for the hidden motives of his behavior, observing his relations with other people, balancing his incongruities, and assaying the gold and the dross in his nature.

Max's first public testimonial to James the writer seems to have been made casually in the *Academy* of 8 December 1900. Various notables had been asked to name the two books they had most enjoyed reading during the past year, and Max chose such dissimilar publications as James's *The*

Soft Side and *An Englishwoman's Love Letters,* then published anony-
mously but later admitted by Laurence Housman. Max was the only person to mention Henry James.

As Max's position in literary and social London became more assured,
he had more opportunities to meet The Master, though he still preserved
his reverent remoteness when James was holding forth in his slow pontifical
measures. James talked much as he wrote, and Max listened and made
mental notes of the unsmiling countenance, the literary phrases, and the
impressive hesitations. He knew James bearded and unbearded: he was
clean-shaven after 1900. With a beard in 1895 he looked to Max like a
grand duke, and later, without it, like a priest. He was usually beardless
in Max's caricatures. Max noted the magnificent head, fine eyes, and strong
voice which could dominate any conversation. James was always a little
withdrawn from the world, Max felt, yet appalled by what he saw of it.
Max was sometimes surprised by the rather malicious way James spoke of
some of his friends.

James became more aware of Max as he read his articles in the *Saturday*
and frequently found his own name mentioned, for Max often compared
James's method or style with that of the man he was considering. On 10
May 1902, Max wrote, "The most salient instance of a writer who could
not be called a 'great' writer, and could not be called a 'mediocre' writer,
is Mr. Henry James, that perfect master of a small method, and accord-
ingly, that perfect type of the modern artist in literature," and decided that
James and G. S. Street, Max's present subject, had much in common. In
their outlook on life both had the "same fastidious coyness, the same unwillingness to stray beyond a certain highly civilized radius." Both were
students, "standing aside to observe life" almost like watching animals at a
zoo. But he saw differences: James was a cosmopolitan, Street an Englishman; and Street became genial in a way James never did.

In comparing James with George Bernard Shaw, Max found them utterly unlike, but he pointed out the similarity of Louis Dubedat in Shaw's
The Doctor's Dilemma to James's Roderick Hudson, suggesting that
Shaw had made use of one of James's earlier themes, that of a youth
endowed with artistic genius but no moral sense. However, the Shavian
and Jacobean (the latter adjective was Max's) methods were different:
unlike Shaw, James portrayed men and women as he saw them, never
pronouncing judgment. He had a sharp moral sense and he loved honor,
but he never let his moral prejudices affect his treatment of his characters.
"The hand of the artist" was held tightly over "the mouth of the preacher."
In Shaw, the preacher always prevailed.

Max's careful study of James the stylist was demonstrated in his parody

"The Mote in the Middle Distance," first published in the *Saturday Review* 8 December 1906 and later included in *A Christmas Garland* (1912). When the book appeared, Max was naturally apprehensive about its reception by the authors he had parodied, especially Henry James. At Christmas of that year, however, Gosse could re-assure him. James had taken dinner with the Gosses, and had brought up the subject; he wanted Max to know that he had read the book with wonder and delight. It was the "most intelligent that had been produced in England for many a day." But he feared that Max had destroyed the trade of writing, for no one could now hope to write without incurring the charge of imitating Max. "What could be more true?" agreed Gosse.

Max hastened to answer Gosse's letter, thanking him for his thoughtfulness in writing him so promptly to send him the good news "that Henry James had not been displeased and was pleased so positively." But that James was not always so entirely pleased with Max is reported in Sir Sydney Waterlow's diary; he said James told him he deplored the cruelty in some of Max's attacks. He found "something unpleasant about a talent which turned altogether to expressing the weaknesses of others. It was indelicate"; and James hated indelicacy. Max once said his favorite line from Henry James was, "Be generous and delicate and pursue the prize."

Max made frequent mention of James and his writing in his letters. In September 1905 he wrote to an American about *The Portrait of a Lady* (1881), calling it "this dear and perfect masterpiece—a classic, yet so fresh that it seems less as though it had been written yesterday than if it were going to be written tomorrow by some one who had at last got the key to perfection in the writing of modern novels." Above all, he found it a "loveable book." And again, "I suppose you have read Henry James's book on America [*The American Scene*]. I haven't yet (only some magazine installments); but I look forward to the treat, loving his mind."

However, he did not always agree with the critical opinions which came from that mind. Max greatly admired the Barchester novels of Anthony Trollope and he could not understand the rather grudging appreciation James gave the Victorian novelist in *Partial Portraits*. In a letter to H. A. L. Fisher, Warden of New College, Oxford, Max said:

> I marvelled that H. J. whose critical sense was so keen and whose power of detaching himself from his own prejudices whenever he set out to estimate the work of good writers, was so salient and admirable, could have allowed himself to indulge in nonsense about "the dull, impersonal rumble of the mill wheel [a phrase James had used to describe Trollope's later novels]—"

James had also spoken of the "lumbering movement" characteristic of Trollope's style and confessed he found his political novels dismally dull and had not been able to read them. "H.J. knew and cared nothing for English politics," declared Max. "But neither did he know or care anything about the Church of England," adding, "He perceived the beauty of Barchester according to St. Anthony but not St. Stephen." Max could find no explanation for James's insensitivity and so he "gave the problem up with much irritation against H.J. and indignation on behalf of A.T."

He thought James's short stories better than his novels because of the confined requirements of the shorter form. James wrote of the life he knew. In a speech on "The Obsessive Upper Classes" before the Playgoers Club, reported in *The Times* of London 8 February 1909, Max said that "neither Mr. Meredith nor Mr. Henry James could have worked his own particular miracle out of any material but the leisure classes." James's tales were linked to the amenities of polite society. Max thought he also understood the life of the artist better than other authors who attempted to write about it, but he showed small concern for the necessities of everyday living, for eating and drinking—such matters were incidental to James's purpose.

Although Max said that he admired the more parenthetical and involved style of James's third period in later years, he thought it began inauspiciously. It was this complex prose which he parodied in "The Mote in the Middle Distance." Shortly after he did this parody he read an article by James which strengthened his belief in the authenticity of his imitation. He wrote a friend:

> The terrible grey eye of Henry James that misses nothing, and that grand brain of his, that understands everything—when I read an article like this one, I feel miserably untalented. My only comfort is the one reservation in my admiration: he can no longer *write*. He who wrote so well—with such elegance and clarity and nicety! Now all these crawling, brokenbacked, inarticulate sentences that have to be actively helped along by the reader . . .

and added, "Now he has spoken the thoughts very much in the manner of my parody."

In spite of this disillusion Max kept faith with his belief in James's ultimate attainment. Although he could not read *The Awkward Age,* he told Reggie Turner he would not hear a word against the rest of James's later manner.

He thought *The Golden Bowl* and *The Wings of the Dove* James's greatest achievements, but he said that reading them "is like taking a long walk uphill, panting and perspiring and almost of a mind to turn back, until, when you turn and look back and down, the country is magically expanded beneath your gaze, as you never saw it yet; so that you toil on gladly up the heights, for the longer prospects that will be waiting for you. I admit, you must be in good training."

When James's story "The Jolly Corner" appeared in the *English Review* for December 1908, Max wrote to congratulate the author. "I could not resist writing to Henry James, about 'The Jolly Corner' and about his writing in general," he told Reggie, "and I have had such a very *lovely* letter from him." Unfortunately James does not seem to have preserved Max's encomium, but Max treasured James's reply to "your beautiful letter" which had left him "quite prostrate and overcome with the force of your good words," and ended:

> You had, and you obeyed, a very generous and humane inspiration; it charms me to think—or rather so authentically to know, that my (I confess) ambitious Muse does work upon you; it really helps me to believe in her the more myself—by which I am very gratefully yours.

Max felt that Spencer Boyden in "The Jolly Corner" was a projection of James himself, who in New York was only a "dim, secondary social success." Later he did a drawing based upon the story, included in his exhibition of "Ghosts" in 1928 and called "An Illustration for Henry James's Eponymous Story," but James was not alive to see the picture or question the adjective.

Max had not seen James's ill-fated *Guy Domville* in 1895, and he feared he was to be denied the pleasure of James's next theatrical attempt, *The High Bid,* which was being performed in the provinces early in 1909; but it ran at His Majesty's in London for five matinées, and Max reviewed it for the *Saturday* of 27 February 1909. He tactfully avoided the issue of whether or not James could write a play, but he testified to the great delight he had always had in James's books and in the man these books revealed. Of all that he loved in James's mind, so little could be translated into the sphere of the drama. The trite conventionality of the story of *The High Bid* was the sort that a man of letters would think the public would understand.

In 1929 when James's story "The Sense of the Past" was dramatized by J. L. Balderston and Sir John Squire as *Berkeley Square* and was having a fair success in London, Max repeated this idea in a letter to Balderston:

> Appalled though poor dear Henry James would be at finding that something of his had actually been made successful in the theatre—

and much though he would wish that the dramatization had been left for him to do and had then resulted in one of those quiet failures which (though they pained him) didn't appall him, I do think that he would feel that the delicacy and ingenuity of your workmanship and Squire's, are so admirable that the public's liking for the play is inexplicable and that you are not to be blamed.

Max chose one speech from *The High Bid* as "the quintessence of Mr. James" and he repeated it in his review: "What are you?" asked Captain Yule of the shabby butler, "I mean, to whom do you beautifully belong?" Max so appreciated the Jacobean quality of this that he used it in 1916 in "The Guerdon," a parody of James receiving the Order of Merit. As Stamfordham (James) reached the gate of the palace, he paused and "all vaguely, all peeringly" inquired of the guard, "To whom do you beautifully belong?"

This adroit imitation was included in *A Variety of Things* (1928), but an unauthorized edition had been "privately printed" in New York in 1925. Max had originally presented Edmund Gosse with the manuscript from which one or more copies had been made, so he did not know to whom to attribute the piracy, but he did not like it.

Max and Gosse shared an interest in James and in 1908 they collaborated on a sonnet to him, Max writing the odd lines and Gosse the even. The sonnet began, "Say, indefatigable alchemist" (only Max spelled it "indefatguable"), and ended

> *Flushed with the sunset air of roseate Rye*
> *You stand, marmoreal darling of the few,*
> *Lord of the troubled speech and single eye.*

But Max admitted "We did not communicate our work to Henry James, thinking he would be too complex to understand our special brand of sincere reverence."

To Gosse Max also gave a revised and expanded version of "The Mote," more in keeping, he said, with the "great dark glow" of James's later manner, neatly collating the addenda with instructions for fitting them into the original. Before this he had made an illustrated copy of *A Christmas Garland* for Gosse, but it contained only sixteen pictures, for he finally had to give up doing James. However, on nineteen other occasions, according to Rupert Hart-Davis, he managed caricatures of James. One of his most telling pictorial comments on the bachelor author who remained aloof from the world is now in the Ashmolean at Oxford. Here James is seen dropped on one knee before a door in front of which a pair of lady's shoes and a pair of gentleman's boots rest connubially. James has his ear at the keyhole. Leon Edel has suggested that this caricature was inspired by James's essay on D'Annunzio in which he made the homely image that a novel which isolated the physical from the art of living had no more dignity than "the boots and shoes that we see, in the corridors of promiscuous hotels, standing often in double pairs, at the doors of rooms."

Not only did the youthful Max and the Max of the *Saturday Review* scrutinize James and his work; in his later years Sir Max continued to read him. In 1937 he was rereading *Daisy Miller,* as he wrote Reggie Turner, "with pangs of longing for the dear delicate, un-panic stricken world of sixty years ago." He thought *Italian Hours* was a "grand and lovely" work, and on 13 November 1949 he reviewed for the *Observer* a new edition of *A Little Tour of France,* which he did not think as good as James's *English Hours,* a book which was so successful because James was by now virtually a native of England, rather than of the land of his birth. James also was better with Italy, for, after the art of fiction, Italy was his ruling passion until 1915, when England usurped that place and he became a naturalized British subject the year before his death. Max wished "he could have lived to know of the final victory; but am, at the same time, glad that he did not live to see other things." Not everyone agreed about James's nationality. In 1912 Max and others tried to secure an honorary degree for him from Oxford, but Lord Curzon, to whom the appeal was made, protested that James's mind seemed to him "to have remained typically American." Then Max gave up, although James ultimately got the degree.

In later years Max was alert to the new criticism of James and was particularly incensed with Edmund Wilson's theory that the governess in "The Turn of the Screw" was a neurotic and the situation merely a projection of her morbidity. It was, he said, ridiculous, as James's *Notebooks* plainly showed. He regretted that the *Notebooks* should be published first in America. He had looked forward to the publication of James's letters, but when he read them he found the references to James's friends hard to understand, even though years before he had written to Reggie of James, "He hasn't a good word to say for anyone." He also deplored James's editing of the *Notes of a Son and Brother,* and his wrath was not turned aside by the inscription in his own copy from the author, "Affectionately and gratefully yours." He thought James had systematically falsified documents in the *Notes* and he carefully cited some twenty instances.

On at least two occasions Max prepared to write about James, and records of these never-completed undertakings are to be found in the Berg Collection of the New York Public Library and in the Houghton Library at Harvard. While the first consists of copious but random jottings in a notebook, the second is the opening chapter of *Half Hours with the*

To Henry James

Say, indefatigable alchemist,
Melts not the very moral of your scene,
Curls it not off in vapour from between
Those lips that labour with conspicuous twist?
Your fine eyes, blurred like arc-lamps in a mist,
Immensely glare, yet glimmerings intervene.
So that your May-Be and your Might-Have-Been
Leave us still plunging for your genuine gist.

How different from Sir Arthur Conan Doyle,
As clear as water and as smooth as oil,

And no jot knowing of what Maisie knew!
Flushed with the sunset air of roseate Rye,
You stand, marmoreal darling of the Few,
Lord of the troubled Speech and single Eye.

Autograph draft of "To Henry James" from the sonnet-game played by Max and Edmund Gosse, with odd lines in Max's hand and even lines in Gosse's. © Eva Reichmann; courtesy of Melville E. Stone.

Opposite, dated 1908, is Max's drawing of Henry James and a fair copy of the sonnet composed with Edmund Gosse. © Eva Reichmann; courtesy of Melville E. Stone.

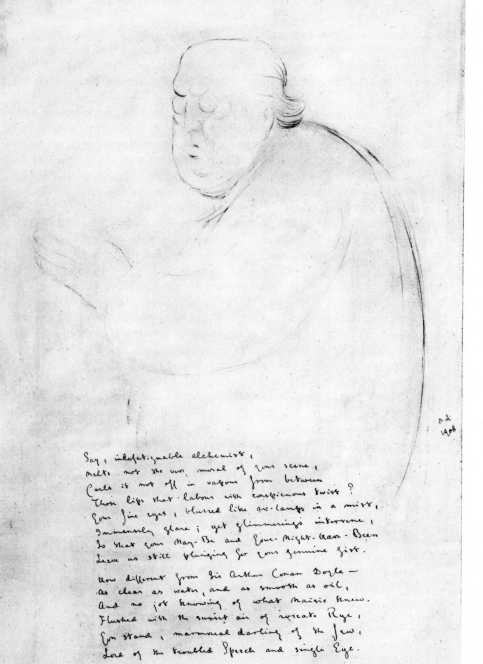

Oct
1908

Say, indefatigable alchemist,
Melts not the very moral of your scene,
Curls it not off in vapour from between
Those lips that labour with conspicuous twist?
Your fine eyes, blurred like arc-lamps in a mist,
Immensely glare; yet glimmerings intervene,
So that your May-Be and Love-Might-Have-Been
Leave us still plunging for your genuine gist.

How different from Sir Arthur Conan Doyle —
As clear as water, and as smooth as oil,
And no jot knowing of what Maisie knew.
Flushed with the sunset air of roseate Rye,
You stand, marmoreal darling of the few,
Lord of the troubled Speech and single Eye.

Dialects of England, printed by J. G. Riewald in *Max in Verse.* The scene is Rye and Miss Peploe, dressmaker, has fallen in love with Henry James at first sight and written a sonnet sequence to him relating her passion in broad Sussex dialect, printed for her friends, "of whom, alas, 'ee do be not for bein' one."

The friendship of Max and James was never close and intimate, with the frank exchange of ideas and confidences such as Max had with Gosse or Rothenstein. They met now and again at receptions or dinners, but there seems to have been no reciprocal hospitality between them; Max never went to Rye, nor James to Upper Berkeley Street. Among the Beerbohm memorabilia are found no invitations from James to dinner or a musical evening; Max never wrote Reggie that "Henry James dined with me last night." Mostly their association was through the written word or as they were fellow guests at some festivity. James never expressed himself publicly in print about Max, though he must often have read what Max said about him. He recognized Max as a bright young man—clever, witty, somewhat to be dreaded—but he seems to have felt no affection for him as he did for the little lame American Jonathan Sturges who was his frequent guest at Rye. Max and James knew each other for nearly twenty years, though in the beginning Max was more aware of James than James was of him. This gap between the two lessened, but it was never closed. Max's early acceptance of *le Maître* was modified year by years as his knowledge increased. He was intrigued by the complexities of the man, amused by his weaknesses, and impressed by his virtues. He respected his integrity and his devotion to his art, but he preferred James the writer to James the man.

This feeling was demonstrated in the last writing he did about James in June 1956 under the encouragement of his American friend S. N. Behrman, though he had recorded the episode earlier in his notebook. This was an incident, included in the later edition of *Mainly on the Air,* which concerned an afternoon in the spring of 1906 when Max met James in Piccadilly just as he was on his way to the Savile Club to read a newly published story by James titled "The Golden Glove." James hoped that Max would go with him to the Grafton Gallery, but Max pleaded an imaginary engagement. He did not tell the author he was leaving him to read his story. Max felt the incident was a theme worthy of James's own handling—"the disciple, loyally—or unloyally?—preferring the Master's work to the Master."

IV

Some Transatlantic Visitors

BESIDES AMERICANS living in London, every steamship brought American visitors from across the Atlantic—novelists, journalists, actors, playwrights, or vacationing tourists, some of whom Max had met in the States and who were eager to renew his acquaintance. That he was not unaware of his duty as host he indicated in an article in the *Saturday Review* (26 September 1903):

> The Englishman who goes to New York needs not so much letters of introduction as letters of preservation—letters of entreaty that he be not killed with kindness outright. As his ship steams into harbour, the very Statue of Liberty seems to be passionately striving to express through her lips of stone the hope that he will have a "lovely time."

The British visitor finds the city agog to please him, to show him around, and prime him with food and wine. Max wonders how an American feels about his reception in England:

> You, for whom on his own soil he really has put himself out, piling kindness on kindness, and grudging no time or trouble that shall secure that "lovely time" for you, take, on your own soil, precious little notice of him.

Some years later in "Hosts and Guests" (1918) he said, "Perhaps if England . . . were a new country, like America, the foreign visitor would be more overwhelmed with kindness here than he is." Possibly it was this feeling about unreturned hospitality that in later years prompted Max to be so kind to American visitors to his home in Rapallo.

The editor of the *Chap-Book,* Herbert S. Stone, came to London in April 1898 and sent back to his co-editor in the States two or three pieces from the *Idler,* though he was dubious about one of them: "Max's Beardsley stuff is merely what we have said already." Stone, like Max, had cherished an affection for the singer Cissie Loftus, but since her marriage to Justin McCarthy he had transferred his interest to Ethel Barrymore.

43

On 9 April he and Miss Barrymore attended the London first night of *The Heart of Maryland,* having dined with the McCarthys. A few nights later Stone reported, "At the theatre last night I sat with Cissie Loftus McCarthy. Behind us were Max Beerbohm, Paul Arthur, Bernard Shaw and Lily Hanbury."

The American transient whom Max most delighted to welcome was Clyde Fitch, the popular dramatist he had met at the Abbey Theatre in New York. Whenever Fitch came to London they lunched together, sometimes at a restaurant, sometimes at Upper Berkeley Street, where the Beerbohms had moved in 1898. Mrs. Beerbohm and Max's sisters Constance and Agnes were devoted to the American.

Although in New York Max had been somewhat abashed because the playwright knew of him as a writer while he had read nothing of Fitch's, he had now remedied this situation and was impressed with the American's achievements. Fitch, seven years older than Max, was already established as a playwright with a number of Broadway successes to his credit and a pleasing bank account. He was gay and dashing and debonair, a little plump, with an olive complexion and oriental eyes. Some people thought him overdressed, but the dandy in Max appreciated his raiment.

Twice a year Fitch stopped in London, once on his way to the Continent and once on his way back. He never stayed long, but he caught Max up in the exciting whirl of his life. To Max he was like a swallow, darting in and out, always on the wing, restless, indefatigable, swift, and Max thought he must seem to Fitch like the common English sparrow, content to hop tamely about on the sooty London branches. They were not birds of a feather, but they found much to like in each other. Fitch's great concern was the theatre; he was always writing a new play or developing an idea for one which he would outline to Max.

"Reckoned by the number of minutes I spent in his company" Max wrote in his notebook, "my friendship with Clyde Fitch might not seem to amount to more than an ordinary acquaintance. But friendship is too quick and spirited a thing to be assessed by an eye on the clock." Max added that friendship wasn't dependent on postage stamps, though acquaintances doubtless languished without them. The record of this friendship as set down by Fitch is more matter-of-fact: on a postcard to a friend dated 22 June 1899 he writes, "Monday—Max Beerbohm is lunching with me tomorrow"; another postcard mentioned that "Max Beerbohm lunched with me yesterday and was very amusing. He is the drama critic now of the *Saturday Review.* But O, he has lost one of his front teeth and *bears* the loss, which I think is a mistake." Max must soon have corrected this flaw in his appearance, for it is not mentioned elsewhere.

When Max had been appointed dramatic critic for the *Saturday Review* in the spring of 1898 to succeed Bernard Shaw—who was temporarily incapacitated by a new wife and a sprained ankle—Shaw had bestowed upon him the epithet "incomparable," from which he never escaped. He thought the assignment might be short-lived, but it lasted till 1910: as Max later said, "I trod in his footsteps and on my colleagues' corns for many a year."

On 10 June 1899 Max reviewed Fitch's *The Cowboy and the Lady,* in which two other American friends of his, Nat Goodwin and Maxine Elliott, had leading roles. Their cakewalk was a hit of the show, Max said, but the murder trial in a Colorado court which looked like a schoolroom, before a judge made up as a combination of Brother Jonathan, Abraham Lincoln, and Uncle Sam, rather puzzled an audience used to the measured dignity of French and English courts. In other ways, Max thought, the local color was of great service: "plenty of good American humour and interesting slang and strange costumes; and the word *damn* used so often that the critics of the town . . . have been throwing up their hands." It was capital entertainment and the fun of it was all the greater, said the traveled Max, "because half the audience, I feel sure, fancies it to be an accurate representation of life lived in the vicinity of New York." But in spite of Max's enthusiastic report, Clyde wrote home to an American friend, "The Cowboy is a bad failure. It comes off next week."

Although Max declared that Fitch had a real feeling for modern drama, he thought *The Masked Ball,* opening on 12 January 1900, a negligible play. In July 1901 Fitch was again in London, negotiating with Beerbohm Tree for the production of his *D'Orsay, the Last of the Dandies.* "I've lunched, dined and supped with Tree, Irving, Alexander, and Max," he reported. All these meals were not taken in vain, for Tree decided to produce the play. Max wrote Reggie Turner:

Clyde Fitch is here, very very successful—eleven companies performing his plays in America. Also, partly owing to me, Herbert is going to produce a new play he has written around Count D'Orsay—really a delightful play. I wish you were here to hear it. You would like it—it is very *du théâtre*—though of a smaller theatre, H. M.'s perhaps. A splendid part for Herbert—D'Orsay, of course.

Fitch wrote Max how pleased he was that Herbert had taken the play, but "much pleased-er and happier that you like it. . . . I shall always look on you, of course, as D'Orsay's God papa! You must remind me to tell you how much Dithmar likes you." (Edward A. Dithmar was the dramatic critic of the *New York Times.*)

D'Orsay was produced in October; for obvious reasons Max did not review it, and at first its future was in doubt, but by the end of the first week it was an acknowledged success. Tree wrote Fitch, "I hope you will be pleased with the production and me: the former is quite beautiful and the latter pretends to be."

When Fitch's last play, *The Truth,* was presented in 1907, Max did not attend the opening. When he saw it later, however, he enjoyed it very much, and he wondered if it was because he knew he did not have to write about it. A conscientious critic, he believed, could not enjoy a play he was to criticize. "The perception of its faults is as pleasing to him as the perception of its virtues." He cannot surrender himself to the story; he has to regard it as a work of art. The best criticism, he said, "is like poetry, emotion remembered in tranquillity." But that was impossible for the dramatic critic; he could not take his time and come back for another look, as could the critic of painting or sculpture. In reading *The Truth,* he realized how dependent the playwright was on his actors. Although he smiled when he read the play, he had laughed when he saw it, and while he had been much moved by the close of the third act on the stage, in reading it his eyes had been as dry as though he were studying a railway timetable. Plays should be acted, not read. But he concluded that Fitch's plays had a "vitality and gay resourcefulness that set him high above ordinary playwrights."

Max's admiration for Fitch extended to matters outside the theatre. On one occasion the American was reading George Moore's *Evelyn Innes,* which had just come out, when suddenly the description of Evelyn singing Marguerite in *Faust* seemed familiar to him. A year earlier he had published in the *Musician* an article on Madame Calvé's interpretation of the part; now he realized that Moore had used the review nearly word for word in the novel. "What are you going to do about it?" asked Max. Fitch said he didn't think he'd do anything. He "was a very good-humoured fellow," observed Max.

Max presented his friend with *The Works,* suitably inscribed and decorated with a caricature of himself, but he apparently later neglected to give him his *Book of Caricatures,* for its inscription reads, "For Clyde, in yearly increasing affection, this book which ought to have been given by me in London instead of being purchased in Paris." This volume contains Max's caricature of Fitch, dapper, balding, jutting chin, impeccably dressed, with a large stickpin in his tie.

In one of his notes Max said

My dear Clyde,

Welcome home. Delighted to lunch with you on Thursday. Have just returned from the country and found your note awaiting me; also your

2 drawings which are fine, though I'm glad you're not like that and I
wish I were.

Affectionately, Max

Although Max might seem to believe that Fitch was at home in London,
once he had to straighten out the visitor's geography. He wired:

Euston? Me friend, you mean Paddington surely. From Paddington
there is a 2:25, but not from Euston and Paddington is the usual
place. Paddington be it.

Yours, A Practical Person

As Max grew increasingly busy with his reviewing, his exhibitions, and
his social life, he and Fitch did not always make connections. In early June
of 1908 Fitch suggested that Max meet him somewhere by "the silvery
sea"; Max wired that he could not, adding, "Am writing." In September
the invitation was repeated, and Max again refused—"Am writing." Fitch
was worried: "From early June till late September, continuously writing.
Have you never stopped?"

The playwright had now become addicted to motorcars and Max thought
this violent mode of transportation suited him. In his new auto, "Pauline,"
he whirled Max off to Rye, where he wanted to visit Henry James, but Max
advised against it. However, Gilbert Chesterton was spending the summer
next door to Lamb House, James's home at Rye, so they compromised on
visiting Chesterton and spent a jolly afternoon, drinking burgundy out of
tumblers and listening to gossip about James.

The summer of 1909 was the last time Max saw Fitch. Although he had
once signed a letter to Max, "Your fat friend," he now wrote that his
"tummy was a thing of the past." He had been frightfully ill and was only
"partly here," but he hoped to see Max, his "uncrowned king." Fitch died
4 September 1909 in France.

Fitch may have been the American friend who gave Max a dog, a
Pomeranian, bought in Italy. Max appropriately named it Dandy, and was
very fond of it. To be sure, it bit him once, but that was because it mistook
him for the hansom cab that had just run over it. Max made a little rhyme
for Ada Leverson's daughter—

If you have anything to ask, ask it—
Where does Dandy like to bask? Basket.

Nat Goodwin, the actor Max had met on his trip to America, also made
frequent visits to London. In 1898 he had married the beautiful Maxine

Elliott and made her his leading lady. They alternated between seasons in New York and London, so Goodwin acquired an English country house, Jackwood, and began issuing invitations for weekends. Max was one of the recipients, as he has related in "Nat Goodwin and Another." He found Jackwood a fabulous estate, staffed by sixteen servants, with an expensive collection of dogs and horses. Goodwin used to take Max dashing down the country lanes in a low-slung, two-wheeled cart he had brought from America. Max had no faith in the horse, who, he felt, would like to kill them both with a couple of well-directed kicks, though at heart the horse was a coward and dared not. "But who am I that I should sneer at him?" asked Max. "He at least had the courage of his conviction; not I of mine. I pretended to be enjoying those drives."

Goodwin was a great story-teller; "barring Charles Brookfield," said Max, "he was the best actor of stories I ever heard." After dinner the actor sat slumped in his chair with ice, rye whiskey, and green cigars before him, telling interminable stories through the long hours of the night. However, Goodwin's account of story-telling at Jackwood differed somewhat from Max's. He said that Maxine "insisted on my entertaining the guests between courses with my supposedly funny stories. Generally after the telling of each one, which occupied some little time, my portion of the feast was either cold or confiscated by the butler. Very little attention was paid to me anyway, except when I was telling anecdotes (and on the first of every month when the bills were due!)."

Max seems to have been only partly aware of the friction in the household. Nat had discovered that his wife was bored unless the house was filled with English guests, and when it was empty she went to visit in other houses, leaving him alone. Perhaps the friends with whom he consoled himself were not welcomed by Maxine. "Off the stage," said Max, "he lived much in the company of prize-fighters, jockeys, professional card players, and other folk whose good opinion is not a passport to the higher circles of life in the land of Emerson and Longfellow." When Nat inadvertently received a love letter his wife had written to another man, he decided it was time to close Jackwood.

Before he managed to sell it, he leased it for a season to Beerbohm Tree, and in the fall of 1902 Max paid another visit there, remembering nostalgically the nights when "Nat Goodwin would ramble on . . . while daylight itself crept in through the windows to listen, and our laughter made inaudible the twittering of birds."

Despite the fact that Max believed plays should be acted, not read, in his reviews the play was the thing, not the actors. Nevertheless he usually managed to say something flattering about Goodwin. When *An American*

Citizen followed *The Cowboy and the Lady,* Max thought nothing of the play but he urged his readers to see Goodwin in it: "Mr. Goodwin is the American of the Americans and a comedian of the comedians. He has, too, a streak of real poetry in him. He is irresistible." Miss Elliott had "charm and distinction." Max had only scorn for E. V. Esmond's "silly play" *When We Were Twenty-one,* but he said, "Mr. Nat Goodwin and Miss Maxine Elliott interpret him with a charm he does not deserve."

In his autobiography, Nat Goodwin indulged in a diatribe against critics, and named the only ones he could trust, omitting mention of Max. He seemed to have changed his mind since he thanked Beerbohm Tree in Philadelphia for his kindness to American actors, now writing, "Acting is a matter of geography. America is the English actor's Mecca; England is our cemetery." But Goodwin was far from buried. In 1913 he married his fifth wife.

Not all Americans in London were masculine; the ladies were represented as well, most conspicuously perhaps by the pretty heiresses married to British peers. At the beginning of his career Max's personal contact with them was slight, but he observed them slyly and found them little different from those he had described in "1880."

> The Professional Beauty was, more strictly, a Philistine production . . . One of its immediate consequences was the incursion of American ladies into London. Then it was that these pretty little creatures, "clad in Worth's most elegant confections" drawled their way into the drawing-rooms of the great. Appearing, as they did, with the especial favour of the Prince of Wales, they had an immediate success. They were so wholly new that their voices and their dresses were mimicked *partout.* The English beauties were very angry, especially with the Prince, whom alone they blamed for the vogue of their rivals. History credits the Prince with many notable achievements. Not the least of these is that he discovered the inhabitants of America.

Max confessed to Reggie Turner that he got along fairly well among the topnotchers, but he did feel a bit quiet in the big houses: his French was bad and he didn't ride. Nevertheless he enjoyed these luxurious establishments, and early in 1901 Will Rothenstein told Robert Ross that Max had "a great success with Mrs. Keppel and other smart reprehensible folk of that kind"—Alice Keppel being the famous hostess and friend of the Prince of Wales, who was soon to be crowned Edward VII. He could not renew his acquaintance with Mary Leiter, whom he had first met in Washington, because, as Lady Curzon, she had gone to India with her husband, who had been appointed Viceroy. Max also knew Lady Cunard, an exotic American whose audacities he dreaded.

More pleasant was his association with Mrs. George Cornwallis-West, the former Jennie Jerome of New York who had married Lord Randolph Churchill and was the mother of Winston. A capable writer, she was one of the founders of the *Anglo-Saxon Review* in 1899, four years after the death of Lord Randolph. She became editor of this miscellany which, bound in tooled leather, appeared on both sides of the Atlantic—very de luxe, very expensive, very short-lived. Two of Max's essays added to its elegance: "The Garden of Love" in 1900 and "The Visit" a year later; both belonged to his "Words for Pictures" series. He wrote Reggie in January 1901 that he was going to see "dear Mrs. Cornwallis-West" at dinner the next night, and he reviewed her play *His Borrowed Plumes* as "very entertaining" in the *Saturday* for 10 July 1909. In 1899, shortly before she married Cornwallis-West, Lady Randolph had published the poetic drama *Osberne and Ursyne* by her friend Mrs. Pearl M. T. Craigie when the play could not find a producer.

Mrs. Craigie, who wrote under the pen-name John Oliver Hobbes, was an American-born novelist who was also a fellow contributor of Max's to the *Anglo-Saxon Review*. Although he had reviewed several of Mrs. Craigie's plays he seems to have ignored publication of *Osberne;* nor could he have known that in 1898 when the play had been given a trial presentation in New York, a pretty auburn-haired actress named Florence Kahn played the leading rôle.

Pearl Mary Teresa Craigie, born in Boston in 1867, had lived most of her life abroad. Her father, J. M. Richards, was a wealthy manufacturer of patent medicine with a residence in London; Pearl had studied at the Paris Conservatory and the University of London, married Reginald Craigie when she was nineteen, had a son, became a Roman Catholic, and separated from her husband. She was a Bodley Head author, considered a "new" writer, and had collaborated with George Moore on a play for the first volume of the *Yellow Book*. Her name appeared frequently in the columns of literary gossip. Soon after Max assumed his post on the *Saturday Review* he wrote of her play *The Ambassador*. He was complimentary, saying she "seems to have achieved through sure instinct for the stage that which most dramatists only learn from years of bitter experience. This makes her play all the fresher and more delightful." He thought she was born to "write perfect little comedies," but he had heard she was now wanting to do something "important." He warned her against it: "Some people are born to lift heavy weights, some to juggle with golden balls, Mrs. Craigie is one of the few good jugglers . . ."

Having explained to Mrs. Craigie her métier, he was naturally disappointed when she did not heed him. Reviewing her *A Repentance* in March 1899, he called it a melodrama which she should not have written. He urged her to repair the havoc she had wrought by doing another comedy forthwith. Nor was he pleased with her next play, *The Wisdom of the Wise* —in fact he was bored by it. "In Mrs. Craigie," he said, "I take always a special interest. She as a dramatist, and I as dramatic critic, saw the light simultaneously; and our conascence has inspired me with the sentimental wish that she should do great things . . . I, divining certain limitations which are set to the talents of women in general, and John Oliver Hobbes in particular, urged her to follow sedulously the fashion she had set for herself in *The Ambassador.*" Max referred to the "unfortunate experience on the first night." Apparently Mrs. Craigie had accepted a curtain call which proved to be unfriendly. Max warned her that "a dramatist who personally courts applause for success must also court execration for failure." But he was confident that "she has the power to do well the good things which on this occasion she has done ill."

Mrs. Craigie apparently took his advice, for in 1902 she and Murray Carson were responsible for *The Bishop's Wife,* which Max declared "quite a delightful and distinguished little comedy," displaying Mrs. Craigie's feminine talent. "When she confines herself to little light things, there is not in England a lady whose work can compare with hers." Other critics complained that the play was too thin.

In 1899 when his *More* came out, Max sent Mrs. Craigie a copy. She thanked him in a brief note: she always read his essays and criticisms with pleasure, she was pleased with his enthusiasm for Ouida whom she considered one of the first women writers of the day, and she was sincerely his.

Mrs. Craigie died in 1906, perhaps by her own hand. Although Max's public criticism of her work seemed tempered and restrained, his private feelings differed. When in 1914 he was elected to the Academy Committee for the choice of new members, he wrote Gosse:

> If George Sand came to life & were English this time, I should vote for her. If Mrs. Craigie were re-incarnated, I should not vote for her. I think genius, or at any rate a magnificent distinction, is needed to enable a woman to add lustre to the Committee and to prevent her from making it slightly ridiculous.

A stronger disparagement of her capability is to be found in the copy of her *The Artist's Life* which is in the Berg Collection of the New York Public Library. Mrs. Craigie had won a reputation as a speaker; in fact, she had made a lecture tour of the States in 1905. Max parodied her with

"An Address Delivered before the Philosophical Institution of Edinburgh, the Literary Society of Glasgow, and the Ruskin Society of Birmingham," on "Isaiah, Watteau, and Strauss," grouping these men together because "each of them has two legs, ten toes, eight fingers, or ten if the thumbs be counted." Her "private motive (between you and me and Papa's Little Liver Pills)," says Max, is that she has nothing to say that has not already been said about them—"that is, nothing above the level of any high school girl who has dipped into a popular encyclopaedia." The travesty gathers harshness as it proceeds; Max's feelings seem to have been so strong that his usual light touch turned ugly. It is one of the few records of Max's divergence from the mores of good taste.

Apparently Mrs. Craigie's father, J. M. Richards, sent Max a copy of the Life he wrote of his daughter, for it is inconceivable that Max would have bought it. In the front of his copy Max wrote in 1920:

> Wherein, painfully, is exposed to us by the well-meaning hand of a devoted father the fact that this pretty and pleasant little woman of the eighteen-nineties was of all climbers the grimest, and of all wire-pullers the most indefatigable and undiscourageable, and of all ladies who ever put pen to paper the most brazenly conceited.

Two other women, both writers, who crossed the Atlantic with frightening frequency, were Gertrude Atherton and Edith Wharton. Indeed, Mrs. Atherton announced she was going to live in England, but she changed her mind. After publishing two small books in America, she had come to London; there she had taken tea with the Whistlers, and had refused an invitation to meet Oscar Wilde. She then returned to the States, but again descended on London in 1895. Before he left for New York, Max had heard of her, for John Lane was bringing out her novel *Patience Sparhawk* and she had submitted a story to the *Yellow Book* which Harland had refused.

On 24 August 1897 Reggie Turner wrote Max from Bois Guillaume, Rouen, of an American novelist staying at his pension there, Mrs. Gertrude Atherton:

> . . . She is the person who reviewed your *Happy Hypocrite* for *Vanity Fair,* a criticism which gave you so much pleasure . . . She is a widow (like Lottie Collins) and has a daughter (in California). It is rather an Ibsen ménage. Do write to me, as having boasted of our intense intimacy it would be awful if I got no letters from you . . . I have never read anything of Gertrude Atherton's except her

criticism of you, and I told her so with engaging frankness, scorning worldly compliments. She has already (I arrived last night) confided to Madame [the proprietor] her hope that she will not like me *too* much. It is a hope I quite reciprocate. She is a friend of Lane's fiancée, and does not like Henry Harland or George Moore.

John Lane's fiancée, whom he married the next year, was Mrs. Annie Eichberg King, a widow from Boston, and a writer herself. Max must have known her, but no record of their contact remains.

Max might well have been pleased with Mrs. Atherton's review, for it was unadulterated praise. *The Happy Hypocrite,* she said, was literature, whether it was a subtle sermon or satire. It was "worth more than all the tomes of historical novels turned out—by machinery—in the last ten years." It was a "perfect little book," she could find no flaws in it. The author was "young, brilliant, successful, and not a cynic."

Max was intensely interested to learn that Mrs. Atherton was under Reggie's roof. "Do tell me all about her and tell her all about me," he entreated. "I had heard she had a daughter over the sea." Then he yielded to wicked impulse, hoping Reggie would inadvertently read his letter aloud at the breakfast table. "She herself started life behind a bar in St. Louis—and then went to San Francisco, where she used to dance naked in one of the dime-shows. Also she was kept for some years by President Garfield. When he was assassinated, she became an authoress. If I possibly can," Max added, returning to reality, "I will come to Rouen for a few days." Apparently he couldn't.

In *Adventures of a Novelist* (1932), Mrs. Atherton related her impressions of Reggie. The proprietress of the pension had been reluctant to accept Mrs. Atherton as a guest because the young men who came to her every summer did not like women in the establishment, but as it was some time before they would arrive, she decided to accept her for the interim. When she had been there three weeks, Reggie arrived unexpectedly. He met her at the dinner table "with a scowl on his gnome-like face, but thawed somewhat before the meal was over. He was a gregarious soul and he liked to talk." They found they had literary acquaintances in common and "exchanged opinions in the parlor until ten o'clock." Within a few days they were good friends and he graciously informed her he would be glad to have her stay.

He confided in her his friendship with Oscar Wilde, whom he now bitterly regretted having known—"he was an evil influence for any young man, and distorted one's outlook upon life." Even so, when Wilde was released from Reading Gaol in May 1897, Reggie and Robert Ross had met him. After Wilde got established at Dieppe he urged Reggie to join him; but Reggie refused. Wilde then came to Rouen, for he was determined to see Reggie. Mrs. Atherton tried to dissuade Reggie from meeting him, but Reggie went off, "dragging his feet, all the jauntiness gone out of him." He returned in despair: he was done for: Oscar said it was Reggie's duty to stand by him and he would stay at Rouen until Reggie went back to Dieppe with him. Mrs. Atherton took a firm position. Did Reggie really want to go back with Oscar? Reggie denied it violently. Then, said Mrs. Atherton, he must run away, leave at once for England. And Reggie did.

Later in London Max met Mrs. Atherton at occasional gatherings. Once at a dinner at William Heinemann's, he recommended Bruges to her as a good retreat for a writer. Then she wrote and asked him to suggest a place to stay there; she was tired of dropping down into a town and trusting to luck. She planned to write her next book there. Whether or not Max could oblige, she went to Bruges where she wrote *Senator North*.

Although by 1901 Edith Wharton had written two volumes of short stories and a novel, her notable literary career was not fully launched until a year later, when her *Valley of Decision* won both popular and critical approval. In 1904 she collaborated with Clyde Fitch in dramatizing her *House of Mirth*. She was a close friend and disciple of Henry James. Max met her first in December 1908, being introduced by Edmund Gosse. She dubbed Max "matchless," her own synonym for Shaw's "incomparable." In *A Backward Glance* she said, "It was not my good luck to meet the latter [Max] often, though he was still living in London and far from being the recluse he has since . . . become. But when we did sit next to each other at lunch or dinner it was like suddenly growing wings." She recalled only one of his "lapidary comments." They were discussing a novelist who was witty in conversation, but whose writing was heavy and dull and overburdened with detail. Mrs. Wharton said she had been told by a friend that this insistence on detail was because he was short-sighted; he had to look at everything closely. "Ah, really," said Max, "I should think it was because he was so long-winded."

Mrs. Wharton was also a close friend of John Singer Sargent. During the First World War she worked actively for the French, sponsoring a hostel for the benefit of which she edited *Book of the Homeless*. To this her friends contributed poetry, prose, or pictures. She was most anxious to have something from Max, but, hesitating to ask him, she enlisted the aid of Sargent. He readily approached Max, who wrote Mrs. Wharton that he would be happy to contribute, though he was a trifle appalled "at being foisted in amidst the work of the hierarchic and august men" named by

Sargent. He thought he could do best the caricature of a single figure. But of whom? Mrs. Wharton replied:

> This is too good to be true! It makes me wish I had asked you myself; now Mr. Sargent has the lion's share of the credit. I have only had two refusals, Mr. Loti and Mr. Kipling, who says he can't write during the war. As Mr. James says, "I kinder see" a portrait of Mr. Kipling explaining the fact to a French refugee who happens to have read his "France"!!? If you're shocked—perish the thought and the picture, and give me dear Mr. Wells—no I'd rather not make any other suggestion, because no other could be as good.

Max ignored the Wells idea but he replied to her other suggestion:

> I wish I could have done the *Kipling* theme—a beautiful opportunity, but one not to be taken by me. For moral reasons—too complicated and tedious to be explained in a letter—I would rather not have a fling at Kipling. I must leave his behaviour to be punished in the next world.

Instead he had done a drawing titled "A Gracious Act" in which Lord Curzon was reading to Emile Cammaerts, the Belgian poet-patriot, a translation (signed with his own name) of a poem by M. Cammaerts. He enclosed a rough sketch for her approval. A series of letters followed in which he worried about the reproduction of the drawing and its transfer to the processors, for he had heard that packages sent from England to France were opened en route, an act that might damage the caricature. It was finally arranged that Mrs. Wharton's sister should personally transport the package; it arrived safely, and the caricature was successfully reproduced in *Book of the Homeless*.

After Max's gracious co-operation in Mrs. Wharton's aid to France, it is surprising to read Mrs. Wharton's denunciation of Max in Wilbur Cross's *A Connecticut Yankee* (1945). In 1924 the *Yale Review* had published Max's cartoons of "Tales of Three Nations, England, France, and Germany." Cross said that Mrs. Wharton had taken him severely to task for printing this group of cartoons "which she denounced as 'abominable caricatures' against England and France by a pro-German artist."

Max must have met many of the American actresses in London about whom he wrote in the *Saturday*, and to one of them, Elizabeth Robins, he had a negative reaction. Considered by Ibsen as his leading exponent in the English-speaking world, Miss Robins was also a writer, and was another of the women devoted to Henry James. Later she chronicled that relation-

ship in *Theatre and Friendship*. Max had met her at a luncheon given by
the Henry Harlands shortly before his visit to America in 1895, and he
wrote his impression of her to Ada Leverson—misspelling her name:

> . . . the Robbins—Do you know her at all? Conceive! Straight, pen-
> cilled eyebrows, a mouth that has seen the stress of life . . . She is
> fearfully Ibsenish and talks of souls that are involved in a nerve tur-
> moil and are seeking a common platform. This is literally what she
> said. I kept peeping under the table to see if she really wore a skirt.

On 13 April 1907 he reviewed Miss Robins's play *Votes for Women*.
Although a year later he was extremely sympathetic in his defense of
Christabel Pankhurst, militant leader of the votes-for-women movement,
he did not seem so well disposed toward Miss Robins's dramatization of
the Suffragette cause. That she was a Suffragist he knew, and as an actress
she had often thrilled him in dramas written by other people; but he was
uncertain whether her play was a satirical comedy or a tract. The second
act, he thought, was a marvelously accurate reproduction of scenes he had
often witnessed at Marble Arch, but he objected to Acts I and III, and to
her handling of plot and characters. He thought the syllogism of the
heroine—"I was seduced. I had not the vote. Therefore all women ought
to have the vote"—showed an "incapacity for clear and impersonal thinking which some brutes have supposed to be the characteristic of all women.
Strange that Miss Robins, one of the cleverest of her sex," should use this
reasoning. Still, "I recognize on her shoulders the mantle of the late Mrs.
Lynn Linton, a campaigner not less strenuous than she, but less subtle, less
formidable."

It is hard to conjecture about Max's knowledge of other American ladies
resident in London. He liked to dine with Mrs. George W. Steevens, a
wealthy American married to a younger journalist, whose good meals he
and Somerset Maugham much appreciated in their early, impecunious days.
Louise Chandler Moulton, like Whistler, whose good friend she was, com-
muted between Boston and London; it was at her invitation that Elizabeth
Robins had come to London. Mrs. Moulton's salons were meeting places
for the literary and artistic of both continents, but Max made no mention
of attending them. When he went to Dieppe he must have seen the beautiful
Misses Kinsella—Louise, Josephine, and Kate—friends of Will Rothenstein, Charles Conder, the artist, and Logan Pearsall Smith. Rich young
American orphans, they had come to Paris to attend school at Saint Coeur
and stayed on to furnish a romantic interest for a number of young men.
They were in demand as models, and Whistler and Conder painted Louise,
said to be the most beautiful of the three. If Max knew them he escaped

falling in love with them, just as he dodged several young British journalists like Ella Hepworth-Dixon, Evelyn Sharp, and Netta Syrett.

Indeed, after his infatuation for Cissie Loftus, Max's affections were until 1904 bestowed on only two young ladies. The first, of course, was Kilseen Conover. Although never announced, their engagement was taken for granted by his family and his close friends, but eight years after he met her in the States it was broken, apparently by Max. The reason for his action was undoubtedly his growing interest in the more glamorous Constance Collier, leading lady for his brother Herbert. In July 1903 he was arranging for Constance to spend the summer at Dieppe, his own vacation habitat; by December he was confiding to Reggie Turner that he was engaged to her. But in April he was admitting to the same friend that it was all over—Constance had decided that neither of them was fitted for the serious responsibilities of life. Max was deeply hurt, though he tried to be philosophical about it; he wished he had been the sober sort of man who would make his way in the world, and he didn't blame Constance for realizing that he wasn't. His generosity must have been a little strained when, shortly afterwards, she married her new leading man, Julian L'Estrange. In 1943, asked by an American editor why her engagement to Max was broken, Miss Collier sighed, "Ah, poor dear Max. He had carpet slippers in his soul."

But in 1904 Max could not foresee this cynical explanation of a broken engagement: he could only grieve at losing the woman he loved.

V

Max Around Theatres

AFTER HIS APPOINTMENT as dramatic critic for the *Saturday Review* in 1898, Max became even more the successful young man-about-town, essayist, artist, critic, social lion, and dandy. His letters to Reggie Turner reveal some amazing sartorial innovations (such as a smoking suit of purple silk and a long yellow overcoat), but he was always correctly attired for the theatre—top hat, tails, white gloves, and tasseled cane.

John Lane brought out the second collection of Max's essays, *More,* in 1899 in London and in New York, where it sold for $1.25. "An Infamous Brigade" especially disturbed some readers, but the *Critic* considered it the gem of the collection. The *Dial* regretted that Mr. Beerbohm had no message to deliver, as "the gifted man whom he so sedulously imitated did have [possibly Whistler?—K.L.M.]," but it recommended the book for summer reading as "of a size suitable for the hammock."

A periodical called the *Living Age,* founded by Eleakin Littell and published in Boston, made a specialty of reprinting foreign literature, and a number of Max's essays appeared in it: "Madame Tussaud's," 3 April 1897; "Pretending," 5 March 1898; "Ichabod," 8 December 1900; "The Humour of the Public," 5 April 1902. His reviews from the *Saturday* turned up now and then in American papers, often enough so Finley Peter Dunne, originator of "Mr. Dooley," the fictional presiding genius of a Chicago saloon, said in the *Bookbuyer* that "English literature was suffering from the Beerbohmic plague."

He also essayed the drama, and in 1900 dramatized *The Happy Hypocrite* for Mrs. Patrick Campbell. It was performed as a curtain-raiser to Frank Harris's *Mr. and Mrs. Daventry* (which Clement Scott labeled "Drama of the Dustbin"). Max's play scored a pleasant success, running from 11 December to 8 February. An anonymous correspondent who signed himself "Gawain" in a London Letter to the American *Dramatic Mirror* thought Max's "little play . . . dainty and delicate and full of feeling as well as fancy, instead of being, like most of his writings and

sayings, crammed with affected and insistent epigrams," adding, "a clever
fellow is this culchawed Oxford scholar . . . although some of his impromptus seem to have been the work of years."

In December 1901 Max wrote Reggie that *The Happy Hypocrite* was
in rehearsal in New York, Mrs. Campbell having taken it with her on
her first American tour; but though it was advertised to precede *Beyond
Human Power* at a Saturday matinée, it does not seem to have been given.
At the close of Mrs. Campbell's engagement the press noted that John
Blair was to become her leading man. One of Max's sketches of Sir George
Hell, "the happy hypocrite," was inscribed, "For John Blair," so the
American actor may have expected to play the part.

In 1901 and 1904 Max had exhibits at London's Carfax Gallery and
from these pictures he chose the caricatures for *The Poets' Corner*. It
was published by Heinemann in 1904, with a thousand copies sent to
the States, where these literary cartoons received scant attention. The
only American poet included was Walt Whitman, encouraging the American eagle to soar.

American journalists often wished to interview Max and though he
declared his doorstep was strewn with the bleaching bones of inter-
viewers who had failed to get anything out of him worth repeating, at
least two of them achieved results—Arthur Lawrence for the November
1901 *Critic* and William Wallace Whitelock in the January 1903 *Bookbuyer,* both American magazines. Lawrence detailed a visit to Max's top-
floor study, on one wall of which hung a pastel portrait of Max at the
age of ten, his heavy-lidded, round eyes looking out "heedless of the
gaze of the world and unperturbed by the uncouth speech of the interviewer." To him Max still seemed as tranquil and undisturbed as the
child had been. He was impressed with the good humor and modesty
of so successful a young man. Recalling Max's visit to the States, Lawrence
said that "those whom he met greeted him as an old friend . . . In fact,
if there is any truth in the suggestion that Columbus discovered America,
the fact is less open to controversy that America discovered Max Beerbohm."

Whitelock averred that Max occupied a very special niche in the
literary world which removed him from the struggle for eminence en-
dured by many writers, so he could be easy and nonchalant. Nevertheless Max spoke disparagingly of Kipling, wondering if Americans were
as tired of him as the English were. He thought Kipling's recent railway
fable was twaddle, but inquired if Whitelock liked it from patriotic
reasons because the engine was American. (Max apparently read Kipling
even if he did not like him, for the reference is to Kipling's ".007" in

which the hero is an American eight-wheeled railroad locomotive.) Max offered his guest tea, one lump or two, bread and butter or cakes? White-lock was pleased with this beverage, saying, "If this were America you would probably insist on my drinking a lot of whiskey and stuff I didn't want; one man would never have the courage to offer another tea in America." Max had noticed that, too. Then he spoke of his trip to the States with his brother eight years earlier, and of the success of the various plays in the different cities. The reporter congratulated him on *The Happy Hypocrite,* then being performed, and while Max admitted it was a clever idea, he modestly gave the credit for its succeses to Mrs. Patrick Campbell. She was the most delightful and sympathetic actress; he was inclined to write another play just for the pleasure of attending rehearsals.

The memories of Max's trip remained clear in his mind, making him quick to perceive the ways in which Americans differed from the British. He was not likely to compare the Scots or the French with the English, but he was ever alert to weigh an American fault against an English virtue, or occasionally the opposite. He was not obsessed by the land across the Atlantic, but he was acutely aware of it and remained so throughout his life. Nowhere in his writings is this concern more evident than in his drama criticisms for the *Saturday Review.*

"It must be because we live in a labour saving age that we English are now so keen to welcome Americans both off and on the stage," he wrote 24 June 1899. "They are as foreign to us (and therefore as surprising, amusing, and interesting) as Italians or even Hottentots." Yet they could be studied or understood "without the galling necessity of either learning a new language or trusting to the tedious interpreter. The very fact that they use practically the same language as we use, makes their contrast more piquant, makes them the less resistible." He thought that as mimes (Max liked that word) they had a new method and that as playwrights they "had just begun to develop a national drama quite unlike ours and yet quite easily intelligible to us."

Max's sensitive ear registered the nonconformity of the American speech to its mother tongue. When George Alexander played the part of an American farmer in *John Glaydes' Honour,* on 16 March 1907 Max thought it a pity that he did not venture to assume an American accent— though usually the accent English actors assumed had little resemblance to any speech ever heard in America. Still, it was accepted as a necessary convention, like the three-walled room in which it was spoken. In a later essay he wrote of the American who comes to England, thinking, "here

The photograph opposite commemorates Max's pleasure on reading a presenta-tion copy of one of Reggie Turner's light novels, *The Steeple,* published in 1903 by Greening & Co., a house specializing in trivial fiction. Below it, Max wrote: "To Reg: Thou trumpet made for Greening's lips to blow!"

For Rag
from
Max
1903

To Reg
Those Ellis trumpet made 5 Baker Street,
& W. Glery Greening's lips to blow!

is the beautiful old cradle of my race"; but this American has quite forgotten, observed Max, "that he himself was never rocked in that cradle. He has a strong American accent."

Max was worried when Clement Scott, one of his rivals in dramatic criticism, went to America, for he had always considered Scott too thin-skinned and sensitive to public disapproval. (Max had on several occasions publicly disapproved of him.) "The Americans," Max said (9 December 1899), "do things on a far larger scale than we. If Mr. Scott could not stand our buckets of hot water, how will he stand the scalding reservoirs of New York?"

Although he thought the British stage in a bad way, the Americans gave it no help. America should be grateful for the plays she got from England, but the English got only Mr. Augustus Daly's farces in exchange, a bad bargain. He did not like William Gillette's *Clarice* (23 September 1905). One subsidiary character, a black cook, seemed to have an air of reality, though this impression might be due to his ignorance of her kind: "I shall not be surprised to hear that she is a stock figure of the American theatre, with no counterpart on American soil. My knowledge of that soil is very superficial; but even had I never scraped that soil's surface, I should be in a position to swear that none of the principal characters . . . bears any relation to reality."

"With all deference to America," began his review 15 July 1899 of DeWolf Hopper in *El Capitan,* Max did not think mid-July the moment "for the glare and blare of such a piece, and the wear and tear of so strenuous a clown." Even Americans, he suspected, would prefer to see it in the winter. "America must deal gently with us, remembering that her civilisation is still new enough to retain strong remnants of healthy barbarism, and that it is further to the West than we, and better able to stand things." He did not like Hopper's monstrous pains to amuse: "It is curious," he continued, "that American stage humour always does seem artificial, not really spontaneous, even when it is expressed in the method opposite to Mr. Hopper's. The quiet, lazy method, used by most American comedians, seems fraught with self-conscious challenge," he wrote, though he hastened to except Nat Goodwin. "The fact is that American humour is still in its infancy. Humour is an outcome of civilisation. The Americans have invented a humour of their own, just as they have invented a constitution and are inventing an Empire. A very good kind of humour it is, and a great credit to them. But, as yet, they are a little too proud of it. . . . They have not had time to take it as a matter of course." Max could not accept Hopper as a comedian, though he acknowledged in an interview for *Cassell's* that the shorter a joke is the better, and that was why "the American jokes—to me at all events—are the most amusing."

Max could be scathing about Britons who wrote of America with insufficient knowledge. On 10 June 1905 he thought James Fagan had a good idea for *Hawthorne, U.S.A.,* with a princess falling in love with an American; it gave a certain freshness to the old Ruritania theme, but he doubted if Mr. Fagan had ever seen an American man: the author had merely taken the old stock figure which had done duty for so many years for an American, "always blatant, always cool, always resourceful, always ready with dreadful funniments." He didn't see how Mr. Fagan could have missed seeing a real American with London so full of them every summer. Shaw, he said, was the only playwright who had made any attempt to portray an actual American; he had given Hector Malone in *Man and Superman* typical American speech and a thoroughly American soul. Mr. Fagan was quite mistaken in his American's reactions, and Max told him what they should have been. When the Princess dismissed Hawthorne because he was not a prince, he made the obvious response: it was a free country, he was as good as anyone. Instead, said Max, he should have been overwhelmed by the sense of distance between them, by the antiquity of her race, and respected the theory of limitations. (Max put this theory into practice with the sentiments he gave Abimelech V. Oover in *Zuleika Dobson.*) He thought Lewis Waller as the hero supplied the comedy omitted by Mr. Fagan, for the actor "spoke as a Briton born, and the effect of stage-American lingo spoken without the stage-American intonation" was really memorable.

On the other hand, in his 21 April 1906 review of *Dorothy o' the Hall*—an American dramatization of the novel *Dorothy Vernon of Haddon Hall,* set in the time of Elizabeth I—he deplored Americans' using the English scene. Titling his article "Dorothy o' the Bowery," he visualized the dramatists, Paul Kester and Charles Major, as standing in tender silence before the ancient edifice that was Haddon Hall and exclaiming, " 'Say, Paul, [or Charley,] we must *use* this!' " and then, with native briskness, mapping out the scenario on their way back to the railroad station. What would America think, inquired Max, if he were to go to the States and visit some showplace of corresponding interest, say Tammany Hall, and write for the New York stage "a play called 'Croker o' the Hall,' showing the famous Boss as an exquisite figure of romance, and involving him in some romantically exquisite adventure?" Americans would say it would not do, but "no Bowery 'tough' could be so crude a character as the Dorothy of Messrs. Kester and Major."

He explored another facet of Anglo-American differences on 28 May

1904 when he questioned the taste of Booth Tarkington's *Monsieur Beaucaire,* which London had folded to its public bosom. England was one country, he said, "where a play with an anti-national basis may have a popular success." He could imagine "New York's fury over a play in which not all the soldiers of King George would be scoundrels and poltroons, nor all the rebels heroes and saints."

He had a word of rebuke for another American playwright, Augustus Thomas, and his *The Earl of Pawtucket.* In America, Max said (29 June 1907), the play had had a great success "by reason of Mr. Lawrence D'Orsay's performance of the hero, who is the latest (and I do hope the last) apparition of the ghost of Lord Dundreary. In America, doubtless, the apparitions of the ghost have not been so constant as here. Possibly, even the ghost is mistaken for a creature of flesh and blood—for a type that really exists in England."

Sometimes he gave to American players the enthusiasm he withheld from their plays. He had the impression (23 September 1905) that "in America the acting is on a higher level than here—that it is more natural and better disciplined." One obvious advantage of the American theatre was its full supply of competent ingenues: "In our theatre ingenues do not begin to approach competence until they have long ceased to seem ingenuous. In America there is, apparently, no such retardment." He thought Marie Doro one of the finest: "But, though I have not seen her match, I have seen many . . . who might be mentioned in the same breath with her. In England, we never mention our ingenues. It would be brutal."

He had mingled feelings about the behavior of an American chorus and its British counterpart. "I remember," he said on 30 October 1909, "when *The Belle of New York* was first produced in London everyone prophesied that the example of that bright, hard-working American chorus would revolutionise the methods of the chorus at the Gaiety. For a while, I think, there was a slight change—a slight semblance of modest effort. But the old local tradition soon resumed its sway, and will never be overthrown"; and all the Tory in Max rejoiced.

He found Ethel Barrymore "a fluttering amateur," but a fascinating person on the stage. Her charm was hard to analyze: it was Protean, perhaps best summed up as Pierrot-like. He did not admire Billie Burke. According to his theory of acting, character should be expressed through the medium of the actor; Miss Burke obscured herself behind a cloud of funny little acquired mannerisms. The nearest parallel he could remember was a performance in a music hall by an American gentleman who described himself as a "child impersonator." He didn't recall the name, but he did identify another "very peculiar" American comedian of the music halls, R. G. Knowles, who invented the concept of the signature tune, using the opening bars of Mendelssohn's "Wedding March." In 1894 Max had caricatured Knowles for *Pick-Me-Up.*

Not in a review, but in a letter to an American, he commented on E. H. Sothern and Julia Marlowe in *Hamlet:* "The latter seemed to me nothing, and the former worse than nothing." And again to the same friend he wrote that he had been to "a very dull farce by Mr. Thomas, a compatriot of yours and personally a very nice and amusing fellow (I met him at dinner a few nights ago) but dreadful as a writer of farces. He wrote 'In Missouri' which I remember seeing and enjoying when I was in Philadelphia all those years ago."

Sometimes all those years ago came rolling back to him from the other side. In 1908 his devastating review of Jerome K. Jerome's *Passing of the Third Floor Back,* reprinted in the Boston *Herald,* was called "an extravagantly ferocious attack quite in the savage spirit of the old *Saturday Review* of Thackeray's day. . . . The present editors could not write more bitterly about the United States and all that is in them." Max was called childish for his rudeness in describing Jerome as a tenth-rate writer; and from the vehemence of his onslaught one might visualize this Englishman as a "huge, black-bearded person." It would be a mistake, for "when Max Beerbohm visited Boston—where he is pleasantly remembered by some—he was smug and amiable, aesthetic and undersized. His face and arrangement of hair reminded one of a learned seal. . . . And in an interview with a reporter of the *Herald* staff he bitterly regretted that local firemen had extinguished a fire the day before and thus deprived him of a beautiful sight. . . ." Thus did fire rise from the embers.

Since American players were so frequently crossing the Atlantic, the impresario Daniel Frohman had the idea of using the companies in transit to present plays on shipboard. Max looked on that suggestion with horror, declaring (18 July 1908) "whenever I go to America I shall choose an unfrohmanized vessel." He recalled his own crossing euphemistically: "Twelve years have elapsed since I was in America. The voyage in those days was a romantic and wonderful experience." One was cut off from the world, with only the sea to watch, "in sacramental detachment from all other things." Marconi had changed all that and now Mr. Frohman wished to add further complications.

His attitude towards Frohman's experiment in the repertory theatre at the Duke of York's was more ambivalent. He had opened with George Meredith's *The Sentimentalists,* scenery and costumes by Will Rothenstein, and on 12 March 1910 Max congratulated him: "Not only has he stepped in (unwanted and eyed somewhat askance) to do what Englishmen, in national conclave, have for so many years, so solemnly, been urging one another to do: he is doing it very well indeed. And, even if, to a patriot's soul, there is anything ugly in the thought that this astute foreigner seems likely to make a 'corner' in all our most vital dramatists, no one will be so sulky as not to thank him meanwhile, for having evoked . . . the great and gracious shade of George Meredith."

After this praise Max was to write only one more review before concluding his career as dramatic critic.

VI

Introducing Miss Florence Kahn

IN MEMPHIS, Tennessee, one summer morning in the early Nineties, a slender, auburn-haired girl held a lighted candle breast-high and recited Portia's speech from the *Merchant of Venice*. Miss Florence Kahn, would-be actress, was practicing breath control.

In 1908, Max Beerbohm, reviewing Miss Kahn's performance as Rebecca West in *Rosmersholm,* wrote in the *Saturday Review,* "She has a voice of great power and resonance."

Florence's father, Louis Kahn, had come to Memphis from Baden, Germany, in the 1860's and set himself up in the dry-goods business. With his marriage to Pauline Freiberg, of a prominent Cincinnati family, two merchandising firms were united, and business prospered. Between 1866 and 1869 three sons were born to them—Henry, Silas, and Joseph —so the arrival of a daughter on 3 March 1876 was welcome; then after Florence, more sons came—Isaac, Lipman, Morris, and Samuel. Mrs. Kahn managed this predominantly masculine household with an easy but capable touch. Although the family was close-knit, each member pursued his own interests, but all had a common meeting-ground in music. Each boy learned to play at least one instrument, and Florence studied piano. In 1896 the Kahn Military Band and Orchestra was accepting engagements for social and civic affairs. The boys all played in it, but Florence was excluded: her absorbing interest was the stage.

In their adult years, Silas and Isaac became professional musicians; the rest chose other callings. Morris was a civil engineer with a degree from Purdue University; Henry went into real estate; Lipman, known as "Mannie," turned to medicine and became a surgeon in New York City; and Sam, with an interest in writing, became Sunday editor of the Memphis *Commercial Appeal.* "The Kahns had ninety percent of the brains in Tennessee," said an old friend of the family, "and Florence was all brains."

During her girlhood Florence's best friend was Martha Michel, and

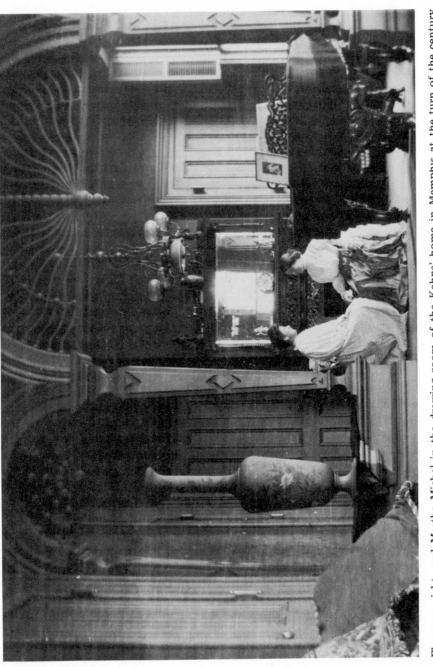

Florence, right, and Martha Michel in the drawing room of the Kahns' home in Memphis at the turn of the century. Courtesy of Constance Kahn Starr.

indeed the friendship lasted until Martha's death in 1933. The Kahns' and the Michels' back yards adjoined and the girls skipped back and forth from one house to the other. They usually walked home from school together, arm in arm, talking of their lessons or their plans for the future. Florence never wavered in her desire to go on the stage. She was not much interested in boys—she saw plenty of them at home—and she was considered too independent to be popular, but she had many friends and admirers in the town. If her strap of books seemed too heavy, she would stop the street-car and ask the conductor to toss them off as he passed her house. Martha thought this rather high-handed, but the books were always on the lawn when Florence reached home. Once, however, when Florence as well as her books were on the streetcar, it collided with a train; Florence, white-lipped and shaking, was lifted out through a window. But she shed no tears. All her life Florence bore suffering bravely.

Like most well-brought-up children of the period, Florence went to dancing school. Here she not only learned the steps of the moment, acquired grace of movement and the niceties of deportment but she also increased her enthusiasm for the theatre. The dancing mistress had been an actress who had studied at a dramatic school in Denver where Douglas Fairbanks had been a fellow student. After a brief career on the stage she had returned to Memphis to open a dance studio—and five Kahn children were included in her first class.

At home Florence glided through the rooms or floated effortlessly down the long stairway, intent on cultivating bodily poise. The family dressmaker who came to make her frocks never had to complain of her uneasy wriggling as a dress was fitted. Florence stood gracefully erect, revolving as directed, and sometimes reciting Shakespeare to the admiring seamstress. On warm summer afternoons Florence used to gather the neighborhood children under the trees and entertain them with stories or act out little plays for them. One member of these audiences still remembers the lovely quality of her voice and the charm of her reading.

As a girl, Florence was not thought pretty, certainly not beautiful, but her features were regular and her eyes expressive. Her hair was red— not sandy or carroty, but a deep, luxuriant auburn. Later, as an actress on the stage, she was called "beautiful" with "glorious Titian hair" and her every motion was "pure poetry."

Memphis was a theatre town and road companies with such distinguished stars as Joseph Jefferson and Lillian Russell came to the old Opera House. Florence saw them all, watching and studying their technique, dreaming of the day when she would stand behind those footlights reciting the lines to which she now listened with such delight. When she was fifteen, she played her first part in an amateur production.

After graduating from the public high school Florence attended the Clara Conway Institute, a finishing school for girls in Memphis. Miss Conway boasted that her pupils were encouraged to think, not to memorize, but every Friday afternoon was given up to readings and recitations; Florence unfailingly presented Shakespeare. She left the Conway School in June 1894, taking her part in the graduation exercises. The élite of Memphis society proudly watched as its daughters, clad in Grecian robes with golden sashes and sandals, presented a program of songs and readings.

The next year Florence studied with Miss Grace Lewellyn, who had opened a studio which was to become the Memphis Conservatory. Although Miss Lewellyn admired Ibsen and a few years later gave the first performance of one of his plays in Memphis, she called her student recitals by such names as "Seasonable Tid-Bits," and it was in "Quaint Conceits" that Florence made her valedictory appearance. A reporter for the *Commercial Appeal* called her recitation of "Irene, Queen of Cyprus" a creditable performance, but Miss Lewellyn declared she was "an undiscovered genius" who must be given an opportunity to develop her talent.

It is a tribute to the good sense and understanding of Louis and Pauline Kahn that they recognized the validity of Florence's ambition and agreed to let her attend the American Academy of Dramatic Arts in New York. Franklin H. Sargent had founded the Academy in 1884 with the purpose of placing the teaching of acting on the same footing with the teaching of any other art by employing similar methods. Julia Marlowe had been an early student; May Robson was on the faculty, and David Belasco was an adviser. The course covered two years, and in both years Florence was at the head of her class. In February 1896 she appeared in the first English performance in the States of Maeterlinck's *L'Intérieur,* before an audience which included William Dean Howells, James Gibbons Huneker, and Edward A. Dithmar, then dramatic critic of the *New York Times.*

When she graduated 27 April 1897 she was already signed to play the feminine lead in the road company of *The Girl I Left Behind Me.* This melodrama of an Indian uprising against an isolated government outpost opened in Buffalo and proceeded westward. As Kate Kennison, daughter of the fort commander, Florence was left behind nearly three hundred times through thirty-five weeks in twenty-six states. In February 1898 she fulfilled a girlhood dream and played in Memphis, and all the Clara Conway girls attended the performance.

The monotony of such repetition convinced her that she did not like long engagements, and in the spring of 1898 she joined Paul Gilmore in *The Musketeers* as Lady de Winter. They opened in New York, then went on tour and ended with another week in New York in June.

After several months of inactivity she was rescued by Paul Kester, the playwright who had dramatized *The Musketeers* (and whose play about Dorothy Vernon would annoy Max profoundly some years later), and John Blair, the actor, who were forming an Independent Theatre for a Course of Modern Plays at the Carnegie Lyceum in New York. This project was more to Florence's liking. European dramatists such as Ibsen, Hauptmann and Sudermann were beginning to ripple the stream of the American theatre and the Independent was dedicated to widening the current. Its declared object was the "improvement of taste, the promotion of sincerity, and the encouragement of art in the drama;" or, as a plainspoken critic interpreted, "giving for the few the plays the multitude does not want to see."

With the opening production of Echegaray's *El Gran Galeoto,* Florence Kahn as Christine won instant acclaim. Said a critic in the *Cosmopolitan:* "When the curtain fell . . . the audience realized that, whatever might be served up to them in the name of art, they would return to enjoy the acting of a young woman who was wonderful to the top of a glorious head of hair."

Another mission of the Independent Theatre was to give trial presentations of plays which professional managers wished to see on the stage before committing themselves to production. Such a performance was given of John Oliver Hobbes's (Mrs. Craigie's) *Osberne and Ursyne.* After the opening performance a writer in the *World* declared the play should now be entitled to a just and eternal rest, but added that it was "a triumph for Miss Florence Kahn, the newly discovered dramatic genius." Edward Dithmar of the *New York Times* said, "Miss Kahn's merits are more than counterbalanced by her faults. She is young and will learn many things if she is not spoiled by ignorant flattery and ribald overpraise." For the remainder of the Independent's season, Dithmar seemed dedicated to preserving Florence from that fate. Of her performance in Hervieu's *The Ties,* he said the part needed an actress of larger experience, but she had at least made the irritating and objectionable heroine intelligible. What she needed was practical experience: a year under the discipline of Richard Mansfield would do her much good.

Other reviewers were not so intent on saving Florence's modesty. Clement Scott, British critic who was in New York, thought she would be one of the leading actresses of the future, and Norman Hapgood said she had lifted her part to a plane more poetical than anything else in the production.

The beginning of the new century found her in Ibsen's *Master Builder,* not seen before in America. Dithmar found her "a mixture of poetic weirdness and conventional melodrama." Still, her acting was the only notable feature of the play. Her personality was strange, almost uncanny, but her career should be very interesting. The friendly Norman Hapgood thought her acting luminous and able. However, *The Master Builder* was soon withdrawn.

In January 1900 theatrical columns carried the news that Richard Mansfield was looking for a new leading lady and had chosen Miss Kahn. Dithmar noted that this engagement had followed close upon his own suggestion; she was not yet a competent actress, but she had unusual gifts—if only she were not spoiled by praise.

Florence now took on added stature in the theatrical world. Richard Mansfield was considered America's leading actor, and to appear with him was a mark of success. She was sought after for interviews and her pictures were seen in leading magazines. On 2 March she played Kate in Constance Garnett's translation of Ostrovsky's *The Storm,* the Independent's last production. Dithmar said she showed glimpses of indubitable power. She was going at once to join Mansfield, and the sympathy and best wishes of her fellow workers would go with her.

During the Course of Modern Plays, Mrs. Kahn had come to New York to be with her daughter and they lived in the same apartment house as Paul Kester, the playwright, his brother Vaughan, the novelist, and their mother. The two families were very friendly. Florence admired the Kester brothers and looked to them for counsel; they liked to be looked up to by such a pretty young girl, whom they sometimes called "Casey." This pleasant and close association ended when Florence left to join Mansfield, whose company was now on tour in New Orleans.

From that city a friend wrote Paul Kester, "I saw the ineffable Florence with swishing skirts on the ferryboat as it took the Mansfield company across the Mississippi Galvestonwise. She was charming and apparently feeling out of place," adding, "I think she will weep before she learns to laugh—the rungs of that ladder are spikes and hurt the feet."

At first Mansfield ignored her, but suddenly she was given the part of Roxane in *Cyrano de Bergerac.* She played it with great triumph in her home town on 28 March 1900, and the Kahns felt justified in their decision to let her go to New York. The tour lasted four more weeks, ending in Chicago late in April when Mansfield's health forced him to cancel further performances. He had chosen *Henry V* for his coming season, and Florence was to be his leading lady.

The spectacular production of this play opened in New York on 3 October with great pomp and pageantry. Florence did not play Katharine of Valois, but made a sensational appearance as the Chorus. Wearing Grecian robes and with her glorious hair spread over her shoulders, she read the opening lines to each act, not from the stage, but from a box over the stage. Norman Hapgood said she was the most beautiful thing in the whole play. He went further and said in the *Bookman:*

> Prophesying about actors is a hazardous amusement, but, if I were to pick out, in the whole range of American players, just one actor under thirty who promised to gain a very high reputation, I should not hesitate a second before naming Miss Kahn. She has a something which makes for greatness.

He looked upon her as "a possibly notable tragedienne of the future." Dithmar said she spoke her lines intelligently and with much grace.

After some weeks in New York the company took to the road, traveling in a special train of ten cars which Mansfield specified should not go more than twenty miles an hour because he dreaded accidents. Thus Mansfield and his leading lady crept regally across the country, being royally received in every city. But behind the scenes Mansfield was a czar and a despot; and such tyranny was not taken easily by a red-haired actress. As the company turned back towards New York a writer in *Munsey's Magazine* hinted at trouble between the star and the girl from Memphis, saying that "the combination of Mansfield and Kahn may be akin to the meeting of Greek with Greek."

It was. After a week in Brooklyn with revivals of *The First Violin, Beau Brummell,* and *Dr. Jekyll and Mr. Hyde,* word went out that the star and his leading lady were separating, Mansfield saying that Florence was now capable of heading her own company. She had no sooner left Mansfield and signed for the next season with James Hackett than she regretted her decision and spent an unhappy summer in New York with Mrs. Kester, trying in vain to secure her release from Hackett. Nevertheless she opened 2 September with him in *Don Caesar's Return* in New York. Her reviews as Maritana were not entirely favorable. Paul Kester wrote his mother that rumor had it Florence was leaving; Hackett was not satisfied with her work. A month later she withdrew from the cast and Kester declared Hackett had behaved very shabbily.

For a while thereafter things went badly for the young actress, and she finally returned to Memphis on the edge of a nervous breakdown, complicated by sorrow over the death of her father. On 1 June 1903 the New York *Telegraph* contained a report that she was seriously ill at her home, the victim of extreme worry and anxiety brought about by

In June 1901 this photograph announced that Florence would be "Mr. James Hackett's leading woman next season." Theatre Collection, the New York Public Library.

her premature prominence, prodigal publicity, and unkind criticism. It was uncertain whether the beautiful Titian-haired leading lady would ever return to the stage.

But she did. Less than a year later she was again in New York, enthusiastically joining the Century Players in another undertaking to uplift the American stage. Sydney Rosenfield, their founder, optimistically hoped they would become the National Theatre, but from the outset bad luck dogged the project. After several out-of-town appearances where Florence had consistently good reviews, the company opened 14 March 1904 in New York with *Much Ado About Nothing,* in which Florence did not have a part. On 22 March, however, she played Rebecca West in the first American presentation of Ibsen's *Rosmersholm*—a calamitous affair for all concerned. Critics could not decide whether the badly cut play, the crude staging, the garish lighting, or the bad acting was most to blame, but Dithmar of the *Times* chose Florence: he said she acted all the time and was never a live woman. The play was withdrawn.

Sudermann's *Battle of the Butterflies* was already in rehearsal but it was canceled. Rosenfield did manage to rally enough of his cast for a week at the Amphion Theatre in Brooklyn, and here Florence played Rose in the Sudermann drama. With this engagement the Century Players' crusade was over.

Now what? She wondered if London might be more friendly to Continental drama than unenlightened New York. Although her brothers were dubious of that, they approved of her having a little holiday and they would help with expenses. Norman Hapgood also encouraged her, saying later in his autobiography, "During my theatre days I had a young friend [Florence] from whom I drew much intellectual comfort. . . . It was partly because she understood so much, especially in the line of Ibsen and the German realists, that she found life in the New York theatre so exasperating." He gave her a letter of introduction to Max.

Florence arrived in London in the early summer of 1904, registered at the Grand Hotel near Charing Cross, and shortly thereafter Max came to call. He was charmed by this American visitor who could speak so knowledgeably of the theatre, of his friend Clyde Fitch, and of Mansfield, whom he had never seen. He invited her to dinner at his mother's house, warning her that the street was pronounced "Barkley," and advising her to take a four-wheeler instead of a hansom, which was not so safe. This was the beginning of Max's unfailing solicitude for Florence's comfort and well-being.

Only a little earlier—on 12 April 1904—Max had written Reggie the news that Constance Collier had broken their engagement. So perhaps it now seemed that solace had been sent him in this shy, pretty girl from the States, so unlike the dominant Constance.

He lost no time in establishing their friendship. He took her to the theatre to see *The Edge of the Storm*. They often dined together at a little restaurant on Jermyn Street where they had a favorite waiter; they walked on Hampstead Heath and had tea at Jack Straw's Castle. In the late summer just before Max left for his annual holiday at Dieppe, Florence went to Berlin; but she could not forget Max, for he wrote her frequently and worried when she did not reply. They both returned to London in September and the pleasant meetings were resumed. Often as soon as he returned home after an evening spent with Florence, he would at once write her a little note to say how much he had enjoyed seeing her, or to suggest a time for seeing her again. They played a little word game together, one in which Max delighted as much as did Florence. On 21 October they were in Trafalgar Square for the Empire Day celebration. In November he took her to Oxford to see Merton College, and the boat races.

What Florence did about trying for a place in the theatre, what help she had from her letters of introduction, what advice Max could give her, remain a mystery. One can imagine the difficulties a young and relatively unknown American actress would face in trying to enter the field of serious drama in London. One can only imagine, but the outcome is known: no chance came to her and in November she returned to the States to try again at home.

As soon as she reached New York, Max's correspondence with his "dear little friend" was resumed. He wrote twice a week, timing his letters to catch the fastest liner. She told him of her hopes and disappointments. Midwinter produced no engagements: she was definitely catalogued as an Ibsen actress and there were few opportunities for such. Then, miraculously, one came.

In early March 1905 Ibsen's last play, *When We Dead Awaken,* was produced for six matinées at the Knickerbocker in New York with Florence as the Strange Lady. Dithmar worried about her deathly pallor but conceded that she read her lines beautifully, while the faithful Norman Hapgood thought her whole embodiment of the character was thrillingly effective.

Her return to the stage won considerable attention in the dramatic columns. A writer in the *Dramatic Mirror* found Miss Kahn like olives: "You have to develop a taste for her and when you have painfully mastered it, you may enjoy yourself with the Kahn cult, for there is one, unhappily for Florence, for to occasion a cult is to stop growing."

James Gibbons Huneker, versatile critic of art, music, and the stage, devoted his May 1905 article in the *Metropolitan* to Ibsen and Florence Kahn. He apologized for the play—Ibsen was over seventy when he wrote it—but in many ways it had been well presented. In spite of Florence's "monotony of diction," he liked her Irene better than her earlier Rebecca. "Her uncanny personality—I hope she will pardon my freedom!—is not so much unlike Irene's." Miss Kahn was given to projecting her temperament "through stained glass . . . America is not her field; we like more modern, more theatric methods"; she might do better in Germany. "A puzzling young woman! A Maeterlinck young woman!" And she was "something to gaze upon."

In spite of Huneker's remarks about her diction, Florence was pleased with the notice and the importance of being featured in a popular magazine. Maeterlinck was one of her heroes and to be associated with him was flattering. She felt rather warmly toward Huneker and told Max so. This confession was to contribute to Max's forthcoming judgment on the American critic.

VII

Beerbohm *vs* Huneker

JAMES GIBBONS HUNEKER, born in Philadelphia in 1857, by the mid-Nineties was well established in New York as a critic of art, literature, drama, and music; he was noted for his wit, his verve, and his unconventionality. Besides a study of Ibsen (1879) he had done gossipy columns for the *Recorder* and the *Musical Courier* before becoming dramatic critic for the New York *Sun* in 1900. He had read Max in the *Yellow Book* and mentioned his presence in the States in 1895 in the *Musical Courier*. When the notice of Max's appointment to the *Saturday Review* reached him, he noted it in his "Raconteur" column, calling Max a clever, insolent person who was a brother of Beerbohm Tree, the actor. Max, he said, was by way of being an actor too. In 1902 he reprinted a picture of Max he had found in the Sunday *Tribune,* saying it was a fair likeness of this brilliant prose master from whom, some day, he expected a wonderful, witty play.

He often made some observation in the *Sun* about Max's articles in the *Saturday*. In October 1903 he cited Max's "A Contrast in Hospitality," agreeing that Americans would fawn over visiting English writers, but the American playwright in London had his troubles. And Yankees, former subjects of Great Britain, would grovel before anything stamped with the words MADE IN LONDON.

Huneker was one of the first Americans to recognize George Bernard Shaw as a dramatist; also, he had met Shaw and found him congenial. Once, in getting ready an article on Shaw for the *Metropolitan,* he had been unable to find a photograph of him and so had sent the editor a caricature by Max, saying he had seen it somewhere five or six years ago and didn't think it had been reproduced in the States; he fancied it would be all right if credit were given.

In 1905 Huneker published his *Iconoclasts,* containing a long chapter called "The Quintessence of Shaw" in which he quoted material which Shaw had sent him as private information and not for publication. He

78

sent a copy to Max, who acknowledged it in the *Saturday* of 29 July 1905 under the heading, "A Yellow Critic." Max wrote that he had received an American book by an author he had been told was much admired on the other side of the Atlantic; otherwise he had no knowledge of him. He hoped he was a young man, a very young man. Apparently he was not a stripling, for he had related meeting Shaw in Bayreuth and drinking beer with him, but American children were very precocious and perhaps such a talker as Mr. Shaw might share his thoughts with one of them. Max noted that Mr. Huneker had written four books, but that did not disprove his youth if they were all written as hastily as this one appeared to have been. Max admitted that the author had vitality and ability, and he might do well in the future, if he worked hard to improve. He was too sensational—

> He writes up the subject of dramatic literature just as his humble colleagues write up the subject of a fire or a murder. "Whim" wrote Mr. Emerson over his study door. "Vim" wrote Mr. Huneker over the door of the cable car in which he presumably does his work.

Max did not find the violence and vulgarity the worst faults. He objected most to the carelessness:

> The writing is so bad that you have to read between the lines to discover what Mr. Huneker means, and when, as often happens, he means nothing, you naturally resent the waste of time.

Max disliked Huneker's journalistic style though it might please the men in Wall Street as they devoured it with their quick lunch. He admitted Huneker's interest in literature, but he disagreed with most of his remarks on Shaw. Huneker lacked training, but perhaps he was young enough to reform. If he wasn't, he might be useful to new writers as a bad example.

Huneker was stunned by this onslaught. He had hoped for a friendly reception by this man he admired and had usually said good things about. The situation drew comment from several literary periodicals. Harry Thurston Peck, editor of the American *Bookman,* printed part of the review in the September number, saying Max had laid bare Huneker's literary vices and those of other American writers given to the practice of uneasy writing; he thought Huneker's book covered a good deal of ground and he took Max to task for writing so infrequently; he urged dramatic critics to fire at each other, and said he wouldn't mind if every shot proved fatal—except for these two men who were among the few who should survive. Percival Pollard, book editor of *Town Topics,* defended Huneker in that paper, and H. L. Mencken later called the *Saturday* article an idiotic assault on Max's part.

Huneker's troubles were not over. He was engaged in editing Shaw's dramatic criticisms, but when Shaw saw *Iconoclasts* and Max's review of it, he wrote the American two long and blistering letters, deploring his breach of confidence and giving him further advice about his writing. When Huneker's *Dramatic Opinions* was published in 1906, the American made no mention of his difficulties; his preface was well tempered and mild, though he referred to Max as a "gentle mid-Victorian."

Then in April the English edition came out, and Max struck again. He began by criticizing the book's format—no title on the pages, no index—but let not the index be compiled by Mr. Huneker, who had no capacity for taking pains as was proved by the misprints and bad punctuation, sources of great annoyance to Max. Again he admitted Huneker's writings were admired in America, and he recalled one sample of them, "a pretentious and loudly muzzy book" which he had "gibbeted" in the *Saturday* a few years before. He had then thought Mr. Huneker was a young man; now he knew he was middle-aged, so it was not surprising that his style had not improved. If Americans were so illiterate as to think well of Huneker they probably needed to have Shaw introduced to them, but in England it was ridiculous to have him introduced by a man so little and so unfavorably known. But Max thought it a rather witty half-truth that he himself was a gentle mid-Victorian. In his conclusion he came back to Shaw and the quantity of his essays in various newspaper files which G.B.S. didn't allow to be republished. Now perhaps something could be done about them.

Huneker did not publicly show his resentment until September 1908 when there appeared in the *Sun* his mock drama called "Blarney at the Box Office," with Shaw, Max Nordau, author of *Degeneration,* and Max Beerbohm as characters; it was later included, with splenetic additions, in his book *Unicorns.* The satire ended with a jibe which Huneker repeated more than once: Beerbohm as "Little Maxie" saying, "Remember, I'm the only living replica of Charles Lamb," and Shaw replying, "You mean cold mutton."

When Huneker's *Egoists* appeared in 1909, the review in the *Saturday* was unsigned, but the Maxian hand was evident. It declared that Huneker wrote in the choicest diction of Wall Street. If it was an American talent for saying a great deal and meaning nothing, Mr. Huneker stood in the front rank of such writers. Max gave the book a very thorough review but could find nothing good to say of it.

That seems to have ended Max's participation in this feud. He did not get a chance at Huneker's next book, for the American gave orders that the *Saturday Review* was not to receive a copy. Max, he said, was itching to get his hands on it—so let him buy a copy; he had given it a preliminary blast two weeks before, which showed his humor. But that blast has not been discovered.

In *Steeplejack,* his autobiography, Huneker had the last word. He related how Max, usually so languid and affected, had bowled him over, possibly because he was an American. He recalled his epithet, "mid-Victorian," and wondered why he had not called Max "Mud-Victorian," for London was clogged with literary mud during the *Yellow Book* period. If he had called him that he could have understood what followed. As it was, he said, Max went up in the air: he had got his goat.

Much of this literary by-play is described by Arnold T. Schwab in his valuable biography of Huneker. In preparing this study in 1952, he questioned Max about his part in the squabble. Max replied that he must have known that Huneker wasn't a young man so his hope for improvement must be presumed a jibe. He didn't think he'd ever discussed Huneker with Shaw or Clyde Fitch; he hadn't known that Huneker had attacked Fitch, but unless he had attacked him unfairly, Max wouldn't have objected. Max apparently answered the biographer's questions honestly, as he remembered the facts after fifty years—but his recollection was at fault, for in July 1905 Max had written Florence from Dieppe:

> I wrote yesterday the last article for the present, a rather virulent attack on Huneker, apropos of "Iconoclasts." And rather disingenuous too, for I have pretended to believe him quite a young man. I really wanted to wound the gentleman. I simply detest his writing. And I think I detest him more because *you* like it. A sort of jealousy enters me! I want to make a fool of him in your eyes I think. I really did enjoy writing the article. Probably you will think the article very unfair (as indeed it is) and not at all damaging (as I hope it *will* be).

There spoke the candid Max. In another letter, written Good Friday 1907, he told her he had much enjoyed reading the book of Shaw's criticism. Its only defect was an asinine introduction by that ass Huneker who took rather witty revenge on him by calling him "mid-Victorian." There was a touch of truth in that, Max admitted.

VIII

The Dear Little Friend

IN THE LATE SUMMER of 1905 Florence joined the Castle Square Players in Boston, not an ordinary stock company, but an endowed repertory company of which Winthrop Ames was the leading spirit. Max was glad she was going to Boston; he remembered the city pleasantly. Here her versatility was put to the test, for she played a new rôle every week. She was scheduled to play Cleopatra, but gave up the part because she distrusted her ability to play it. Max was intrigued with the idea of a red-haired Queen of the Nile; he promised he would now read the play, but gave up the idea when she gave up the part, writing to her, "so my education suffers through your wrongful hesitancy."

During the day Florence often went to the Boston Public Library where she admired the Sargent murals, and Max said he would tell Sargent of her approbation. One of her letters Max said was really in blank verse; and he so transcribed it for her:

> *And though the rhododendrons look forlorn*
> *The grass is green, and if you do not mind*
> *The splashing of the fountain (I do not)*
> *You may read here in comfort*
> *With the reference library just upstairs.*

He insisted she must be happy to break into blank verse.

As usual not everything went smoothly for Florence, and Max was amused by the accounts of her troubles; still, he thought the company must be well managed. However, on 4 December 1905 Florence left the Players and returned to New York; she had had enough of stock.

Her next experience was even more distressing. The last of January 1906, Winchell Smith signed her to play with Arnold Daly in a road production of Shaw's *You Never Can Tell,* opening 4 February in St. Louis. She studied the part on the train and had only one rehearsal before the opening. The audience liked her and the press was good, but after three performances Daly called her in, saying he had grave doubts as to her suitability for the part. Under those circumstances, Florence said, she would withdraw from the cast, and did so. (Daly had hired and fired ten leading ladies in the past two years.)

Once more Florence returned to Memphis, where Max wrote her in February, "It is nearly two years since I called at the Grand Hotel and met the dear little friend. I can hardly believe it."

Florence apparently thought two years was long enough for dear friends to be separated and in the summer she returned to London and a happy reunion with Max. The little dinners were resumed, the walks on the Heath, the evenings at the play, and now he introduced her to Reggie Turner who feared she did not like him. When the *Daily Mail* commissioned Max to go to Italy and record his impressions, she went as far as Paris with him and he loved seeing her see Paris for the first time.

This visit to Italy first convinced Max that here would be a desirable place to live. He saw Rome, Verona, Padua, Florence, Venice, and Siena —to which he lost his heart because it was so "cosy." The sight of so many American tourists staring at the antiquities awakened in him the fear that eventually all the treasures of Europe would be seized by predatory Americans. He had already in the *Saturday Review* indulged in a fanciful account of J. Pierpont Morgan buying Anne Hathaway's cottage for two million pounds and taking it to America, duty free. A few months before his Italian journey he had discussed for his readers this acquisitive habit:

> [It is] very natural that the Americans, having no history of their own, should be so much keener than we on the "antiquities" that abound in Europe. It is very natural that they, having no art worth mentioning, should eagerly covet for their own country the objects of art that we take as a matter of course and hardly notice. I have never been inclined to join in the outcry that is raised whenever some famous work of art . . . is in danger of being spirited across the Atlantic. Why . . . should we play the dog in the manger? . . . Why grudge this or that morsel of beauty to our starving "cousins"? Especially too, when these poor relations are prepared to pay so handsomely for the transfer.

Now when he saw the green-bronze horses of St. Mark's in Venice, he wondered about their fate:

> They have caught the eye of this and that American magnate. For a time they are held captive by the law that forbids exportation of

Florence as the Chorus in Richard Mansfield's production of
Henry V—the part for which she received her widest acclaim in
America. Theatre Collection, the New York Public Library.

works of art. But modern Italy is very commercial, and, as soon as it is in a position to dispense with the money brought in by tourists, will gladly dispose of its masterpieces to the highest bidder. Two or three generations of American magnates may have passed before that time comes. . . . And so they are already restive, these pawing horses, these passengers; restive for the Atlantic and for the cornices of the Capitol at Washington. Yes, it is there they will air themselves—for a while. And afterwards where? In the midst of some yellow race, maybe. All empires perish.

Florence returned to London before Max, and, with no prospects of an engagement, decided to sail for home. From Italy Max protested: why didn't she wait till he was there? Perhaps Granville-Barker (Harley Granville-Barker, playwright and producer) would have a part for her. So Florence waited, but when the Granville-Barker possibility came to nothing she went back to New York. Her mother was at the boat to meet her, and reporters, too, for she was still a theatrical personage. The *New York Times* said she was back with a lot of Paris evening gowns and a new play, the identity of which was not revealed.

She settled in with her doctor brother Lipman—"Mannie"—at 73 West 116th Street, an address Max had trouble in remembering. He thought the system of calling streets by numbers was as unpractical as it was hideous, asking her, "Who can remember a number? Names have a meaning—something the memory can catch hold of." But his uncertainty did not prevent the steady flow of his letters.

In January 1907 Florence saw Paul Kester again, and one of her letters to him is preserved in the Kester Collection at the New York Public Library.

> My dear Mr. Kester:
>
> Your letter with all the old dear kindness made me feel for a moment as if nothing had happened, as if the years had not gone by. . . . But much has passed, though in a way, nothing is changed. I am still trying—and shall try on—for a while longer . . .
>
> Yes, I, too, love England and the people I know there. If only my own folk or some of them were there I should not have returned. I have been there twice now, each time for about five months. I only returned in November. Unfortunately, I came away at what, it seems, was a wrong time, for if I had stayed a while longer I might have had work there, but I heard of that opportunity only after I returned. . . .

Your letter, though it did make me sad in a way, was a real pleasure to me—and I thank you for it.

I send my love to you all and my wishes as always for your happiness.

Faithfully, Florence Kahn.

When no suitable part developed in New York, Max tried to console her, saying:

So few actresses have any real humanity or any intellectual interests outside of their art. You *are* rather an exception . . . that is a certain fastidious idealism in you, a shrinking from contact with dull, false people—a disinclination to meet them halfway—an incapacity for those little compromises and amenities and that "push" which is so horribly necessary in this world—prevent you from being at the moment on the little pinnacle that is being reserved for you.

Florence was cheered by Max's diagnosis of her difficulties and his faith in her ultimate victory. She, too, felt more hopeful, for during her absence the American public had grown more tolerant of Ibsen. Minnie Maddern Fiske had been well received as Nora in *A Doll's House,* but a more startling success had been scored by a diminutive Russian actress, Alla Nazimova, in *Hedda Gabler.* Suddenly the part of Mrs. Elvsted became vacant and Florence stepped neatly into the rôle alongside Nazimova. John Blair was in the cast and he may have suggested Florence, who was now happy to be again embarked on what the critic William Winter had called "the murky sea of Ibsenism." Max wrote her in support of her conception of the part, "Mrs. Elvsted is a normal, well grounded, human person, definitely a foil to the hysterical and inhuman Hedda." He was so glad she was acting again, but was prepared for the worst; "I suppose Ibsen doesn't run much longer in New York than in London."

Before Florence left London, Max had been working on some more chaplets for his "Christmas Garland," seven of which appeared in the *Saturday Review* during December 1906. On 23 and 30 December the New York *Herald* reprinted six of them with illustrations in its Sunday magazine. Florence quickly sent them to Max, who studied the accompanying pictures critically. From the parodies of Shaw, Kipling, Henry James, Maurice Hewlett, John Davidson, and George Moore, he chose the illustrated parody on James, "The Mote in the Middle Distance," and sent it to Edmund Gosse, saying, "The compatriot artist has preserved in his drawing something of the mystic quality of H. J.'s narration—though the

lettering above is not happily chosen, I think." An unusually kind comment for Max.

His parody of Chesterson, titled "Some Damnable Errors about Christmas," came out in the American *Bookman* for January 1907, and in
February he wrote Florence he was struggling with "A Morris for Mayday"
—which bore no sign of such effort when it appeared in *Harper's* the
following October.

IX

The Actress and the Critic

FLORENCE'S ENGAGEMENT to play Mrs. Elvsted with Alla Nazimova in *Hedda Gabler* began 11 March 1907, and was terminated 7 April by a black-bordered telegram with the news of her mother's death. Shocked and grief-stricken, Florence bade a hasty goodbye to the company and started for Memphis. Had she known it, she was bidding farewell to her acting career in the United States, for never again was she to appear on an American stage.

It was a sad homecoming. In spite of the distance which often separated them, mother and daughter had been very close, and Florence knew she would feel this loss all her life. Aware of the uncertainties of an actress's life, Mrs. Kahn had bequeathed her daughter one hundred dollars a month for her lifetime. This legacy was to take precedence over other bequests and her brother Isaac was to see that she received it. In 1907 a hundred dollars was a generous amount and this inheritance was always conscientiously paid by her brothers.

In April Max had his largest and most successful show at the Carfax Gallery. He had worked hard to obtain scope and variety in this exhibit and the caricatures represented the current celebrities of the London scene —men of letters, artists, musicians, statesmen, diplomats, social lions, and such personal friends as Reggie Turner, Clyde Fitch, Edmund Gosse, and the poet John Davidson. The press notices were good and Methuen wanted to bring out the caricatures in book form. Socially and financially Max's stock was going up. Busy as he was with attending the theatre, writing his reviews, taking tea with Mabel Beardsley, Aubrey's sister, or Ada Leverson, and dining with ladies of title, he did not neglect his letters to the dear little friend in Memphis, keeping her informed of all these activities. In June he wrote her that he had met her fellow American, Samuel Clemens.

Clemens had come to England to receive an honorary Doctor of Letters from Oxford University; he had crossed on the same boat as

Hitherto unpublished drawing of Mark Twain by Max, undated. © Eva Reichmann; courtesy of the Wadsworth Atheneum, Hartford, Connecticut, the Ella Gallup Sumner and Mary Catlin Sumner Collection.

Professor Archibald Henderson, who was on his way from North Carolina to see Shaw, whose biographer he was to become. Shaw met the boat train and Henderson introduced him to Clemens. With a little prompting from Henderson, Shaw asked Clemens to lunch at his flat in the Adelphi, where Max was invited to join them.

In 1899, writing about DeWolf Hopper, Max had said that he could not laugh at his jests, "even as I cannot laugh at Mark Twain. I admire both gentlemen as phenomena testifying to the determination of the young country which has produced them; but I can accept neither Mr. Hopper as a comedian nor Mr. Twain as a humorist. I admit their jests to be good intrinsically. But the manner in which their jests are made—the manner of Hercules in his twelve labours—prevents me from delighting in them."

But when Max met this particular Herculean jester face to face, he delighted in him, if not in his jokes, and was deeply incensed by what he considered Shaw's rudeness. Unfortunately Shaw had had an appointment at the dentist's and therefore dashed off as soon as lunch was over, a procedure which shocked the punctilious Max. He wrote Florence that he had lunched last Wednesday with Shaw to meet Mark Twain and described Shaw's hasty exit. "I wondered what Mark Twain (with an American's idea of hospitality) must have thought of this! Certainly Shaw has the defects of his qualities!"

Forty years later in a letter to Cyril Clemens Max described Mark Twain as he remembered him: he was "very old, but very beautiful to look at, and to listen to. A lovely voice, lovely manners and among other attributes, wonderfully eloquent hands." At this luncheon Max gathered the details he needed for one caricature he did of Mark Twain—now in the Wadsworth Atheneum in Hartford, Connecticut—slim, sharp-faced, cigar-smoking, with a halo of white hair; but Max did not attempt the eloquent hands; they are hidden in the trouser pockets. However, in another caricature, which he presented to Shaw, Mark Twain holds a long black cigar in one hand.

Although in 1910 Max wrote in a letter, "I only once met Mark Twain . . . I have not yet read any of his books," he must have remedied the lack or changed his mind about their humor, for when the *Mark Twain Journal* awarded him the Mark Twain Gold Medal in 1955, in thanking Cyril Clemens, the editor, he signed himself *K.M.T.,* "Knight of Mark Twain," and sent him *Around Theatres,* "inscribed with fond reverence to the great memory of Mark Twain."

In August 1907 Max made his annual visit to Dieppe, where he saw his former fiancée Constance Collier, and assured Florence that his love for Constance was completely ended. Perhaps this was a declaration Florence was waiting for; at any rate she was soon on her way to London. Max welcomed her with tender warmth and she took up residence at Elm Lodge in Hampstead, not far from his friends the Rothensteins. Will admired her red hair and girlish figure but wondered how so shy and elusive a personality could dominate a stage. The Rothenstein children were fond of her and considered her an honorary member of their household; she liked to entertain them, and John (later Sir John, and Director of the Tate Gallery), remembered a really stupendous tea to which she had treated him.

Although she was glad to be back in London, enjoying the companionship of Max and his family, Florence grieved for her mother and felt lonely and depressed. She had made few friends in London, for which, Max told her, "you had only your dear little self to blame. You never would have known even me if I hadn't gone out of my way to insist—to 'thrust' myself; a thing I had never done before." She wrote frequently to her brother Morris in New York, who declared he could "feel the charm of Elm Lodge way over here." Apparently there was some prospect of her playing Ibsen's *When We Dead Awaken,* and Morris hoped for it, but he advised against repertory in Manchester, saying, "Even Castle Square was better."

About this time Max did a drawing he inscribed "Florence Kahn recovering from boredom at Hampstead, 1907"; the title seems ironic, however, for in the picture Florence sits dejected with bowed head and folded hands while a dapper, derby-hatted Max with cane and boutonnière walks away. Perhaps Max's walking away symbolized his November departure for Italy where he visited his friends the William Nicholsons at Portofino on the Italian Riviera and carried on a flirtation with the Baroness von Hutten, formerly Bettina Reddle of Erie, Pennsylvania, and at the time a popular novelist. He did not confide this affair to Florence, but perhaps she sensed a lessening in his devotion, for she seemed unusually despondent. Many years later when the Baroness proposed to visit them in Rapallo, Florence protested vigorously against it.

Max returned not visibly altered by his recent philandering, and pleased with the reception of his new *Book of Caricatures,* from his Carfax exhibit. Then things took a turn for Florence. Alfred Wareing, once stage manager for Beerbohm Tree, agreed to present her for a limited engagement in *Rosmersholm.* She was pleased to have a second chance at playing Rebecca after the play's fiasco in New York in 1904.

Max was anxious to help in every way. He asked William Archer, critic and exponent of Ibsen, to give his advice, and he tried to bolster Florence's waning courage. How would London greet an American actress in an Ibsen play? Max was reassuring; she mustn't doubt herself; he had every confidence in her. He volunteered to help with the properties, but his offer elicited this response from the manager:

> I really think I shall not want Mr. Beerbohm's help. I am afraid that really he is not the sort of man that would have been of much use, though I am dreadfully sorry to say so. He has not turned up this evening (6:40 P.M.) so I think really I would rather not see him now, if you will explain that the post is filled.

Max was more successful in his approach to William Archer, for he wrote Florence four pages of criticism and comment. Max urged all his friends to attend the play, sent tickets to the Rothensteins, and thought his little niece, Viola Tree, was not too young to appreciate the beauty of Florence's acting, even though she wouldn't understand much of the play's meaning.

When the curtain went up at Terry's Theatre on 10 February 1908, Max was too nervous to take his seat but stood in the rear of the dress circle. He watched the audience, noting absentees, and the next day he wrote Bernard Shaw:

> Have you gone to see *Rosmersholm*? If not, do so. Two years or so ago I wrote Mrs. Shaw, telling her about Miss Florence Kahn who was then in England and who (I thought from what Norman Hapgood and other Americans had told me) would shine in one of your plays. Now that I have seen Miss Kahn act, I think Norman Hapgood and Co. did not say half enough. A true tragedian with a quite extraordinary beauty of "style." Do go and see for yourself.

Florence was no longer just the dear little friend from Memphis; she was now an actress of proven ability. When Max had corrected the proof of his article for the *Saturday,* he wrote Florence a note. He feared his review was rather like a bad copy of the performance itself, suppressed emotion. It might have been more flattering if he had not known her, but she would like it, because he had done his best, such as it was.

Max's best was very good. Florence could not fail to be pleased. Unfortunately the *Saturday* did not come out till the day the play was to close, but Max urged his readers to attend the last performance. He said he found it difficult to write about Miss Kahn, for it was never easy to analyze the merits of great acting—but he did it. As Rebecca, Miss Kahn showed actual understanding, skillful control, and genuine emotion; her voice and facial expression revealed her soul. He did not find a tone inharmonious, a movement without grace: "in its appeal to the emotions,

Miss Kahn's acting is not more remarkable than its appeal to the sense of beauty."

Not all the reviewers were as moved as Max had been. To the critic of the *Athenaeum* Miss Kahn did not at all convey the personality of Rebecca; she underplayed throughout the play. But the *Pall Mall Gazette* thought her "the essence of Ibsen," and her work "extraordinarily touching and beautiful . . ." Reggie Turner sent her enthusiastic congratulations, and Will Rothenstein realized the force in her he had not perceived before. One disinterested opinion is preserved in *Figures in the Foreground* (1963) by Frank Swinnerton, who saw *Rosmersholm* at Terry's and thought it "the most fascinating play I'd ever seen."

If Florence had expected to be at once sought out by managers, she was disappointed. The only opportunity which came was in a one-act play by Alfred Sutro for a benefit matinée. She was not enthusiastic about this playwright, and Max warned her, "Don't give Sutro the idea that you don't like him. I mean, don't live up to the letter you had intended to write him. He really is a nice and appreciative creature." When Sutro wrote asking her to take the part, and adding, "Be quite frank with me if you'd rather not," Florence took Max's advice and accepted at once.

On 21 March she appeared at the Aldwych Theatre in a benefit for the Jewish Children's Penny Dinner Fund. Although such stars as Marie Dressler and Lena Ashwell took part in other of the one-act plays, Max devoted his review to *The Man on the Kerb* by Sutro, asserting, "The woman was beautifully played by Miss Florence Kahn who showed again, though in a very different style, the intense emotional gifts that she showed in *Rosmersholm* a few weeks ago."

Max now turned to Laurence Housman, known as the author of *Prunella, Or Love in a Dutch Garden*. He and Max had once caricatured each other for the London *Illustrated News*. Max wrote him:

> If in your new play, there is an important woman's part that has not yet been filled provisionally,—if that is, you are in need of a really poetical actress—do give your attention to the idea of Miss Florence Kahn. I saw her the other day, and she said she was going to write to you. And, as you may not have seen her act, and as you may credit me with being a more or less good judge, I write to tell you that I am sure she is a person who is "worthwhile."
>
> I have seen her in "Rosmersholm," also in a short play of Alfred Sutro's: her acting, in both of these things, was of a quite extraordinary beauty and power. With the exception of Mrs. Pat Campbell, there is no actress to touch her in the sense of poetry, or style

for poetry. (She is an American, of course, but with nothing American in her voice or ways.)

He hoped that Housman could give her a chance: he would ever after be glad he had. But if Housman had the chance he did not offer it to this un-American American. Florence stayed on at Hampstead.

In April and May 1908 Max had another much talked-of exhibition at the Carfax Gallery from which a number of his subjects bought their own likenesses. Just as Florence's performance had enhanced Max's regard for her, so his success at the Carfax increased her admiration for him. Their relationship grew warmer and more intimate; they exchanged confidences and they flirted; and, though Florence had first rebuffed Max's attempts to kiss her, it is not probable she could have continued so unyielding toward the dear Max who said he cared for nothing but her happiness. Still, the tie between them remained equivocal, and the love that leads to marriage had never been mentioned. They saw each other frequently, but Max never seemed to include her in his social contacts outside his family and the immediate circle of his friends, though he told her with whom he was dining or where he was spending the weekend. Florence must have felt excluded from one part of his life as well as from one place in his heart.

As usual Max went to France in midsummer, leaving Florence in London; but in the autumn she left Max in London and went on tour with Mrs. Patrick Campbell. The company opened in London and then played Scotland and Ireland. Max's letters followed her from theatre to theatre. He wished he might have seen her as Chrysothemus; he was sure she was beautiful. He hoped she would like the Irish when she was in Dublin; he thought they were dears, especially the shop people. He wrote:

> How awful that they should all be driven to emigrate as fast as they can to America—there to lose their own souls by gaining the whole world—there to become the most blatant and successful type that America has. What a pity there isn't any scope for their genius in their own place, so that they could be prosperous *and* sweet.

Then the engagement with Mrs. Campbell ended and there was nothing else. With sudden resolution Florence made up her mind—she told Max she was going home and would not return. Max protested. Surely she might go and visit her brothers, but she must not expatriate herself; she belonged in England. But this time Florence was adamant and she booked her passage. Perhaps she felt Max's noncommittal attitude no longer endurable.

She was not a young woman. London had brought her no great success in her career, it had provided no eager suitor urging her to abandon that career for his sake. She must look elsewhere for her future. The dear brothers who adored her, the exciting aura of New York, even the loyal friends in Memphis, seemed preferable to her present life in London.

Max, too, was giving the situation serious consideration. He was tired of his job on the *Saturday,* he was tired of the endless round of social engagements, he was even tired of Reggie Turner—but he was not tired of Florence, and life without her looked very empty, even desolate. His financial standing was improving every year; he should soon be able to afford a wife, especially one who had a modest but regular income. So, after four years of devoted friendship, Max mentioned love and marriage.

He proposed in person—hence no record remains of his declaration—but Florence did not say Yes or No, so he had to write at once, urging her to consider carefully, not to marry him just through kindness, but only if she were sure she would be happy. Still Florence took a few days to consider, then she said Yes. Now Max wrote:

> Dear sweet, I feel so much happier than I have felt for a long time. A sort of feeling of peace—of being able to look into the future, hand in hand with you . . .

The dear little friend now became "My own darling," or "My dearest one," and neither of them could understand why this had not happened long ago. However, Florence's plans to return to her brothers were unchanged, only now the reason was altered. She must tell them of the new disposition of her life, her coming marriage. Not that it was to be immediate, for no date had been set. Both wanted time to make their preparations; Max must save money for his new responsibilities. He thought it might take a year. Actually it took a year and a half.

X

"Not at Any Price"

FLORENCE STAYED in America from late December 1908 till June 1909, being treated as something of a celebrity in Memphis, though her failure to pursue her career was regretted. She and Max corresponded vigorously and missed each other very much. She told her brothers and Martha Michel, her best friend since childhood, of her engagement; otherwise it was a secret. Max may have told his family, but he did not tell Reggie, to whom he had usually confided his affairs of the heart.

At various times during Max's life the question was raised of his returning to America. He was more tempted by this idea when Florence was there. In 1907 he wrote her that "an American named Hamburg" had asked him to go to America and make drawings of prominent people who would pay him twenty-five pounds each for the privilege of being caricatured. Max did not think the scheme was sound: "The people who could afford to pay for the advertisement, would not need it," he told her, "and conversely." Once when Alfred Sutro was going to the States he urged Max to go with him; the idea was alluring, but Max decided he couldn't get away. His reluctance to journey across the Atlantic became so well-known that Hampton's *Broadway Magazine* invited him to do an article on "America Unvisited." He reported to Florence, "They say they will pay anything in reason," and he wondered what that would be.

At least twice, perhaps oftener, he was invited to go over on a lecture tour. His answers left the promoters in no doubt as to the sincerity of his refusal. In 1921 Lewis Hind sent him an offer from Pond's Lecture Bureau. Max was sorry to be churlish and stodgy, "but there the plain fact is: I'm not in the least degree tempted." He had no "desire to spout before an American audience," and he would have to have terms so "utterly monstrous" as would "leave you in a very heavy financial loss over me. So forbear!" But he was gratified by the notion.

Some years later he refused an offer of $12,000, minus 35 percent—

> . . . for "Hard travel" plus the horror of "wide-spread newspaper publicity" in your "beautiful country" for a "period of three or four months"—oh, dear Mr. Reid, how little you know me!

After the Second World War, Sam Kahn, Florence's editor brother, urged Max to come to the States, promising he could make $50,000 a year there. "Yes," answered Max, "but I'd have to go to the States to do it." He even refused an opportunity to appear there by telecast, as S. N. Behrman related in his *Portrait of Max.* The television agent told Max how simply it could be done. "You will sit, if you like, as you are sitting now. You will simply say, 'My dear friends, I am happy to be addressing you!' " to which Max replied courteously, "Do you wish me to start with a lie?"

He had no show at the Carfax that spring of 1909, but in the summer fifteen of his caricatures were shown at the New English Art Club, and he was getting together essays for *Yet Again,* to be published by Chapman and Hall. In June came a visit from an American he had met in Washington in 1895—Thomas Nelson Page, author of *In Old Virginia.* Max was able to put him in touch with Mrs. T. P. O'Connor, whom Page wanted to see, and, on embarking for home on the *S.S. Cedric,* Page wrote to thank Max for his kindness. He could not leave English waters without expressing the pleasure he had felt at seeing him. He had gone to Mrs. O'Connor's and they had talked of Max. The letter ended, "I wanted to send you one of my books, but thought it would be rather hard on you on so short an acquaintance. But if you ever come to America again you may take your pick and meantime I will write the inscription and subscribe myself with highest regards, Yours very truly . . ." Then he discovered that he didn't have Max's address, but he hoped simply "London" would do. It did.

Max had made no secret to Florence of his dislike for many American customs and habits, and though he sometimes adopted a propitiating or bantering tone in his letters to her, his public pronouncements remained unchanged. When he told her of the offer the British artist Roger Fry had received to join the Metropolitan Museum in New York he applauded the chance because Fry would have to spend only four months a year in that city. "Not that America isn't nice," he hastened to add, but Fry had a wife and children in England. In another letter (which contained a mysterious reference to the American Shoe Company) he apologized, "I would not say anything not nice about the country that produced you." When Florence played in Dublin, he hoped she would like the people "who are as much more civilised and charming than the English, than the English are than the Americans." After attending a lecture by an American at Prince's Restaurant, he told her he saw many Americans there, but "I didn't see the only one American who matters to me at all. They were all very unlike you."

On the other hand, he seemed to strike out more violently against some person she liked or admired: her friend Paul Kester, whom he had ridiculed for his play *Dorothy o' the Hall,* or James Gibbons Huneker. But consistency was never important to Max.

In his writings he treated American politics and government with scorn. In "King George the Fourth" he hoped that the English would some day "place politics on a sound commercial basis as they did in America." In an article for the *Saturday* of 8 July 1905 he blamed the corruption of American politics on the respectable people who held themselves aloof. That was the trouble: if these respectable Americans would realize their duty to "redeem American politics by dashing into them in the full armour of their respectability" the situation would be improved. He saw America as "racked with growing pains," and he sometimes wondered if it could make anything of itself.

He had no belief in the wisdom of the people. G. K. Chesterton once chided him for not cherishing in his heart the ideals of democracy, and Max replied, "I will not stake a sixpence on the people's capacity for governing itself, and not a penny on its capacity for governing me. Democracy, where it has been tried, has failed as a means of increasing human happiness." In "Porro Unum" (*Saturday Review,* 25 July 1908), he discussed the relative merits of kings and presidents. In France and America, he said, the president is "of an extrusive kind." The office had been

> . . . fashioned on the monarchic model and his whole position is anomalous. He has to try to be ornamental as well as useful, a symbol as well as a pivot. Obviously, it is absurd to single out one man as a symbol of the equality of all men. And not less unreasonable is it to expect him to be inspiring as a patriotic symbol, an incarnation of his country. Only an anointed king can be that. . . . In America, where no kings have been, they are able to make a pretense of enthusiasm for a President. But no real chord of national sentiment is touched by this eminent gentleman who has no past or future eminence, who has been shoved forward for a space and will anon be sent packing in favour of some other upstart. Let some princeling of a foreign State set foot in America, and lo! all the inhabitants are tumbling over one another in their desire for a glimpse of him—

a desire which showed "their unsatisfied inner craving for a dynasty of their own."

Max shuddered at the hustle and bustle of American life, with its emphasis on making money. He thought America had invented the millionaire. In England, he said, the common greeting is "How are you?" This implies that the most necessary element to well-being is physical health. But in America "the struggle for wealth is so fierce that no one is well. Everyone there—every man, at least—is suffering from overstrained nerves," and when two male acquaintances hurry by each other on the street, "their greeting is a perfunctory, 'What have you?'"

He had made one pictorial comment about the relations of the United States and England in his series called "The Second Childhood of John Bull," exhibited in 1901 but not published until 1911. Here John Bull is kneeling behind a cigar-smoking Brother Jonathan (Max preferred the old Yankee representation to Uncle Sam), pulling at his coattails as he pleads, "O Sir, please Sir, do let us young Hanglo-Saxons stand shoulder to shoulder agin the world. Think of our common tongue. Think of that there Mayflower. O, Sir, ain't blood thicker than water?" etc., etc. (Brother Jonathan guesses the Atlantic is not com-posed of blood.)

He often had a barb for rich Americans who bought works of art abroad, saying he experienced a thrill of delight when he heard that J. Pierpont Morgan had "acquired Lord So and So's priceless collection of this and that." When the royal collection of Whistler's etchings was bought by an American, Max thought it only right that America should have the chance of "gathering to her wide and wistful bosom, at last, the works of him who basely deserted her in order that he might achieve them." And again, "You must be an American if you want to be filled through and through in every fiber, with an intense sentiment for the past of Europe." And if you have had President Roosevelt (Theodore) bawling "moral platitudes at you for many years from the roof of the White House, you will more fully savour the culture of the old world."

If Max looked with such disfavor upon Americans who carried home the material belongings of Britain, he should have felt more kindly to those who came only for knowledge. Yet he reacted nervously when Cecil Rhodes, the British financier who had made a fortune in the diamond mines of South Africa, left a large bequest to establish scholarships at Oxford for American, as well as for Colonial and German, students. Max, ever jealous of new and foreign influences which might change his beloved university, looked askance at Rhodes's generosity. Might Oxford in time come to curse its benefactor? He wondered if these young Americans would adapt to the environment, or "will they produce atmospheric disturbances unsettling the traditions of a place whose whole charm and use is in the placid maintenance of its tradition—whether, in fact, the newcomers will or won't be a great nuisance . . ."

He illustrated this situation in *A Book of Caricatures* (1907) with "Mr. Charles Boyd receiving a Rhodes Scholar." (Mr. Boyd was Secretary of the Rhodes Trust.) The Scholar is a stereotyped minstrel-show black, wearing a plaid suit topped by an abbreviated student's gown, and carrying a mortarboard in one hand. Mr. Boyd holds the other in both his, as he welcomes the newcomer. So did Max demonstrate his concern; he was to give the subject of Rhodes Scholars further consideration in *Zuleika Dobson* in 1911.

Max caricatured two American Presidents—Theodore Roosevelt, as "Permanent Prince of Bores"; and Woodrow Wilson more sympathetically, at first as a thin, ascetic figure addressing a beefy, paunchy Senate, and then, in "Woodrow Wilson's Peace," with the ailing President seated in an armchair, while Lloyd George and Clemenceau whisper furtively, "Thought he was going to get the better of you and I."

Sometimes Max gave grudging credit to the New World. He disliked the attempts to modernize London. The tearing down of the old, he said, "will filch from Englishmen the pleasant power of crowing over Americans, and from Americans the unpleasant necessity of balancing their pity for our present with envy of our past. After all, our past is our trump card. Our present is merely a bad imitation of what the Americans can do much better."

When the poet Richard Le Gallienne, his friend of the Nineties, went to the States and apparently planned to remain there, Max chided him gently on a postcard:

> *O witched by American bars!*
> *Pan whistles you home on his pipes.*
> *We love you for loving the stars,*
> *But what can you see in the stripes?*

Max's last thrust at the U.S.A. before he retired from the *Saturday* was aimed at the critics and press of America. The sally was occasioned by a most unfriendly and personal attack upon Laurence Irving, son of Sir Henry, who was in New York playing in *The Affinity* by Eugène Brieux. The critic of the *New York Times,* Alan Dale, had so insulted Irving and his choice of the play, that Irving had denounced him from the stage. Max thought Irving had lacked judgment but he had no respect for this critic. "Base indeed do I deem a dramatic critic," said Max, "who makes it his business to attack actors and actresses, be they good or bad, in such language as shall cause them the greatest possible amount of pain. . . .

But the fact remains that a great part of American journalism is unseemly, a peril and a pest. Why do you stand it?" he asked the American people. "You deplore the corruptness of your politics just as you deplore the vulgarity of the 'yellow press' . . . You are a vital and vigorous people. I have an immense admiration for your immense potentialities." He would feel desperate indeed if England had such politics and such a press, because she was growing old and could not cast off such maladies. "But you, the young and buoyant, the aquiline and star-spangled, very surely you have the power to set your house in order. Apparently you have not the will."

XI

Life Begins at Rapallo

IN THE SUMMER of 1909 Florence came back to London, this time to Craven Hill Gardens, while Max was preparing to leave for his holiday in Dieppe. He did not forgo this last playtime with his friends of the old days, but he found it strangely dull. Already he seemed set towards a new pattern of living from which everyone except Florence was excluded. When he returned, Florence was with Max's sisters at Bognor, on the Channel coast, and he took every possible chance to be there too. She was suffering from rheumatism and he was solicitous about her bathing: she must not go in if the water was cold. He said whisky was better for rheumatism than wine. Her affliction did not keep her from riding and he thought she looked "a great darling on horseback." She must take a nap after lunch every day and, when he came, she could sleep in his arms quite soundly. How wonderful it would be when they could always be together.

Yet sometimes Florence worried about Max. Although he declared he was tired of the social whirl, he carefully enumerated to her his week's engagements: dinner tonight with Lady Desborough in Grosvenor Square; last night with Lady Lewis, wife of Sir George and friend to many artists; the night before with the author Violet Hunt at the Writers Club. Would he be happy away from London and his absorbing friends? Max tried to allay her fears: she was all he wanted. "You will be the whole population of my globe," he told her. "We shall be brilliant for each other, wherever we are"; and, "Darling, it will be lovely, won't it, being together? I am sure we shall be so happy."

In October 1909 Max's third book of essays, *Yet Again,* was published, coming out in the States the next spring under the aegis of John Lane. The *Nation* gave it a most flattering and appreciative review, praising Max for maintaining his own qualities unimpaired, but adding, "This art will mean little to a world that wants reading for the train. To the few who still care for quality in letters, it is a delight." A critic in the *New*

York Times inquired, "Yet which of us moderns may deny to Max Beerbohm the possession of that degree of talent which is so close to genius that only posterity may be trusted to decide whether or not it actually crosses the line and enters the 'golden realm'?"

Florence's brother Morris had been hoping to come to England and he arrived in November. Florence was glad that one member of her family was to meet Max. He and Morris got on well together; Max thought Morris a charming fellow and Morris found Max a fascinating talker. He was taken to lunch at Upper Berkeley Street and quite lost his heart to Mrs. Beerbohm in her black silk and white lace.

Max was now thirty-seven (Florence, thirty-four), and he had been on the staff of the *Saturday Review* for twelve years. He had warned Harold Hodge, Harris's successor as the *Saturday*'s editor, that he would soon be leaving, but he was chary of any advance announcement of his wedding. Twice before he had been engaged and twice the commitment had not led to the altar. Now he was thankful for his escapes, but understandably he wanted this marriage to be a *fait accompli* before he talked about it. For many years Max's bachelorhood had been under feminine attack until it had been deemed impregnable, but George Egerton, the pseudononymous female author of *Keynotes,* had told him, "You'll settle down to a decent wife and a chop somewhere"; and when she saw him at *Rosmersholm* in 1907 she thought he was on the way to fulfilling her prophecy.

By March of 1910 Max was more financially solvent than he had ever been. He was not having a spring exhibit at Carfax, but the Leicester Galleries had negotiated with him to show there next year and had made a substantial down payment. George Alexander, the actor-manager who produced several of Oscar Wilde's comedies, had given him an advance on a play he was writing, and Kegan Paul was asking to publish his next book. Although he did not consider himself affluent, Max felt reasonably secure; he thought he and Florence could manage if they lived simply and not in England. In mid-April he swore Reggie Turner to secrecy and told him the news:

> Florence is the one woman with whom I could be always and wholly happy, and the woman apart from whom I could not be happy. . . . To me she represents the achievement of happiness, happiness for good and all.

Florence also wrote him, "a sweet and delightful letter" which Reggie said he would always treasure. He was very, very glad that Max was so happy, and pleased that he would now have two good friends instead of one.

Will Rothenstein and his wife, Alice, were also pleased when they heard the news; Will said that Alice had suspected this outcome for some time. They would love Florence as they loved Max.

On 4 May 1910 Florence and Max were married at the Harrow Street Registry Office in Paddington, to which Max drove safely in a four-wheeler, accompanied by his mother, his sister Constance, and Reggie, who had returned from Paris for the event. The bride, with Max's sister Aggie, followed in a "second conveyance, Miss Kahn wearing a stone-coloured dress of classical design, with an unpretentious hat trimmed with feathers shading to green," according to a report in *The People*. After the brief ceremony the party returned to Upper Berkeley Street for lunch. One reporter declared that the wedding was so sudden that a special license had been required, and the wedding cake was late in arriving.

After joyous goodbyes, the couple left for Chesham in Buckinghamshire, not far from London; there the first part of the honeymoon would be spent. Reggie's present had been a check of such generosity that on the first evening in Chesham Florence wrote him a letter of thanks, which Max amended by changing all her first-person singular pronouns to plural (identifying italics supplied):

> My dear Reggie,
>
> Just a note to say goodnight, for *we* would not feel as if the day had come to a right close without saying that *we* will not try to thank you nor would you want *us* to but *we* send *our* love.
>
> > Goodnight, Reggie,
> >
> > Affectionately,
> >
> > > Florence *and Max*
> > > [Italics Max's]

The Kahn-Beerbohm nuptials did not go unnoticed on either side of the Atlantic. A day or so previously the *New York Times* had declared that this marriage would occur within a few weeks. The bride-to-be had recently retired from the stage: "It was during Miss Kahn's tour of England which included readings before King Edward that she met Mr. Beerbohm." (No record of these readings has been found. Surely Max, with his scorn for the deportment of the former Prince of Wales, would never have sanctioned this proceeding.)

The New York *Review* reported the marriage of the brilliant critic and

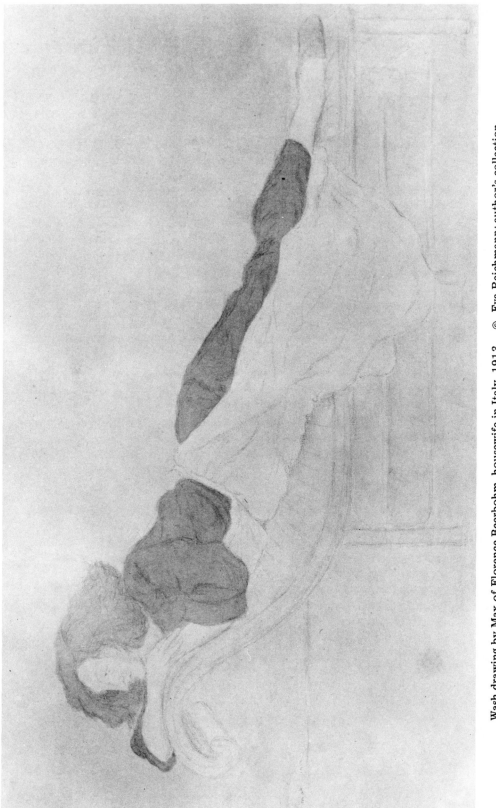

Wash drawing by Max of Florence Beerbohm, housewife in Italy, 1913.　© Eva Reichmann; author's collection.

the intellectually fascinating woman, and everyone agreed that the couple made an ideal match. Errors sometimes crept in: the Memphis *Commercial Appeal* identified Mr. Beerbohm as on the staff of *The Times* of London and the New York *Morning Telegraph* identified Miss Kahn as the daughter of Congressman Kahn of California. The London *Academy* wished the couple happiness, saying it would be hard to find such a nice, quiet, respectable, and urbanely civilized little gentleman as Mr. Max Beerbohm. (Would this have been from the pen of Lord Alfred Douglas?) The *Daily Mirror* described Max as a "homey man."

The account which inflicted real pain on Max and Florence did not reach them till they had been married more than a dozen years. In 1923 Frank Harris, once Max's editor on the *Saturday Review,* related in *Contemporary Portraits* a version of the wedding which he said had been given him by Max's sister Agnes, then Mrs. Ralph Neville:

> "Oh yes," Mrs. Neville began, "Max was married, you can take it from me, legally married, in church even, to a very charming and very pretty girl, and they've gone off to Rapallo and the Italian Riviera for the honeymoon. Max went through the ceremony beautifully as such a dandy would, omitting nothing not even the first kiss to the bride. I could not help telling him how proud I was of him, and now I said, as we were all leaving the church and the bride was getting into the carriage, I must say 'Good-bye, dear Max.' Suddenly his marvellous self-possession broke down; frantically he seized me by the arm: 'You're not going to leave me *alone* with her,' he cried. And when I replied, 'Indeed, I am!' he looked at me reproachfully, muttering, 'It's hardly decent!' "

Max and Florence did not see the book until it had been out some time, but when they did, they were much disturbed. Max wrote to the *Times Literary Supplement* in "deep annoyance" to deny any such conversation had ever taken place, as anyone who knew his sister would be certain. He was pained and distressed by such a false account.

No one had a chance to meet husband or wife during their honeymoon for, after leaving Chesham, they stayed in seclusion at Hythe, one of the old Cinque Ports. Florence cooked delicious meals, they sat in the sun in the garden, and though the view of the sea was somewhat obscured, they didn't mind as long as they could look at each other. Early in June they crossed the Channel en route to Italy, stopping first in Paris, where Max saw Rostand going into a shop and was amazed at his likeness to Clyde Fitch in figure, movement, and face. The resemblance was painful; Max could not help wishing it was the author of *Cyrano de Bergerac* who had died, and "dear old Clyde who had been spared to flutter and shine and to write new plays and buy new ties." They went on to Italy and after some days at Santa Margherita, where the only English-speaking person they saw was the novelist "Dodo" Benson (E. F. Benson), who didn't see them, they came to Rapallo, where they found a charming little villa on the coast road to Genoa, and decided to take it temporarily and stay longer, if it pleased them. And it did.

The small, two-storied Villino Chiaro above the blue Mediterranean became home to them for the rest of their lives. The living quarters were on the second floor, reached by a winding stone stair from the road below, but the villa was so fitted into the hillside that the doorway was level with the garden. Although they had no car (and indeed never did have one) they decided to rent the garage beneath as a place to keep the ice-box. In the center of the flat, deck-like roof stood a square third-story room with French doors facing seaward, reached by an outside staircase. It would make an ideal retreat for Max.

So began the married life of Florence and Max, the American and the Briton, far from their families and friends, in a land strange to them where a foreign tongue was spoken—a new Eden where they could be all in all to each other. The sun shone, the bay sparkled; lemons, oranges, and camellias grew in the garden, and every hour was a delight. Two people had never been so happy. Each afternoon they walked down the hill to Rapallo, twenty minutes down, twenty-five back, with no traffic to challenge their right-of-way. They bathed in the sea, they climbed the neighboring mountain, they had all their time for each other.

Gradually they began the work of settling the villa and rejuvenating the garden. Max arranged his books and pictures in his upstairs study, the walls of which he later painted blue. Florence undertook the training of two Italian maids, so that food was cooked and served exactly as Max wanted it. She had begun to study Italian before her marriage and soon grew proficient in it, but Max never learned to speak it. When Viola Tree, Max's favorite niece, visited them in December 1910 she reported that Florence was an amazing person, who managed everything perfectly. She admired Max's roof-top study where his working utensils were all shipshape—"six perfectly sharpened pencils and his cream-laid foolscap paper."

Now that he was free from the pressure of London, Max was working in good earnest, writing and drawing, though since he had promised the Leicester Galleries a spring exhibition, he gave preference to his caricatures. He went to London early in April 1911 to arrange for the exhibit, leaving Florence in Rapallo. They hated the separation, but money had to be considered. Florence counted the days of his absence. She watched eagerly for his letters, writing him, "You are in my heart, in my mind, in my soul, in everything I do—in everything I think." When he returned she met him at Genoa, and a little later the receipts from the exhibit allowed them to take a second honeymoon in Venice.

That summer Max's sister Dora, who had become an Anglican nun, came to Rapallo from St. Saviour's Priory to pay the first of many annual visits. They always delighted in her presence; she was so gay and witty and worldly. The maids, too, looked forward to her coming.

In August Will Rothenstein wrote that he was going to New York, and Florence promptly alerted her brothers Morris and Mannie. She was pleased when Morris wrote that he had liked Will and Will reported he had enjoyed knowing her brothers. He and Max compared notes on their impressions of the U.S.A., Will complaining that no standard of knowledge or intelligence was taken for granted in America: it was as if, in playing tennis, one must mark out the court anew for every game. Max agreed, and wished that he had thought of that truly superb metaphor.

In September, Florence and Max went to Milan where Viola Tree was to make her singing debut. She had been married the preceding June to Alan Parsons, a writer. But Viola developed a bad sore throat, and her appearance had to be canceled. Much disappointed, Florence and Max returned to Rapallo, but Florence could sympathize better than Max at this lost opportunity.

Now they were awaiting with some impatience another important debut, that of *Zuleika Dobson*. The publication date was 26 October 1911, and on that day Max presented an inscribed copy to Florence "without whom this book would never have been written." They had a gala luncheon at the Villino, and drank Asti spumante to celebrate.

XII

Abimelech V. Oover

MAX'S FIRST MENTION of *Zuleika* seems to have been in a letter to Reggie Turner in 1898, thirteen years before the appearance of the novel. In June, after reviewing Maeterlinck's *Pelléas and Melisande,* he wrote Reggie, "I am going to write *Zuleika Dobson* and cut Maeterlinck out." He had taken Kilseen Conover to the performance and she was one of the first to know his intention. That he was awake to the difficulties of writing an Oxford love story is evidenced in his article on a melodrama by Cecil Raleigh with Oxford as a background, appearing in the *Saturday* 4 October 1902:

> Poor Oxford! Will she, I wonder, ever be made successfully the background for a play, or for a novel? What is it that prevents the serious novelist from catching the spirit of the place? I suppose it is his fear of eliminating sex. Without sex, he is sure, there can be no human interest . . . It is true that since the Fellows have been permitted to marry, and to take unto themselves little red-brick villas . . . and since the foundation of Somerville and Lady Margaret Hall, Oxford has in itself quite a large feminine element. But the spirit of the place . . . is still the ancient spirit of celibacy. . . . Sport, athletics, books, and, above all, good fellowship—these are the things that make up the lives of the undergraduates, these are their true interests. The instinct of sex is dormant, and even if it happen to be stirred in vacation, it quickly relapses in term.

Therefore, thought Max, novels about Oxford do not ring true, but what a chance "for the novelist who shall accept the limitations of Oxford as a milieu, and write sincerely in the plenty of room left to him." He himself could not write a realistic novel about Oxford; his own feelings for the place would be inimical to such a presentation. He could use the actual town and towers, the patterns of life, but his characters must be exaggerations and his plot wholly fantastic. He must be whimsical, satirical, seemingly reasonable, yet quite unreasonable—that was the idea.

In December 1899 Will Rothenstein asked him about *Zuleika* and hoped she was finished, and in December 1902 the American *Bookman* announced that Mr. Max Beerbohm had written a novel, a whimsical comedy of Oxford life and love, *Zuleika Dobson*. But this was premature, for Max did not begin working seriously on it until 1909. Then his letters to Florence refer to it frequently. "I was able to do some Zuleika after writing my article because I don't find Zuleikaing a strain . . . knowledge that one has time to make all sorts of corrections sets the mind at rest, and then, of course, there is the difference of being interested and not interested." And again, "I wish I could read you the new part of Zuleika." Later, "I have copied out half the chapter of Zuleika. I will post the whole to you tomorrow." In December he informed her he had just introduced a Rhodes Scholar, an American. Just before Christmas he was going to send her about six thousand words; he feared it was a small amount for the time he had spent on it, but he thought the quality was good. "Darling, it will be lovely to do the later chapters with *you*. I feel it will be all easier then."

So he put off Zuleika until he and Florence were together at the Villino, where he finished his Oxford love story with Florence at hand to suggest and criticize.

Zuleika, his heroine with the beauty of Helen and the magic of Circe, comes to Oxford to visit her uncle, the Warden of Judas College, and becomes the *femme fatale* of the undergraduates, who commit mass suicide in the River Isis to demonstrate their hopeless passion for her. Among those who share in this fatal immersion are the Duke of Dorset and Mr. Oover, the Rhodes Scholar.

As Miss Dobson arrives at Oxford and is driven past the Sheldonian Theatre, the busts of the Roman Emperors surmounting it look down upon her and great beads of perspiration glisten on their foreheads. (These Emperors, say Max, are frequently mistaken by American visitors for the Twelve Apostles.)

Before she came to Oxford, Zuleika had made a triumphal tour of America with her performance of magic. Max's description of this experience has the ring of remembrance: she was much praised by the American press, her picture in nineteen colors being sprawled over front pages—

There she was, measuring herself back to back with the Statue of Liberty . . . peering through a microscope held by Cupid over a diminutive Uncle Sam; teaching the American eagle to stand on its head; and doing a hundred and one other things—whatever suggested itself to the fancy of native art.

In America, Zuleika had also been photographed in more realistic poses, such as

> . . . finding a split in the gloves she had just drawn on before starting for the musicale given in her honour by Mrs. Suetonius X. Meistersinger, the most exclusive woman in New York; chatting at the telephone to Miss Camille Van Spook, the best-born girl in New York; laughing over the recollection of a compliment made her by George Abimelech Post, the best-groomed man in New York . . .

She went West in a private railroad car owned by an admiring millionaire, and her reception in Chicago eclipsed the fanfare in New York.

The Duke of Dorset, the hero, belonged to the Junta, a club so exclusive that for a year and a half he had been the only member, having felt obliged—so exacting were his standards for eligibility—to black-ball, on the actual evening of election, all candidates previously proposed by himself. Eventually, however, he accepted two, lest the Junta die out.

Thus it is that, shortly after Zuleika's arrival, the club meets for dinner with three guests, one of them being Abimelech V. Oover, the American Rhodes Scholar. Now Max was presented with the opportunity to annotate the query he had raised nearly five years earlier about the impact of Mr. Rhodes's generosity: as he is presented to the Junta, Mr. Oover makes a little speech:

> "Gentlemen . . . Like most of my countrymen, I am a man of few words. We are habituated out there to act rather than talk. Judged from the view-point of your beautiful old civilization, I am aware my curtness may seem crude. . . ."

He is interrupted by the summons to dinner. Then:

> The President showed much deference to his guest. He seemed to listen with close attention to the humorous anecdote with which, in the American fashion, Mr. Oover inaugurated dinner. . . . He found these Scholars, good fellows though they were, rather oppressive. . . . The Americans were, to a sensitive observer, the most troublesome—as being the most troubled . . . The Duke was not one of those Englishmen who fling, or care to hear flung, cheap sneers at America. Whenever anyone in his presence said that America was not large in area, he would firmly maintain that it was. He held, too, in his enlightened way, that Americans have a perfect right

to exist. But he did often find himself wishing Mr. Rhodes had not enabled them to exercise that right in Oxford.

For a page and a half Max analyzes the American through the Duke's eyes, finally summing up Dorset's opinion:

Altogether, the American Rhodes Scholars . . . are a noble, rather than a comfortable, element in the social life of the University.

Since this is the Duke's last dinner on earth—he has already decided to die for Zuleika, his loved one—he finds it hard to take pleasure in his guest. He is perfect in his manner towards him, however, though he finds Oover's aura "even more disturbing than that of the average Rhodes Scholar."

In the room where they dined, a portrait of Humphrey Greddon, founder of the Junta, hung on the wall, and Humphrey's ghost in pale brocaded coat and lace ruffles stood by the mantel and watched the diners. Below his portrait was a miniature of lovely, ill-starred Nellie O'Mora, whom Greddon had loved, wronged, and deserted. The Duke tells his guest the story, usually taken placidly by English listeners; but Mr. Oover's moral tone and his sense of chivalry are of the American kind, and the ghost is surprised to hear him say, "Duke, I hope I am not incognisant of the laws that govern the relations of guest and host. But, Duke, I aver deliberately that the founder of this fine old club, at which you are so splendidly entertaining me tonight, was an unmitigated scoundrel. I say he was not a white man." Greddon sets upon the Scholar with his sword to avenge this insult, but, when no blood is drawn, remembers he is only a ghost—"But I shall meet you in Hell tomorrow," he promises. However, the author assures us he is wrong: there is no doubt that Oover went to Heaven.

After dinner the Duke rises to propose the first of the two toasts traditional to the club. "Gentlemen, I give you Church and State." Oover drinks the toast with a richer reverence than most, "despite his passionate mental reservation in favour of Pittsburg-Anabaptism and the Republican Ideal." But the Duke, now that he is in love with Zuleika, cannot bring himself to propose the second toast to Nellie O'Mora, and another member takes the outrageous liberty of proposing Zuleika in Nellie's stead.

Mr. Oover, too, looked grave. All the antiquarian in him deplored the sudden rupture of a fine old Oxford tradition. All the chivalrous American in him resented the slight on that fair victim of the feudal system, Miss O'Mora. And at the same time, all the Abimelech V. in him rejoiced at having honoured by word and act the one woman in the world.

When the Duke discovers that the other five present are, like him, resolved to die for Zuleika, he tries to dissuade them. Mr. Oover, who has been sorely tried by the English custom of not making after-dinner speeches, now rises to his feet with a sigh of satisfaction.

> "Duke . . . I say that your words show up your good heart, all the time. Your mentality, too, is bully, as we all predicate. One may say without exaggeration that your scholarly and social attainments are a by-word throughout the solar system, and be-yond. We rightly venerate you as our boss. Sir, we worship the ground you walk on. But we owe a duty to our own free and independent manhood. Sir, we worship the ground Miss Z. Dobson treads on. We have pegged out a claim right there. . . ."

And Oover declares he will love Zuleika to his last breath.

The American appears in one more scene. The next morning the Duke meets him in the High Street and hopes he has dismissed the notion of the night before. "Duke," says Oover, "d'you take me for a skunk?" The Duke is not quite sure what a skunk is, but he takes Oover to be all it isn't. He says, "And the high esteem in which I hold you is the measure for me of the loss that your death would be to America and to Oxford." Oover thinks that is "a bully testimonial. But don't worry. America can turn out millions just like me and Oxford can have as many of them as she can hold. On the other hand, how many of *you* can be turned out, as per sample, in England? Yet you choose to destroy yourself." He again affirms that the Duke is a white man, and they shake hands on the bargain of mutual suicide. When the Duke tries to detain him, Oover hurries on: "Sorry, unable. It's just turning eleven o'clock and I've a lecture. While life lasts, I'm bound to respect Rhodes's intentions."

Some of this conversation will have a familiar ring as a repetition of Max's advice to the author of *Hawthorne, U.S.A.* in his 1905 review of the play for the *Saturday*. Another echo in the novel concerns J. P. Morgan. In the last hours of his life the Duke writes an appreciative poem to his landlady. Mrs. Batch greatly prizes this poem, Max tells us—"(witness her recent refusal of Mr. Pierpont Morgan's sensational bid for it.)"

In England *Zuleika* had good, bad, and indifferent press notices. The London representative of Charles Scribner's Sons advised his firm against taking it, explaining, "I did not think it would interest us. The author is more highly esteemed by himself than by anyone else." However, John Lane published it in the States. Critics there were undecided on its classification: just what was Mr. Beerbohm's intention? C. M. Francis in the June 1912 *Bookman* called it a "literary burlesque of nothing in particular," saying of the author, "if he could be cut open, it would probably be found, as Emerson unjustly said of Hawthorne, he had no insides. His soul, if he has one, is entirely composed of literary layers." The book proved the author's "delicate belief that to feel is vulgar and to think is rather coarse." He took the Duke to be modeled after Sir Willoughby Patterne in George Meredith's *The Egoist*. The New York *Sun* called Max "a bright young man who flits with equal assurance from music and drama to art and literature." The *Dial* termed it a "masterpiece of parody" which "should prove a solemn warning to our ultra-romantic young writers."

American resentment at the character and speech of Abimelech V. Oover was voiced by Louis Kronenberger in the *Saturday Review of Literature* 21 June 1947.

> And this is as good a place as any (since in "Zuleika" we meet the Rhodes Scholar, Abimelech V. Oover) to touch upon Max's treatment of America and Americans. His aversion, real or assumed, for America would trouble me very little if it did not so consistently coarsen his touch. Certainly nothing lends itself more to burlesque than a certain type of Rhodes Scholar. But Abimelech is a burlesque of a burlesque—or rather a parody of a parody, since it is his lingo that chiefly matters. How the greatest parodist alive could have gone so startlingly wrong with the American language is not easily explained.

The Kronenberger charge is true, but perhaps an explanation is needed. Abimelech's speech is parody of parody, but the original parody was not created by Max; rather, it was the stage-American used by English playwrights and believed, as Max often remarked, by the English to be an accurate reproduction of transatlantic talk. Max had had enough experience with his American friends to be familiar with their language. If he had lapsed, Florence would have told him, for she was ever alert to point out errors in his writing. No, Max intended Abimelech to be the burlesque of the stage American seen in the London theatres. He spoke the platitudes, the clichés, the slang, heard by a London audience.

Undoubtedly Max got some impressions of American students when he visited Harvard, for there were no Rhodes Scholars at Oxford while he was an undergraduate. But following Kronenberger's essay in the *Saturday Review of Literature,* Ronald Mansbridge of the Cambridge University Press wrote to the editor, identifying the original of Abimelech as a Rhodes Scholar at Oxford in 1907, whom he called "Steve." "Steve" was an athlete who broke the record in the hammer-throw against Cambridge in 1907; he was socially and intellectually brilliant, and he belonged to the circle of Max's later Oxford friends at the time he began writing *Zuleika*. Max expected Americans to be odd, so "Steve" deliberately fulfilled his expectations: his first name was Albert, but he gave it to Max as Abimelech, saying all his family had names from the Bible. After Oxford, "Steve" taught at Hotchkiss, then took an M.D. degree and practiced in New York. He served in the Navy in World War I, and was a prisoner of the Germans. After the war he returned to his practice, serving not only as a doctor, but as a guide, philosopher, and friend to his patients. But he was too much of an idealist for the modern world and in 1934 he withdrew to an island in the Pacific. He "died suddenly" on 7 August 1945, the day after Hiroshima. "Steve never wasted any time when it came to expressing his opinion," said Mr. Mansbridge.

If Mr. Mansbridge is right in his conjecture, then the original of Abimelech is Dr. Albert M. Stevens, Yale '05, who died in Kaneohe, Oahu, Hawaii, and whose record exactly corresponds to that of "Steve."

Although is has usually been assumed that Florence was the woman most evident in the creation of Zuleika, in his later years Max told S. N. Behrman that the model for Zuleika was a young girl he had known who died of tuberculosis. He might possibly have meant Lily Hanbury, a member of his brother's company on the trip to America, who died young of tuberculosis. Max spoke of her in a letter to Ada Leverson but mentioned no attributes which might suggest Zuleika. Mabel Beardsley, Aubrey's sister, is another possibility, though she died of cancer. At least three other ladies have made their own claim to being Zuleika: Kilseen Conover, who wrote Max about the book when it came out, saying he had given it a different ending; Constance Collier, who once told William Rose Benét, "I was Zuleika Dobson"; and the actress Lillah McCarthy, who played *The Sign of the Cross* at Oxford when Max was an undergraduate. Years later he told her that she was Zuleika. Although she questioned his sincerity, she admitted it was pleasant to hear, even in jest, that she was the model from whom he drew his immortal heroine.

XIII

America Discovers Max

MAX AND FLORENCE did not cut themselves off completely from London, and in 1912 and 1913 they spent Christmas at Upper Berkeley Street. Florence enjoyed these visits and appreciated being accepted as one of the family. When they all gathered for the Sunday dinner of roast beef and Yorkshire pudding, it was a large group: the Beerbohm Trees and their three daughters, with Viola's husband, Alan Parsons; Julius's wife and son and daughter; Agnes, now separated from her husband, Ralph Neville; Constance, who had never married; and Dora, when she could leave her convent. Mrs. Beerbohm presided with a gay dignity.

Max's superb parodies in *A Christmas Garland,* published October 1912, came out in New York the following month, where they had mixed reviews. Several of the parodies had already been available to American readers in the *Chap-Book* and the New York *Herald*'s weekly magazine section. The *Outlook* explained the parodies were by a "well-known English humorous writer and caricaturist," and decided that "such a book has no lasting value, but if it is well done, as this most certainly is in many respects, it affords an hour's enjoyment." The *Independent* thought it added to the merriment of the season. On 13 January 1913 a critic in the *New York Times* who had previously wondered, in his review of *Yet Again,* whether Max was a genius, now decided in the affirmative. In a lengthy article he said the writer had reached the "Olympic Heights of great satire."

At the same time that New Yorkers were reading *A Christmas Garland,* they had the chance of seeing an exhibit of Max's caricatures at the Berlin Photographic Company. Seventeen drawings were listed in the catalogue, including one of Sargent, two of Clyde Fitch, and two of Max—one a self-caricature and the other done by Oliver Herford and lent by Martin Birnbaum. Another early collector, A. E. Gallatin, lent a caricature of Lord Chesterfield. The *New York Times* art critic said that Max was "not an interesting artist on the aesthetic side. His color

116

is dull and meaningless; and his line is flaccid and inexpressive, but he manages to put together his poor line and stupid color in a way to convey often an excessively humorous impression." He was a literary artist, not an intellectual one: his mind was more on the perfecting of his story than of his method. "The collection . . . provides an agreeable half hour for the pleasure seeker not too exacting as to the quality of his amusement."

In January 1913 Max's play *A Social Success,* on the advance payment for which he had risked getting married in 1910, was performed by George Alexander at the Palace, and Max and Florence stayed in London for the opening. Max was pleased when it ran long enough to clear up his financial involvement. He carried back to Rapallo with him in February many unfinished caricatures for his next show at the Leicester Galleries. In April, it was his most successful exhibit so far, and the sales exceeded £ 800.

That summer Max did a number of wash drawings of Florence: Florence in the garden with her red hair blowing in the breeze, Florence on a chaise longue with her hair tucked up like a page boy's, and Florence, the housewife, in a dull blue gown and white apron. With a little box camera he also took pictures of her, which she helped develop and print. When Compton Mackenzie visited them Florence snapped a picture of him and Max on the terrace; Max had now grown a rather heavy mustache and he labeled the snapshot "A Major of the Volunteers in Conversation with a Faun." Mackenzie said he and Max sat on the terrace and drank Sicilian wine brought to them at intervals by Florence with her "mass of golden red hair and rose-red complexion."

In January 1914, after spending six weeks with Max in London, Florence went to visit her brothers in America and the transatlantic correspondence was resumed. In New York she could read Max's spoof of Russian literature, "Kolynatch," in *Harper's.* Her brother Sam was married and had an infant daughter. She told Max how delightful it was to be with Martha Michel again; no friendship had ever been so satisfying. Max wrote her of the people he was seeing in London, including Henry James:

> I did so wish for you here last Wednesday, for on that day I lunched at the Lewises' [Sir George and Lady Elizabeth Lewis], and oh you ought to have been there: Henry James was; and so amusing and interesting—nothing much to *repeat,* but delightful at the time. His heart seems to be bad; he looked ill when he came in.

Florence replied, "So glad you saw Henry James again. Meeting him meant so much to me."

Florence's brother Silas died later in the spring, so she was glad she had gone home.

Then came the fateful August of 1914. Florence and Max were in a quandary—should they leave Italy or wait out the war there? Max felt a sense of guilt at being absent from his country in time of crisis, and in 1915 they returned to England, where they remained four years. After visiting the Rothensteins at Far Oakridge, Gloucestershire, they settled into a cottage near by. Max hoped he might find something to do in the war, but when nothing seemed feasible, he tried to resume his own work. Florence knitted, cared for Max, and did some work for the Red Cross. At Oakridge in June 1915 Rothenstein painted Florence, a profile portrait in a blue gown with her auburn hair drawn into a bun at the back.

Max found the light touch and the amusing caricature difficult to achieve in wartime. He wrote John Singer Sargent, "The Comic Muse, who helps me in time of peace, sits nowadays, with ashes on her head, wailing, and having nothing to say to me." And again to Edith Wharton's request for a contribution to her *Book of the Homeless:*

> In times of peace—I am by way of being a cartoonist—a dealer in symbolic groups with reference to current events—But now there is only one current event: and it, the war, is so impossible a theme for comedy that one cannot (unless he is on the staff of a comic paper and *has* to) do a cartoon touching the remotest fringe of it. My cartooning days are thus over for the present.

So he turned to the past and developed what he called in a letter to Robert Ross, "a bad case of Rossettitis—(a malady that, like measles, is serious when it attacks you for the first time in middle age)." From this infection came the inspired drawings for *Rossetti and His Circle* in which the pictures of Elizabeth Siddall, beloved of Dante Gabriel Rossetti, were thought to look very like Florence.

They lived quietly; evenings they often played games with the Rothensteins, and sometimes they went up to London to see Max's family or dine with friends. In April 1917 Agnes, who had been for some time a widow, was quietly married at the Church of the Annunciation in Bryanston Street to Edmond Francis Vesey Knox, a barrister, whose son, Collie Knox became a well-known journalist. Max gave away the bride; Mrs. Beerbohm was not well enough to attend and Herbert was on tour in America.

After he returned to England in late May Herbert had a fall, tearing the cartilage in his knee so that an operation was necessary. He was well on the way to recovery when a blood clot developed, and he died 2 July.

A Comprehensive View and a Friendly Estimate of One of the Most Brilliant of English Humorists

By Robert B. Macdougall

IT is unfortunately possible for many Americans to consider themselves mature in appreciation of this century's literature and yet remain ignorant of Max Beerbohm. He writes little these years, and secure in his native England lives ostentatiously in Rapallo, one of Italy's fragments of beauty. No coterie on this side of the Atlantic does the service of aggressively bringing his works before the public; fresh admirers are of necessity recruited by word-of-mouth praise or by the chance reference. So admire Max wholeheartedly the pleasurable responsibility of now and again relating to the world at large our love for his genius, our delight in its accomplishments.

In all likelihood, the creative powers of Max Beerbohm are as varied and well balanced as those of any contemporary artist. He has chosen forms that make him a veritable minister to the wandering moods and yearnings of mankind. He is not a metaphysician or a philosopher in disguise. There is a quality, though, in his cool sanity and balance, in his absurdly credible illogic, which makes us conscious of contact with an intelligent man of the world—a man who knows what he is doing with life, and precisely why.

Why, therefore, with these qualities, has Max Beerbohm remained a hobby to a few in this country, rather than the familiar of the many. Chiefly and bluntly, the reason is that he is for the sophisticated, the reader who prefers subtleties of insight, imagination, and an intelligent artist. He appeals to those of the reading public who can appreciate his reactions to the world, and who, by intuition, by sensitive sympathy, can by with him when he leaves solid ground, drops ever so lightly, and embarks, as in his most fascinating of modern fairy tales. Stand not on ceremony...

Max Beerbohm

A full-page article—the notation "Boston Evening Transcript 1925" is in Max's hand—extols his essays, ending with *And Yet Again*, and awards high praise to *The Happy Hypocrite* and *Seven Men*.

The entire family was shocked and grieved; Max was most helpful to Maud. He and Florence were becoming increasingly aware of death, not only in the war, but in their circle of family and friends. They had sorrowed at the death of Henry James in February 1916, and a few months later Mabel Beardsley had lost her long fight against cancer. Now grief came closer: Evelyn Beerbohm, only son of Julius, was killed in action; and in March 1918 Mrs. Beerbohm died at the age of eighty-six. Florence mourned with Max at this parting.

Before they left Rapallo in 1915 Max had begun compiling the biographies of his *Seven Men,* imagined friends of his past; three of them appeared in the American *Century:* "James Pethel," illustrated by Dalton Stevens in January 1915; "Enoch Soames," illustrated by George Wright in May 1916; and "A. V. Laider," with the same illustrator, in June 1916. "James Pethel" had come out in the *English Review* a month earlier than in the *Century.* Max wrote Reggie:

> I am so very glad you liked my "James Pethel." It appeared also in the *Century* in America with surprising and delightful illustrations: James Pethel and myself in the motor-car, both of us extraordinarily keen, noble, square-jawed Amurrican men, simply vying with each other in strenuousness and vim and grit. . . . I have been writing another and longer essayish story, called "Enoch Soames: A Memory of the Nineties."

Although Max reacted favorably to the "James Pethel" pictures, when he received the proof of "Enoch Soames" he complained bitterly to the *Century* about the illustrations. He detested illustrations of imaginative work, disliking good ones almost if not quite as much as bad ones. He knew Americans did not share his horror. They considered pictures good for the commercial value of a book. He said he was quite willing to observe the *Century Dictionary* spelling—*envelop, honor, defence* and so on—but he would not accept the "crude and asinine interference with my punctuation," nor "the rough and ready standardizing methods of your proof readers." In "A. V. Laider" the paragraphs had been subdivided; he admitted that doubtless this was advisable, as magazine readers "are so easily tired—they must be humoured—their meat must be cut up small for them." Any change in his copy was a heinous sin to Max.

Philip Littell, having read "James Pethel," made it the subject of an essay in the *New Republic* for 30 January 1915. He had looked up Max in the eleventh edition of the *Encyclopaedia Britannica* and discovered he was given one and a half lines in Caricature and four lines in Criticism, making a total of five and one-half lines in all; yet Littell could safely predict that Max's prose would have the same immortality Max had predicted for Whistler's, that he "would have those few constantly recurring readers." An editor of the *Bookman,* who had assumed Soames was drawn from the poet Ernest Dowson, received a letter of correction from Max:

> I didn't draw Enoch Soames from anybody. I ventured to invent him, and having done so I ventured to adorn him with this and that slight point of resemblance to several persons—quite half a dozen—whom I knew in the nineties. Nor will I reveal who those persons were . . . Enough that Ernest Dowson was not one of them . . . I gather that he (Dowson) was a particularly modest and amiable young man, which Enoch Soames was *not.* . . . It is true that both Dowson and Soames went often to the domino room of the Café Royal and drank overmuch absinthe, and it's true that both of them (in reality and imagination) were drawn by Will Rothenstein in Glebe Place, Chelsea. . . . So please mix no more the dust of Enoch Soames with the ashes of Ernest Dowson.

"Hilary Maltby and Stephen Braxton" did not appear in the *Century* until February 1919, and "Savonarola Brown" was reprinted from the *London Review* in the American *Living Age* for 12 April 1919.

November 1918 brought the Armistice, but Florence and Max spent nearly another year flitting about England, trying to find a place that suited their taste and their pocketbook. In September 1919 Florence entrusted Max to the care of Maud Tree and returned to Rapallo to investigate the condition of the Villino. She found it little changed, and in December, after the publication in England of *Seven Men,* Max joined her, and life resumed its blessed and peaceful way.

Heinemann brought out *Seven Men* the last of October 1919, but no American edition was immediately forthcoming. Max offered the copyrights to the Century Company, but it did not accept, and Alfred Knopf became Max's American sponsor. The two editions were very different. For the special American edition of two thousand numbered copies, Max did an Appendix and six plates depicting the six men (the "seventh" being himself as narrator). He also departed from his avowed preference for unillustrated stories by making six additional drawings, which, however, were not used and became part of the Knopf collection. Six months later —in April 1921—Knopf did a second printing of a popular edition.

Herbert S. Gorman took the occasion of the first printing to review all of Max's writings in the *New York Times* for 2 January 1920. He disagreed with the contention of some critics that Max's true fame was as a draughtsman and caricaturist. He was more enchanted with Beerbohm's prose—each essay was an adventure. This evaluation was later included in Gorman's *Procession of Masks*. Carl Van Doren in the *Nation* found that Max, "the experimenter of the Nineties," was luridly up-to-date, "no matter what extinct creature he exhibits." Philip Littell, one of Max's earliest lobbyists, praised him again in the *New Republic,* but raised a question: "Will *Seven Men* . . . bring more readers than he has ever had in this country to Mr. Beerbohm, who has long been the classic case of reputation without popularity? I hope so. I am betting that this time the 'finer meat,' although as fine as ever, will make its way to more markets." Indeed the office of the *New Republic* was a forum for tributes to Max, addressed by Littell, Stark Young, and Francis Hackett.

William McFee, an expatriate Englishman, did an article on Max as the "Seventh Victorian" in an article in the New York *Evening Post,* later transferred to his *Swallowing the Anchor* (1925). One of the first scholarly studies of Max was done by Harold Newcomb Hillebrand in the April 1920 *Journal of English and Germanic Philology,* but it was accessible only to a limited public. Hillebrand called Max the "most completely artistic of English literati," and found "elegant diction, splendid wit, and lively fancy" to be the trinity of his art.

During 1919 and 1920 Max could be read in a number of American magazines: "A Relic" in *Harper's* of May 1919 and "Hosts and Guests" in August 1919; "The Golden Drugget" in the *Century* of January 1920, and "William and Mary" in December 1920. *Living Age* reprinted "Servants" 10 April 1920, "The Crime" 21 August 1920, and "Homes Unblest" 23 October 1920. The *New Republic* also printed "The Crime" 25 August 1920.

Max was now reaching the period of his greatest creativity, the 1920's. He was constantly sketching, writing, and projecting work. He was at the height of his fame in England and reaching towards that pinnacle in America. Few critics there failed to recognize his importance in the dual world of art and letters. Most gave prolonged and careful consideration to his work; others by more casual comment indicated familiarity with it. His prose was judged by American intellectuals to be of a unique and special sort, and admiration for it was a criterion of good taste. If his caricatures did not evoke quite the commendation that they did in England, this was understandable, since his subjects, mostly British, had more appeal in the land of their origin. Some American readers who did not undertake published criticism expressed themselves informally in letters to friends.

H. L. Mencken, although a friend and supporter of James Gibbons

Huneker, did not lack appreciation of Huneker's antagonist. Writing to Harry Leon Wilson in 1913 about his *Bunker Bean,* he called it a first-rate comic novel, "save *Zuleika Dobson,* the only good one in years;" and later he linked the two as "genuine satires, both wholly free of the Wallingford-Earlderrbigger's species of whimsicality." When he was consulting with Ellery Sedgwick about the new *Smart Set,* which he hoped would be a frivolous sister to the *Atlantic,* Mencken named Max as an ideal author to be sought. Willard Huntington Wright (S. S. Van Dine), an editor under Mencken's influence, prided himself, though erroneously, on having given Max a first printing in the United States with "The Mobled King" in the April 1914 *Smart Set.*

George Jean Nathan, who co-sponsored the *Smart Set* with Mencken, did not always agree with his partner. He wrote Mencken: "I consider you, old cock, an utter ass when it comes to Beerbohm. The essay is mere fla-fla—Max trying to grab some easy money in the gullible American magazine market. Let him sell it to Tom Swift for the *Century.* Tom admires Beerbohm because Beerbohm's brother, Beerbohm Tree, was a celebrated actor-manager and wore silk spats. Moreover the readers of the *Century* will like this sort of thing. Such stuff always fetches school teachers. I doubt that it would interest our customers. . . . As you know, I esteem Berbohm highly, but it seems to me that he hasn't turned out a decent piece of work for five years."

John Macrae of Dutton's, an enthusiastic admirer of Max, was disappointed when Knopf got his *Seven Men,* but Dutton published *And Even Now* in 1921. Macrae believed that Max had attained the prestige requisite for a Collected Edition of his work; he proposed the idea to Heinemann and an agreement was reached. In his letter, he called Max "that splendid old lion." Max was startled: "That I was old I knew," he said. "That I was splendid and leonine was a revelation: dazzled by the light of which I made a feebler resistance than I should have made to the whole scheme." This Collected Edition, which did not include the caricatures, took Max through *A Variety of Things* (1928).

XIV

Happy Days on the Coast Road

WHILE MAX'S professional life was progressing so satisfactorily, his personal happiness was not lagging behind. He and Florence were delighted at returning to the idyllic existence at the Villino, though they disagreed slightly about the desirability of their new neighbors, the Edward Gordon Craigs, who had taken the Villa Raggio near by. Craig—artist, designer, theatrical producer, and son of actress Ellen Terry—had been a friend of Max's youth, and now Florence feared he might be a disruptive influence, luring Max from his necessary endeavors. She soon became reconciled to the newcomers, however, and recorded in the family diary, "All went over to the Craigs where it was delightful as it always is."

When they had first come to the Villino Chiaro, Max had begun to keep a journal with which Florence sometimes helped, and it was continued from 1911 to 1932, with more lapses than entries. It was a matter-of-fact record of daily events: "Walked to Rapallo . . . Tea at Verdi's . . . Florence undertook sending off caricatures . . . Max watered roses and lemons . . . Colefaxes here . . . Max had a slight toothache . . . bouillabaisse at supper, best I ever tasted . . . Reggie here . . . Mr. and Mrs. Charles Morgan coming." "Bathing at the *spiaggia* [shore]" was a frequent item. There is little mention of Max's work, though on 16 October 1921, he noted, "In evening Florence typed Whistler-Hethway correspondence."

Friends were appearing more and more often at the Villino: gone were the days when Max could say they did not hear a word of English spoken except by themselves. The visitors were graciously and hospitably received. When the poet and critic R. Ellis Roberts, an Oxford friend of Max's, married an American girl, Harriet Keen, and took her to Italy on their honeymoon in 1920, they were warmly welcomed by Max and Florence, so warmly that on their first evening together Ellis was reported to have declared, "I'm not so think as you drunk I am!" From then on the two Anglo-American couples were close friends, visiting each other in England and Italy.

Terrace of the Villino Chiaro, high above the Coast Road.

Ada Leverson, witty fascinator of Max's salad days, now grown older and unfortunately deaf, often stayed near by and came to lunch. She brought the Osbert Sitwells in 1924, and Osbert grew lyrical over Florence's cooking. Mary Annette Russell, author of the celebrated *Elizabeth and Her German Garden,* rented a castello at Portofino and liked to descend on the Villino where she could be sure of good conversation. When Harley Granville-Barker came to Rapallo with his American bride, Florence felt a little strange; she had liked the actress Lillah McCarthy, the play-wright-producer's first wife, now divorced. Somerset Maugham, luxuriating in his Villa at Cap d'Antibes, tried to entice Max and Madame to visit him, but Max said privately that nothing could induce him to accept the invitation; still, Maugham came to see him. Max was gladly at home, too, when the Americn drama critic Alexander Woollcott motored over from the Cap.

Bookmen and editors from the States felt a call on Max to be a duty and a pleasure when they came to Italy. One of the earliest of these, A. Edward Newton, the famous bibliophile, explained:

> Who that knows him would not spend a day or two with Max Beer-bohm, if he could? He lives in one of the loveliest places in the world, Rapallo. From the deck of the Villino Chiaro, he watches year after year, the ever changing and always beautiful Mediterranean, heedless that the world passes his door; let it pass. His talk is as whimsical as his writing, and his writing is—must I say, was? the most subtle of his day and mine. Far be it from me to say that Max, "the incomparable Max," is no longer young; he is not so young as he was thirty years ago, when I first met him, but he is—in a way —immortal.

Newton seemed to arrive every year, explaining the reason for his absence if he did not come. He presented Max with most of his books, and they were included in the posthumous sale of Max's effects: Max had made several notes in the margins, and, in accordance with a pastime he enjoyed increasingly—that of altering photographs—he had changed a like-ness of Walt Whitman to a likeness of the Prince of Wales in 1875.

Newton collected Max, writing him from London that he had just paid an unwarranted price for *More* and had heard that *The Works* recently sold for eighty-five dollars. Again, he had just bought two caricatures, a Kipling from *The Poets' Corner* and an unpublished Oscar Wilde. When he sent Max his *Greatest Book in the World,* he mentioned that it was now worth ten or twelve dollars and he was not just trying to get rid of a copy. "I suppose you will never come to America again," he said, "so I will have no opportunity to repay your courtesies. You might, however, kiss your wife for me and thus add to the obligation I am under."

Newton named *Zuleika Dobson* among the one hundred best books, saying it would never have the success of *David Harum* "but it will be read when David Harum is forgotten." He urged his readers to collect Max, who reciprocated by doing a caricature of Newton titled "On the Riviera di Levante," inadvertently naming him "Arthur" instead of "Alfred."

Since his brother Herbert's death in 1917, Max had been occupied with a memorial volume to him, for which he had asked contributions from Herbert's wife and daughters, Edmund Gosse, and George Bernard Shaw, among others. Max had to make several trips to England before the work appeared in 1920. His own essay, "From a Brother's Standpoint," was one of the easier tasks in preparing the tribute. Dutton took twelve hundred copies for the States from Heinemann, but it was of more interest to people of the theatre than to the literary public. "Simon Pure" (Frank Swinnerton), writing in the American *Bookman* for December 1920, said that the difficulty of biography had recently been felt "by one of the quickest brains" in England. He found Max's essay on his brother charming, full of affection and humor, but the only chapter in the book which had value as a portrait was done by Shaw.

When, in September 1921, Dutton published the American edition of *And Even Now,* the book had been out in England for nine months. Under the heading "Puck on Piccadilly" in the *Nation* for 12 October 1921, Joseph Wood Krutch deplored Max's lack of recognition in the States. He had entered a fairly intellectual bookstore on Fifth Avenue and inquired if it had anything by Beerbohm, to be asked by the clerk whether he wanted it in the original German or in translation. At the New York Public Library he could find neither *The Happy Hypocrite* nor *Zuleika Dobson* in the catalogue. Krutch felt this American lack of perception was regrettable: he enjoyed Beerbohm's mocking spirit; it was a check on ponderosity and it prevented English art and letters from becoming too British. He repeated this idea in the New York *Evening Post.*

Gilbert Seldes did little more than mention *And Even Now* in the *Dial* along with eight other books, of which he said Max's and Logan Pearsall Smith's were least known in America. (The *Dial* had made one attempt to remedy this lack by printing Max's "T. Fenning Dodworth" in August 1921.) One of the less pleasant notices of *And Even Now* was given by Burton Rascoe in the *Bookman*. He contended that American essayists were superior to British, saying that to prove it one only needed to read Max Beerbohm. His latest book gave evidence that "his patrimony is running low. He is a gentleman and he would not have you know that he has turned his linen and put cardboard in his shoes. His manner is as cultured as before . . . but this only serves to remind us that he was always a little bogus and that his snobbery is rather cheap."

Max had not had an exhibit in London since before the war, but in 1921 he had two, one in the spring and another in the fall. Both were highly successful. The May show contained several cartoons of interest to Americans. In "The Churchill-Wells Controversy," Churchill is saying to H. G. Wells, "You were only fourteen days in Russia," and Wells replies, "Your mother was an American;" also in this exhibit were "Woodrow Wilson's Peace," and caricatures of Henry James, Logan Pearsall Smith, and Ezra Pound. Most of these were included in *A Survey* (1921). The September exhibit was largely devoted to the colorful Rossetti cartoons to be published in 1922 as *Rossetti and His Circle*.

In late August 1921 Florence came home from a visit to the States, bringing her fifteen-year-old niece, Alexandra Kahn, the daughter of Mannie and his wife, the former Helen Irwin, a Canadian. Alexandra, called "Dody," was to spend six months at the Villino. Mannie Kahn had stipulated that his daughter must write home every day, and these letters, recently edited by Dody's daughter, Marion Bagshawe, offer an intimate picture of the Beerbohms at home: their cat Strachey; Max in the nerve-racking process of writing an article on drama critic A. B. Walkley for *The Times;* preparing a miniature book for inclusion in a doll house to be presented to the Queen; drawing caricatures; Florence typing, reading proof on the American edition of *And Even Now* (very bad!) and cooking wonderful meals. On her arrival Dody wrote home that Uncle Max was rather bald, though not unattractively so, and his remaining hair was nearly white. She could understand why he was said to be the most attractive man in England. She got on famously with him; he was a great tease, playing jokes on her, such as making an apple-pie bed, poking fun at her American ways, and imitating her American accent. When she spoke of the Fourth of July, he said it should be celebrated in England too, as Good Riddance Day. They sang folk songs together while Aunt Florence plucked at a guitar. Max said folk songs were all made of sad words and rollicking tunes. Although Florence encouraged Dody to read *Hamlet* with her, Uncle Max was excluded from the readings because he said, "Oh" in a disappointed tone when one of the minor characters left the stage in an early scene, adding, "I'm sorry that man is gone. I'm going to miss him frightfully."

Dody thought Aunt Florence most kind, but a little strict: she wouldn't let her whistle, face powder was taboo, and she mustn't talk too freely with Teddy Craig, Gordon's son. In Rapallo people greeted Florence like a long lost friend and seemed to adore her. When Sir James M. Barrie received the Order of Merit in 1922, Aunt Florence thought Max should have had it—and an earldom and the Nobel Prize as well, added Dody.

In November Max sent Mannie Kahn the verses, "The King is duller than the Queen." Because Dody much admired the Prince of Wales, Max teased her by doing a drawing of the Prince marrying a boarding-house keeper's daughter. While she was there several noted people came to visit—the Granville-Barkers, Miss F. Tennyson Jesse, William Archer and Reggie Turner. The Baroness von Hutten, with whom Max had flirted briefly in 1907 at Portofino, was in Rapallo, but Aunt Florence wouldn't invite her to the Villino.

Dody was much missed when her father came and took her home. A year later Uncle Max gave her the local news in a long typewritten letter:

> The family Craig is in great force and thrivingness, playing soft-ball cricket on their terrace, cataloguing and printing and pricing and archivising and wood-cutting and being as picturesque and beautiful as ever. Florence and I have become globe-trotters: we have recently returned from an extended tour, embracing Carrara, Lucca, Pistoia, and Florence. . . . I have become a percher aloft on precarious ladders, a painter of domestic frescoes. I have done a fresco in the embrased arch over the green door of the spare bedroom, and another above the high-up fanlight in the hall. I think they look very jolly and Giottesque [sic]. Florence is not so sure about them; but there they are to impress posterity. . . . Have you ever worked on the top of a ladder? It is exhilarating, bracing, and great fun. One may fall and be fractured or killed at any moment. One faces death but one sees only one's art. And one *sings* all the time.

He then recalled their singing and his difficulty in getting the words right to "I didn't raise my boy, etc." Then he added a postscript: was this nearer the right thing?—

> *I didn't raise my boy to do a fresco,*
> *I brought him up to be my pride and joy;*
> *I wish I were Elizabeth Bibesco,*
> *Who doesn't yet possess a darling boy.*
> *These horrid ladders ought to be prevented,*
> *These brushes all should confiscated be—*
> *There'd be no walls today*

If mothers all would say,
"I didn't raise my boy to do a fresco!"

So went Max's joyous account of the painting of the famous Villino frescoes: Zuleika and the Duke and Katie, the serving maid, in a rounded arch just inside the front door—and profile caricatures of twelve of Max's contemporaries above the door leading to the bedroom. After his death the Zuleika mural was taken to the Max Beerbohm memorial room at Merton College, there to "impress posterity."

In 1922 Knopf brought out Bohun Lynch's *Max Beerbohm in Perspective,* and in May the *Dial* reviewed it, together with *A Survey* (caricatures), and *And Even Now,* with most attention given to the book of essays. "If Mr. Beerbohm intends to contribute anything substantial to our civilization (or whatever it is), he had better begin at once," decreed the reviewer.

> I notice an unusual exasperation in the reception of his latest work, and it is clear that the world which has been indulgent to his frivolities for such a long time is at last demanding that he put his gifts to proper use. . . . Can anything solid come out of Rapallo? The turning of the tide gently against Mr. Beerbohm is as interesting as anything in his career. One English critic irritated by the Labour cartoons accuses the artist of vulgarity; an American remembers that in his writing, he was always bogus. And even those who are favorable to the later work show signs of strain . . .

The reviewer saw two reasons for this dissatisfaction: first, the resentment against the legend of Max, the "neatness too long drawn out"; and second, his identification as the aristocrat, not the artist—the patrician, not the individual. Notice was given of the forthcoming Collected Edition, and the review concluded with a right-face turn, "One hopes that by the time it appears, in all its completeness, people will recall, that in spite of reviewers, Mr. Beerbohm is a very entertaining man."

In the *New Republic* of 10 May 1922 Rollin Kirby characterized Max's style as too restricted, too cerebral, to appeal to the man in the street: "His gifts are like a vintage wine of a year when the yield is small. Such liquor is not for the taverns."

In February 1922 Dodd, Mead announced it had acquired all John Lane's copyrights, including those of Max Beerbohm, and to prove it issued *A Defence of Cosmetics,* originally part of *The Works,* as a separate edition of one thousand copies at one dollar each; the edition seems to have vanished with little trace. Dodd, Mead also gave Haldeman-Julius at Girard, Kansas, permission to print it in the latter's Little Blue Book series, selling for five cents.

Doubleday Page received a thousand copies of *Rossetti and His Circle* in October 1922 for distribution in the States. In the *New Republic* for 21 February 1923, the art critic Thomas Craven declared that these caricatures of the Pre-Raphaelites were in Max's most felicitous vein. Max had returned to his natural home, the past; the drawings would be extremely fascinating to an audience who knew the Pre-Raphaelites. The effect of Max's drawings was literary rather than artistic, for "his drawing is arbitrary and conceited, he applies colors as a tinted texture; he has no sense of design and no ability to relieve his flat areas by strong black-and-white contrast; in short, his work is devoid of formal beauty"—but he was a genius, if not an artist.

One caricature in *Rossetti and His Circle* reflected Max's feelings about American culture. In it Oscar Wilde, plump, long-haired, wearing knee breeches and holding a long-stemmed lily, is lecturing to an American audience with the caption, "The name of Dante Gabriel Rossetti is heard for the first time in the United States of America. Time: 1881, Lecturer: Mr. Oscar Wilde." The stolid bewhiskered men to whom he speaks could best be described by the old New England term "hayseeds." In the background is a picture of Abraham Lincoln, with American flags behind it; the President looks unimpressed.

Max and Florence went to London for Max's exhibit at the Leicester Galleries in 1923, but perhaps with reason were not present on opening day, for next morning the London papers exploded with shocked and aggrieved comment at several cartoons of the Royal Family. After some discussion the drawings in question were withdrawn. The most controversial one, "Long Choosing and Beginning Late," was Max's Miltonic observation on the continued bachelorhood of the Prince of Wales (later Edward VIII), which he had first done to tease Dody. An American novelist who was visiting England was much more incensed by another cartoon. Sinclair Lewis, whose *Babbitt* had been a success in Britain as well as America, was now in London, working with Paul de Kruif on *Arrowsmith* when he wasn't being entertained by literary folk or lecturing critics on their gross underestimation of American writing. He had been so outspoken on this subject that Philip Guedalla warned George Jean Nathan that if America didn't recall Lewis at once there would be war between England and the United States. Lewis had been invited to the opening, but his temper flared when he came to Number 51, "Reciprocity," in which a cigar-smoking Brother Jonathan faces a cadaverous Dame Europa before a background of packing cases labeled Monet, Rembrandt, Gainsborough, with this dialogue:

> DAME EUROPA: "And now, young man, that you've bought up all my art treasures, I shall be happy to acquire all yours and I am willing to pay a generous price."
> BROTHER JONATHAN: "Name it, Marm."
> DAME EUROPA: "Twopence-halfpenny."
> (Brother Jonathan is slightly hurt, but like a sensible fellow, closes with the offer.)

"Where the devil did he get his idea of America from?" Lewis demanded. "Why is he authorized to insult America in this way?"—good questions from the author of *Main Street*.

Had he seen two other cartoons Max did in 1924, "The Poor Relation" and "Marianne's Creditors," Lewis's blood pressure would have soared again. These were Max's comments on the role of the United States in the matter of war debts. In the first drawing, a corpulent Brother Jonathan is receiving money from an apologetic John Bull, in the second, from a petite France.

"Reciprocity" was the only shaft aimed at the States in *Things New and Old,* published October 1923, with seven hundred fifty copies to Doubleday in November. Perhaps the most significant result of its publication was an article in the January 1924 *Yale Review* by Wilbur L. Cross, later governor of Connecticut. Cross thought that although Max's care for style might have its defects, they were lost in its virtues. Reproduced with the article were Max's cartoons "Tales of Three Nations, England, France and Germany," which Edith Wharton scolded Cross for publishing, saying that they were "abominable" and that Max was "pro-German."

Alexander Woollcott used *Things New and Old* to present to the readers of the *Ladies' Home Journal* a brief sketch of Edward VII and his relations with his mother, Queen Victoria, with a mention of Max's unpublished verse, "The King is duller than the Queen." He said that in Rapallo Max devoted a good bit of his time as an expatriate to sticking out his tongue at Royalty. "The Poor Relation" and "Marianne's Creditors" were included in *Observations,* of which Doubleday took seven hundred fifty copies and later fifty of a limited edition. One other caricature had reference to America—"The Prince of Wales in New York." Here the slender, perplexed son of George V is surrounded by fat, overdressed

American dowagers, who are scrambling to curry favor with the heir to the Throne.

Helen MacAfee said in the *Yale Review* that *Observations* would appeal only to the most discriminating public and would never be widely popular. She felt Max's medium was too delicate for political caricature—he was more successful when he dealt with art and literature. Other American critics agreed.

Florence paid her last visit to the States in 1924 when Isaac, always called Ike, the dearest of her brothers, was to undergo surgery in New York. Long a bachelor, he had married a bright pretty girl seventeen years his junior, whom Florence liked. In New York Florence spent much time with her doctor brother Mannie, Dody's father, driving with him in his car and seeing a great deal of the City. Max confided to Will Rothenstein that she thought the city greatly improved, and though she would not admit publicly that there was room for improvement, she admitted it to herself. After Ike's operation, which was successful, Florence went to Memphis to be with her younger brother Sam.

In 1925 Will Rothenstein introduced Max and Florence to the Gerhart Hauptmanns, living in Rapallo but hitherto unknown to them. Hauptmann was grateful for this new friendship, saying the Beerbohms added much to the charm of Rapallo. He thought theirs a perfect form of existence and he appreciated his visits to the Villino. Florence, who had long admired the German dramatist, expertly fostered the friendship with her fluent German, for the Hauptmanns spoke no English and Max no German. She was delighted that Max and Hauptmann seemed so congenial in spite of the handicap of language. Elisabeth Jungmann, Hauptmann's clever and pleasing secretary, became one of Florence's dearest friends, and a sincere admirer of Max. From now on, she was to be an increasingly important figure in their lives.

Often, if not every year, they could count on a visit from Reggie Turner. He and Max played chess together, talked over old times, discussed their current literary productions, and sometimes got on each other's nerves. Reggie admired Max's books and Max admired Reggie's, though he was one of the few people who did. Florence made Reggie welcome, worried about his health, and gave him advice about it. Max's sister Dora, sometimes with a friend, came every summer for her holiday. One spring Morris Kahn and his wife, Myrtle, came to stay at the Villino and he and Max renewed their friendship after twenty years. Morris listened enchanted to Max's conversation and noticed that Florence listened with as much delight as anyone.

Florence saw her brother Mannie more frequently now, for he and his wife, Helen, had bought a villa down the hill from them and came there whenever he could get away from his hospital post in New York. Florence was always glad when they came and sorry when their stay was ended.

Mannie was not there, however, when she really needed him. In the spring of 1927 she developed what Max termed a whitlow on her right index finger, and after several painful, but ineffectual, lancings, the Italian doctor removed the tip of the bone. From then on she had to wear a flesh-colored stall on that finger. She was, as Max said, frightfully brave about it, and refused to let it make her self-conscious or hamper her freedom of gesture, but she had always been proud of her hands and it was hard to have Mannie say afterwards such extreme treatment had not been necessary.

In the mid-Twenties Max was spending more time at his drawing board than at his writing desk, yet his reading public in the States was increasing. A new American reprint magazine, *Golden Book,* begun in 1924, and edited by H. W. Lanier, with William Lyon Phelps and Stuart Sherman on its staff, frequently used his essays or quoted from them. In the first number, with the caption, "What the Well-dressed Heroine Has Been Wearing," Zuleika's appearance was described, and a year later Abimelech V. Oover was presented. Clever quotations from Max often filled out columns, and under "How I Became a Success" Max's Letter to Bohun Lynch beginning, "My gifts are small, I've used them well and discreetly, never straining them," was quoted. Several of Max's pieces were given in entirety, including *The Happy Hypocrite,* "Enoch Soames" from *Seven Men,* and his early play, *A Social Success.*

Three other American reprintings of his work did not please Max, and for them Max Harzof of the G. A. Baker Company must be held responsible: *A Peep into the Past* (1923), *The Guerdon* (1925), and *Leaves from the Garland* (1926). In his Introductory Note to the English edition of *A Variety of Things* (1928), Max spoke of *The Guerdon,* which he had done at the time the Order of Merit was conferred on Henry James:

> I wrote it . . . without any thought of publication. I gave the MS. to a friend; and to another friend I gave a copy I had made of the MS. One of the receivers asked me whether somebody, who liked it much, might make a copy of it. I said, "Oh, by all means. And let anybody who likes it make a copy." No doubt the copyists were equally compliant to others; and I don't at all blame them for not foreseeing that a booklet entitled "The Guerdon" would be pub-

lished, with my name and without my knowledge, by an American firm.

In the Note to the first American edition of two thousand numbered copies of *A Variety of Things,* published by Alfred Knopf, he was more explicit:

> A little later, a friend wrote that he was posting the book to me. I did not, however, open the parcel when it arrived. I put it into the fire, not wishing to run any risk of being arrested as a receiver of stolen goods.

He went on to say that the same firm had published a squib about Oscar Wilde, *A Peep into the Past,* and some five or six parodies, which he had discarded as crude stuff, in *Leaves from the Garland.* He feared that people would think he was responsible for the republication of some rubbishy parodies and of some gibes against a distinguished writer whose life was to end in disaster. He asked why he should have his negligibilia foisted upon the public, and answered himself:

> . . . anything hitherto unpublished, or published only in a newspaper, ranks as a "first edition" when it comes out in the form of a book or pamphlet. . . . If I chose to offer to the public, as book or pamphlet, any little old thing, however stupid, I could make some money by so doing. But I prefer to go without such emolument, and am, on the other hand, mean enough to grudge it to whatever less sensitive person may at any moment rush out and do the trick in spite of me.

He suggested that American collectors should not buy any book whose issue was not sanctioned by its author, since the reason for desiring a first edition was the sense of nearness to the author it gave.

> "This is the binding *he* chose—perhaps. This—perhaps—is the fount of type that *he* insisted on. Here certainly is a typographical error which *his* eyes overlooked—bless his noble spirit!" . . . I urge there is nothing like piracy to give one a sense of remoteness from one's favorite . . . "This is the book *he* didn't know was going to be published. . . . What wouldn't one give to possess, on a velvet pad, under a glass case, the one single cent *he* never received for his work! Here is a marble bust of the publisher. The brow is magnificent, isn't it?"

Max cannot be blamed for this resentment towards unscrupulous publishers, inspired though they might have been by a desire to spread his fame and do him honor. The parodies taken from the early *Chap-Books* were by no means rubbishy, and today's reader may be glad they were rescued to become collectors' items, but that is no excuse for piracy. How *The Guerdon* reached the U.S.A. probably will never be clear. Max gave the manuscript to Edmund Gosse and a copy to his friend Mrs. Charles Hunter; others undoubtedly read it, but who carried it across the Atlantic?

The American and English editions of *A Variety of Things* differed, "The Happy Hypocrite" and "A Note on the Einstein Theory" being omitted from the Knopf edition. More than half the material in this collection was of older vintage, written in the Nineties or in the early days of the twentieth century, perhaps giving some basis for Burton Rascoe's charge, already mentioned, that Max was beginning to turn his linen. One essay, written in March 1927, bore reference to the acquisitive tendencies of Americans in the book trade.

"Not that I Would Boast" is an account of three literary men, Felix Argallo, Walter Ledgett, and Max Beerbohm, who tells the story. Max has contrived to boom Ledgett's work through faked letters written in his praise by Argallo, who holds an assured place in letters, partly through a big success in America. Max describes that success:

> Within a month of its publication . . . "Last Shadows" . . . had come out in America too, of course. America in such crises is less self-controlled than England. There were strange doings. The principal literary critic in Pittsburgh lost his reason and had to be placed under restraint; and the number of suicides here and there was so large that in some of the states the sale of "A Bare Bodkin" was banned by the authorities. And during the summer months in Ermyntrude Road the crowds of American tourists standing outside Argallo's exposed refuge were too great for his endurance.

The day after he has written these commendatory letters on Ledgett, Argallo dies, and Max now waits the publication of his *Letters*. In the meantime he buys up every possible edition of Ledgett's books, Ledgett, too, having died. With the publication of the Argallo *Letters*, Ledgett's fame begins. Max is approached by Mr. Nat Heinz, a famous "Firsts Agent" from America; when the small dark eyes of Mr. Heinz alight on treasure after treasure, they gleam uncontrollably though he tries to pretend Argallo doesn't mean much to him; he'd handled him extensively at one time, but he had greatly depreciated. However, he eagerly gives Max nine hundred pounds for the books. Max cannot resist telling the story of his hoax to a friend and refuses to be dashed when the friend

reminds him he has put that sum, or more, into Heinz's pocket. "I never
want to get the better of anybody," says Max. "Enough that for once
Europe had held her own!"

"But she hasn't!" my friend retorted. "America has got the books!"
This, I confessed, was a point I hadn't thought of. But perhaps also
(not that I would boast) it is a point which Mr. Heinz's clients, when
these pages shall have appeared, won't think very much of.

Felix Argallo and Walter Ledgett became the "Two Others" in
Seven Men and Two Others (1950).

Heinemann extracted one story from *A Variety of Things* and printed
it separately in 1928 as *The Dreadful Dragon of Hay Hill,* a fantasy, or
perhaps an allegory with a deeper meaning than Max imparted to his other
fairy tales. The story, set in the past—not the immediate past, but the
prehistoric past of the human race—concerns the Homelanders, the hero
and heroine, Thal and Thia, and the dreadful dragon. All the people are
united against the menace of the dragon, but when the beast is killed
their morale deteriorates. Since Max wrote at least part of the story
during the First World War, J. G. Riewald's interpretation seems valid:

To me it seems that this story is . . . a parable or allegory, on the
fact that war brings out all sorts of virtues in the people which are
latent at other times, and a satire on the human race to the effect
that it requires a war to accomplish this.

The *Dragon* was not published separately in the States.

Although in 1924 Heinemann had issued *Around Theatres,* two volumes
of Max's reviews collected from the *Saturday,* and dedicated to his Rapallo
neighbor Gordon Craig, six years elapsed before Knopf risked their publication, fearing perhaps that articles about the London stage of nearly
a generation earlier would have small appeal to American readers caught
up in the Roaring Twenties. However, not a drama critic in the States
failed to read and comment on *Around Theatres.* Harry Hansen of the
New York Times admitted on 8 November 1930 that he had sat up well
into the night reading the reviews, and decided that Max had an independent point of view and took his reviewing seriously. Mark Van Doren
in the *Nation* for 17 December 1930 declared that the present articles
proved once more that not only was Max perfect—he had always been
so—but the reader must not suppose because Max had a gentle style that
he had a gentle heart: he could murder a playwright, maul an actor, and
massacre a whole cast. But Stark Young in the 31 December *New*

Republic asserted that four-fifths of the volume was not worth reprinting; in the remaining fifth, however, he said Max's native shrewdness was joyously apparent. Young found Max at his best about Shaw (most critics agreed), capital on Henry Irving, and not so good about Eleanora Duse and Sarah Bernhardt.

In 1954 a one-volume edition of *Around Theatres* was brought out by Simon and Schuster; Wolcott Gibbs, who acknowledged he had been much influenced by Max's writing, gave it a ten-page notice in the *New Yorker* of 3 October 1953. Walter P. Kerr observed in the *Commonwealth* of 2 July 1954 that the play being reviewed was more frequently Max's irritation than his inspiration, but found the essays very fresh and funny. Within the past few years Rupert Hart-Davis has collected the rest of Max's reviews from the *Saturday* into two volumes, *More Theatres* and *Last Theatres,* published in London by Rupert Hart-Davis Ltd., and in New York by Taplinger Publishing Co., Inc.

XV

Again the Actress

THE RISE OF Mussolini and the growth of the Fascist party in Italy disturbed the transplanted Britons, and during the Thirties they spent more time in England, either separately or together. In 1930 with some reluctance Max left Florence at the Villino and went to London, two reasons prompting the move. He was to receive an Honorary Doctor of Law degree from the University of Edinburgh, and his sister Constance was facing an operation. Florence anxiously awaited his bulletins and was relieved when the news was good.

The following spring Florence was tempted by an offer to return to the footlights. Alfred Wareing, who had been responsible for her appearance in *Rosmersholm* in 1907, had established a repertory company in Huddersfield, Yorkshire, to compete with variety shows and movies. He offered Florence the part originally played by Duse in Pirandello's *The Life You Gave Me*. The part, the play, and the purpose appealed to her; perhaps, too, the money, for with the Depression times were harder at the Villino and checks from her inheritance did not always arrive on schedule from America. Max urged her to accept, and they departed for London, where Max stayed while Florence went north to Yorkshire. Their friends Ellis and Harriet Roberts were keenly sympathetic with the undertaking and tried to ensure that leading London critics would go to Huddersfield for the first performance, even though Paul Robeson was opening in London with *The Hairy Ape* the same night. Undoubtedly, though, it was the loyalty they felt for Max that drew Charles Morgan of *The Times* and W. A. Darlington of the *Telegraph* to Florence's opening; their reviews made pleasant reading for Florence and Max. Ellis Roberts in the *New Statesman* said Miss Kahn united rare beauty with spiritual intelligence only seen once or twice in a century. The most enthusiastic, though briefest, verdict was Max's cable to brother Sam, "Florence—magnificent."

Although Florence maintained that she was happier as a wife and home-maker, she must have been secretly still hoping for a success in the theatre. In the autumn of 1934 she went again to London, ostensibly to recover from an attack of the 'flu, but covertly hoping for a chance to act. Alfred Wareing was sympathetic and thought her presence in London desirable. Nothing seemed to work out, but Florence enjoyed herself, even away from Max, staying in a flat in the Adelphi which Mrs. Thomas Hardy had lent her and seeing her old friends. The friendship of the Beerbohms and Hardys had grown during the Twenties and after the novelist's death in 1928, the two women had kept in touch. Florence had been pleased when Mrs. Hardy went to Huddersfield to see her in the Pirandello play. Now Mrs. Hardy wrote Florence, "How lovely if Max could come and stay in my flat. Garrick's shade would rejoice."

But Max was now the stay-at-home, and Florence could write him of her social engagements. She had gone to a dinner at which William Butler Yeats had been a fellow guest. Years earlier Max had written Florence that though Yeats was a genius, geniuses were usually asses, and Yeats's particular asininity bored him, querying her sharply, "Have you seen him again?" Now Florence wrote she was quite won over by Yeats; his talk was extraordinary, sometimes profound, sometimes gay, and without malice. It had been a pleasant evening.

George Freedley, Curator of the New York Theatre Collection, who was in London that summer, was taken to see Florence by Wareing. He found her quiet and reserved until she learned that he was a friend of Paul Kester's. At once the coolness melted and she plied him with questions, for she had lost touch with this old friend; Freedley had to give her the news of his death. She hoped Freedley could come to Rapallo and see Gordon Craig's theatre collection, but he was unable to do so.

Florence felt awakened and stimulated by her stay in Mrs. Hardy's flat with its view of the Thames, and she thanked Max for encouraging her to remain. The love between Florence and Max which their letters reveal was always a love of kindness and consideration. They never took each other for granted; if one did a service for the other, it was always gratefully acknowledged.

Although no work resulted from this visit to London, the following year brought Florence an offer to play at the Old Vic. When she was at Huddersfield, William Cass had been in the company. Now he was producing at the Old Vic, and remembering Florence's interest in Ibsen, he asked her to play Åse in Ellis Roberts's new translation of *Peer Gynt*. Again this was a rôle which tempted her, and she and Max went to London. On opening night, 20 September 1935, the stalls were filled with West End society, literary and artistic personages, and as many students as standing room would allow. Again the critics came and Florence's triumph was undeniable, though James Agate unnecessarily referred to her "hurt finger." A young actor, William Devlin, was warmly praised for his portrayal of Peer.

Many years later, by then an established figure in the theatre, Devlin described this early experience. He had taken over the part when Maurice Evans had to give it up. On opening night, Devlin recounted, he had a bad case of stage fright. As he stood in the wings, nervous and shaking, waiting to go on with Florence in the scene of their quarrel, she suddenly spun him around, delivered a ringing slap across his cheek and pushed him on-stage. The scene, he said, went like a bombshell.

Peer Gynt was so popular it could have run for months, but it had to be withdrawn after five weeks to make room for *Julius Caesar*. Conditions in Italy still alarmed the Beerbohms and they decided to remain over the Christmas holidays in London. This decision led to Florence's last appearance on the English stage. She was offered the part of the Duchess of Gloucester in John Gielgud's production of *Richard II* for the Oxford University Dramatic Society, familiarly known as OUDS. She would not receive any salary, only expenses, but it was an honor to be asked, and pleasant to be in Oxford.

Just before Christmas Max had a performance of his own. He had been asked to broadcast for the B.B.C. on "London Revisited," and, pleased by this new challenge and by the generous fee, he had accepted. He gave the preparation of his talk the same meticulous care he used in writing an essay and getting it ready for the printer, and again his capacity for taking pains won him the approval of the broadcasting authorities and his audience. He was asked to speak again; on 16 April 1936 he did "Speed," and on 16 July 1936 "A Small Boy Seeing Giants." Of course these were not heard in the States, but some years later Angel made a recording of Max reading "London Revisited," and "The Crime," and this record, carried home by tourists, demonstrated to Americans Max's well-modulated voice and the nicety of his diction.

In February 1936 Florence went to Oxford, and Max followed shortly, finding joy in returning to that magical city. While Florence was in rehearsal Max found no lack of company; he drank morning coffee with the dons, lunched at the Mitre, and dined in hall at Merton, his old college. As he sat at the high table, the Junior Common Room sent him up an honorary sconce of beer and he was genuinely touched by the compliment. He raised his sconce, beamed mistily upon them, and drank. Those present insisted they had seen Max the Incomparable weep in his beer. As another mark of esteem the Merton Floats, the college dramatic society, presented *Savonarola Brown*. He also made the speech of the evening at the OUDS banquet.

Visitors to Florence's dressing room at the New Theatre found prints of fourteenth-century England hanging on the walls and a Shakespeare Variorum on her table. She believed that such surroundings helped her to get the mood and feeling of a play (when she played *Peer Gynt,* her walls had been bright with pictures of Norwegian mountains and fjords). She was surprised that Vivien Leigh, who was to play the Queen, seemed to feel no need for such atmosphere: her room was filled with undergraduates, all set to the music of the wireless.

Florence's presence in *Richard II* again rated the attention of London critics. Opening on Monday, 17 February 1936, the play ran a week with matinées on Wednesday and Saturday. The *Spectator's Notebook* for 24 February reported, "On the first night of the O.U.D.S. production of *Richard II* many recognized Max Beerbohm in the stalls. He was paying one of his rare visits to the theatre to see his wife Florence Kahn as the Duchess of Gloucester." For the *Spectator,* the excitement of the evening was Florence's amazing performance. She gave the play "an intensity of life, a richness of colour otherwise lacking."

This lack of color was felt by an American Rhodes Scholar, John Espey, who is now a professor at the University of California in Los Angeles. He recalled the opening night:

> I don't think Gielgud made any attempt to direct Flo Kahn; or if he did, he certainly had no effect on her. The whole languid attitude of the production triumphed from the beginning, though it is difficult to believe that of the first scene. But the contrast of the duchess's voice and action in the second scene was truly dramatic. There she was, speaking with passion and resolution . . . as she broke through all the quietness and the not very successful underplaying, with her style. . . . It was such a wonderfully positive thing —she had given the speech everything she could—that on the first night . . . we all broke into spontaneous applause.

During this stay in England Florence made her one essay into the cinema, playing in the Gaumont British production of *The Secret Agent,* directed by Alfred Hitchcock. Her part, as the wife of a German suspected of being a spy, was small and she played in the rather overwhelming company of John Gielgud, Peter Lorre, Madeleine Carroll, and Robert Young, but she had one poignant scene in which she waited the return of her husband who does not come. This she played with great feeling and skill. The film is now a part of the collection of the British Film Institute and offers incontrovertible testimony to Florence's ability to act. But *The Secret Agent* marked the end of her acting career.

XVI

Americans at Rapallo

WHILE THE BEERBOHMS were staying in the Roberts's house at Stroud in 1931, Max did a series of caricatures of men in the public eye for the *Spectator*. He also did the *Bitter Sweet* cartoons, commissioned by his old friend C. B. Cochran to celebrate the success of Noël Coward's musical comedy. Both of these sets demonstrate the change in Max's approach to his art. As a young man he had once set forth his theory of caricature: "To seize mercilessly upon the points of his subject's features, expression, and general appearance which lend themselves to burlesque, and to emphasize them for all they are worth, with a frank disregard for the feelings of his victim, or the remonstrances of his friends." Now, however, the drawings which he did were calculated not to offend; they were likenesses rather than travesties. The once impervious lampooner had become kind and amiable. When the *Bitter Sweet* pictures were published in a portfolio labeled *Heroes and Heroines of Bitter Sweet,* Max called them "sentimental." He seldom attempted women; however much he might slash with his pen at the mentality of the literary ladies, some innate sense of chivalry forbade his distorting their appearance with his pencil. When he went to see Miss Peggy Wood to portray her as Sari Linden in *Bitter Sweet,* he warned her that he did not draw pictures of pretty women. Miss Wood thought he was rather a shy person and she was grateful to Cochran for commissioning such a distinguished artist to do her likeness. The *Bitter Sweet* portfolio was the last collection to be published during Max's lifetime, although Penguin Books reprinted *The Poets' Corner,* edited by John Rothenstein, in 1943. No publication resulted from the 1928 exhibition, "Ghosts," at the Leicester Galleries.

In 1933 Florence's brother Mannie died at his home in New York. He was only fifty-three, and she could not be reconciled to the loss of such a useful and needed person. His charm and wit had made him welcome among her friends at Rapallo and now he would never return to the Coast Road.

When Mannie died, his daughter Dody's baby daughter was six months old. After her visit with the Beerbohms in 1922, Dody had returned to New York to finish her education at Columbia University and then at the American Academy of Dramatic Arts. She had come to England in October 1930 seeking a place in the theatre and Florence was instrumental in her being accepted as a member of the Leeds Civic Playhouse, under the name of Alexandra Aubrey. She was considered by a local reporter to be "a lady of elfin charm with an elusive quality of gaiety," but her promising career as an actress was cut short by her marriage to George Bagshawe, an amateur actor with the Civic Playhouse. He was taken to be inspected by Aunt Florence and Uncle Max, then in England. As he had attended Charterhouse, Max's old school, the ice was broken and he was happily accepted as a new member of the family. Dody and George were married in October 1931 and their daughter Robin was born in New York in January 1933.

In this decade before the Second World War, Florence took over more and more of the details of their life at the Villino. She ran the house expeditiously, she helped Max with his correspondence, and she packed and sent off his manuscripts and cartoons. Max admitted that he was helpless in such matters. Because of her fluent Italian all negotiations with tradespeople, workmen, and servants were Florence's responsibility. If tickets were needed for a concert or a railway journey, she bought them. Circumstances had changed the shy, retired dreamer into a person of down-to-earth practicality. Not least among her duties was the hospitality offered to all guests. American callers were frequent at the Villino, sometimes known to Florence and Max, sometimes sent by friends, and sometimes just coming to pay homage to Max. Invited for lunch, the happy guest often discovered he was expected to stay for tea as well. He would return to the States warmed with the glow of a new and understanding friendship. Occasionally the pilgrim recorded his experience in print as "Tea on the Terrace," or "An Afternoon with Max."

In November 1934 John Barrymore arrived to discuss with Max his desire to make a movie of *The Happy Hypocrite*. Barrymore was one of the ephemera on Max's list of American friends, yet a bond existed between them. David Cecil, the authorized biographer of Max, has said that Barrymore was at Dieppe in the summer of 1903 when Max and Constance Collier were there. It seems likely, as Barrymore had just left the Slade School of Art in London and was considering the stage. He had hoped to become a caricaturist before he turned to acting, so naturally he and Max had much in common. In the spring of 1925 when Barrymore was in London playing *Hamlet* with Constance Collier, Max was

Max on the terrace, *circa* 1930. Courtesy of Morris Kahn.

there too, setting up his exhibit, and, though he had forsworn the theatre, he could not resist going to see Constance again. Max invited Barrymore to come to the opening day of his exhibit, but the actor did not appear and wrote on 25 April to explain the reason. He had prepared to arrive full face (he was often called "The Profile") but he had lunched with Hillaire Belloc in the country, a ritual "Sacerdotal and Epicurean," and he "rose from the board with the glutinous dignity of a fatted lamprey at five o'clock, just in time to arrive at the theatre and hurriedly arrange my cosmo into the stark and ascetic exterior of a Danish vegetarian." But he had found it great fun to see Max and looked forward to another meeting, perhaps in sunny Italy, where over Asti spumante they would talk of Aubrey Beardsley and the kippers of England.

When Winston Churchill visited Barrymore in Hollywood in 1929, a press photograph in the *Tatler* caught Max's attention, and he sent it to the actor, inquiring, "Who are these gangsters that they must be photographed together?" Barrymore cabled his delighted thanks, saying he had entered suit against the photographer, the motion picture studio, and Churchill, whose insensate desire for publicity was to blame. In a later letter he wrote Max that his *Tatler* picture, chastely framed, entranced all who saw it. When Barrymore died in 1942, the columnist Louis Sobel said that he had prized above all other possessions a picture clipped from a London weekly with a note from Max Beerbohm on it. Max also gave Barrymore a caricature of himself in classical robes.

Early in 1935 Phyllis Bottome, the English-American novelist, staying with her husband, Captain A. E. Forbes-Denis, in Rapallo, came to call on Max and Florence. She was a friend of Miss Masie Murray, the Beerbohms' next-door neighbor, who had lent Max some of Miss Bottome's books, about which he had written the author appreciatively. Miss Bottome found Florence somewhat remote and withdrawn, not as approachable as Max, but she felt they were two deeply civilized human beings, who knew the art of living (perhaps Florence's food convinced her of that.) She was glad that Mussolini had had the sense to leave them alone, but she thought it must annoy Il Duce sometimes to know that famous people from all lands came to see the Beerbohms when they would have died rather than visit him.

Neither Florence nor Max could believe that May of 1935 brought their silver wedding anniversary, but the calendar confirmed it, and so did a cable from Sam. Dora, too, was there to help them celebrate. They now had a guest house, for they had bought a small adjoining cottage which Florence transformed into a charming "casetta," known to Max as "Kahn's Folly."

A Kahn occupied it in the autumn of 1937 when Sam came on a visit en route home after reporting the American Legion Convention in Paris. Florence was delighted; she was proud of this big, handsome, fun-loving brother and pleased that Max liked him too. At the end of his visit, Max insisted that Florence travel with him to Florence and Rome. On her return home she sent Sam a card, announcing her safe arrival: Max had met her, having taken down to town with him the Ezra Pounds, who had been there for tea.

Sam was interested in the mention of Ezra Pound, for during his visit to the Villino he had hoped to meet the expatriate American in Rapallo, since Pound and his wife, the writer Dorothy Shakespear, were living above a restaurant in a flat with many balconies overlooking the harbor. Pound, who had left the States in 1907, was one of the founders of the Imagist school of poetry before passing on to Vorticism and even more obscure theories of prosody. Before settling in Italy he had lived in London and then in Paris, where he had known W. B. Yeats, James Joyce, Ernest Hemingway, and T. S. Eliot; indeed, he was one of the first critics of international stature to praise the work of Joyce and Eliot.

Although their circles were very different, Max and Pound may have known each other in London, because the poet arrived there in 1908, two years before Max married and left England. David Cecil says Max noted that Pound would be a good subject to draw, and in 1914 caricatured him with Dante, using as a caption the lines from Pound's "To Guido Cavalcanti." It was shown at his 1921 exhibition at the Leicester Galleries, but was not included in any published collection.

Meanwhile Pound must also have had opportunity in London to observe Max, and, being one of those who believed the Beerbohm family to be Jewish, he no doubt meant the "impeccable Brennbaum" in his *Hugh Selwyn Mauberly* (1920) to be Max:

> *The sky-like limpid eyes*
> *The circular infant's face*
> *The stiffness from spats to collar*
> *Never relaxing into grace;*
> *The heavy memories of Horab, Sinai*
> *and the forty years*
> *Showed only when the daylight fell*
> *Level across the face of Brennbaum,*
> *the Impeccable.*

In 1925 the Pounds took up residence in Rapallo, but just when the two couples began exchanging social calls is not clear. The first written evidence of their knowing each other is a note from Pound to Florence on the death of Mannie in 1933. He expressed the sympathy of his wife and himself for the loss of her brother (whom he called "Colonel Kahn," undoubtedly meaning "Doctor Kahn"), and said he would come to call when she was ready to see visitors. The note is dated *18 Sept. XI*—as an ardent supporter of Mussolini he had devised a calendar system based on the year the Fascist leader came to power (1922), so the letter actually was written in 1933. A year later he gave her an inscribed copy of his new prose work, *The A.B.C. of Reading.*

Max drew Pound again in 1934 as a burly, green-coated figure against a blue Mediterranean background. After her meeting with the Beerbohms in 1935, Phyllis Bottome, a long-time friend of Pound's, quoted Max as saying he felt the poet was out of place in Rapallo: he belonged in the great forests of his native land, swinging an axe against a gigantic tree; could she persuade him to return there?—Pound was enthusiastic about Mussolini, Max was not.

Mrs. Pound, asked in 1963 by John Espey for her memories of the Beerbohms, replied that she and her husband used to go to the Villino for tea, and found Max's separate studio very interesting. At one time Pound apparently had thought of writing a book to be called *The Life and Times of Max Beerbohm,* saying that an American firm had offered him a good sum for it, but no British publisher was interested; anyway he was too absorbed in political matters to write that book, and was becoming an increasingly vociferous supporter of the Fascist régime.

After Sam failed to meet Pound in 1937, Florence and Max wrote him a joint letter when he returned to Memphis. Florence began:

> The Ezra Pounds came today. I had met him in Rapallo and told him laughingly what you said, that you had traveled across Europe to talk with him. Well, I (Max is speaking—Florence has handed me the pen) rather fear Ezra may have been inclined to take these words rather less "laughingly" and lightly than they were meant, and that the words may have raised hopes rather higher than hopes ought to be. He is writing to you. If there is anything you can do for him . . . do please do it, dear Sam, for he is a good fellow, and a gifted one, and disinterested, and not (who is?—who that matters, I mean) rich. *But,* oh *but,* of course you mustn't do for him anything . . . difficult for you or prejudicial to you or shocking to the *Commercial Appeal.*

Then Florence added that the Pounds had been there for luncheon, and Max had explained it all better than she could.

Pound, hoping the Memphis editor could provide him with a pulpit for his pro-Mussolini message, wrote Sam, saying he would like the chance to make his opinions known, for there was much that America did not know, and should know; but Sam was not willing to fill that lack. Max probably felt much as Phyllis Bottome did, that Pound would not have accepted the dictatorship of Mussolini if he had not felt the Fascist leader to be the agent who could bring about universal social credit.

Because of Pound's broadcasts from Italy during the Second World War, he was brought back to the States at its conclusion to be tried for treason. On 12 November 1945 Miss Bottome wrote Max asking if he would be willing to sign a petition if the present threat to Ezra should become a death warrant. She said T. S. Eliot thought the petition should be made ready and held in reserve. She re-iterated her belief that Pound had merely blundered because he hoped to make the world a better place. Two copies of this petition, asking clemency for Pound from the United States on behalf of English literature and the institution of intellectual freedom, are among the Beerbohm papers at Merton College. Does this mean that Max did not sign them? At any rate, Pound was judged insane, so the petition was not needed.

Strangely enough, Max had no contact with one American residing in Italy, Bernard Berenson, art collector and critic, who lived with his wife and secretary at Villa I Tatti outside Florence. Sylvia Sprigge, a later friend to both men, said Berenson had a mistaken idea of Max, disliking him and his writing. However, S. N. Behrman said Berenson admired Max and told the story of the Berensons' going to the Villino Chiaro when Max was in London, being graciously entertained by Florence, but going away believing Max was hiding because he did not want to see them. Max always affirmed that visitors stopped to see him on the way from Somerset Maugham's to Berenson's, or from Berenson's to Maugham's.

Mrs. Berenson was a sister of Logan Pearsall Smith, so that old friend of Max's could easily visit him en route to the Berensons'. Smith, son of Philadelphia Quaker parents, had gone to Oxford in 1888 to complete an education begun at Haverford and Harvard; his time in Oxford overlapped Max's, though they had not been close friends there. In 1895 Smith published a book of Oxford stories and then retired to live with his family at Friday's Hill in Haslemere not far from Tennyson's Aldworth. Will Rothenstein was there in the summer of 1894, painting a portrait of Logan's sister Alys, who later married Bertrand Russell. Another Smith sister, who lived near by, was to become the wife of Berenson. Max came to know Smith as a man of letters when his "Trivia" pieces began appearing in the *Observer* at the turn of the century. He did a cartoon of Smith in 1921, which shows the noted paragraphist handing a miniature-sized manuscript to the editors of the London *Mercury*. Before he saw himself as Max saw him, Smith met Edmund Gosse at a dinner party and Gosse warned him:

> Logan . . . I feel it my duty to tell you that something has hap-
> pened to you that sooner or later happens to us almost all. Max
> has got you. We don't like it and you won't like it, but you must
> pretend that you do. You can console yourself at any rate with the
> thought that it will give uncommon pleasure to your friends.

Max also "got" Smith on the flyleaf of Arthur Bendix's copy of the collected pieces, *Trivia,* with apologies to the owner for defacing a delight-ful book.

Smith always thought Max an unlikely person to have championed the cause of Christabel Pankhurst in the Suffrage arrests of 1908, but Max had visited her at the Bow Street Lock-up, written sympathetically of her clash with Lloyd George, and later attended a banquet in her honor.

Smith was glad to see Max whenever the latter came to London, hunt-ing him out at whatever railway hotel he was patronizing if Florence was not with him. However, Max and Florence were staying at William Nichol-son's studio in Apple Tree Yard late in 1928 when Smith asked him to subscribe to a fund for Augustine Birrell, the author and statesman. Max sent him a pound, saying he wished all pounds were as well spent as in doing honor to Birrell. When Max sent him a copy of *Seven Men,* Smith thanked Max, affirming he had seen himself in the book as Enoch Soames, as Braxton, as "Savonarola Brown," but without, alas, the talent of any of them.

After he had assured Florence that he was not an American journalist doing an assignment, Stephen Greene, one year out of Harvard, where his honors thesis was on Max, was welcomed at the Villino in the summer of 1938. He found Max stouter than he had expected, but impeccably dressed in a white suit with a flower in his buttonhole. Florence was gracious, but rather silent as she offered tea or wine under the grape arbor. (Max took wine.) Since Greene was an American, that country was occasionally mentioned in the conversation. Max inquired if people were still being inoculated for everything in America; and speaking of the war in progress between China and Japan, wondered where Japan found the money to fight with—were rich American syndicates allowed to back them? Some remark about dark glasses drew from Max the

"Seeking inspiration" in the Italian landscape the year after Florence and Max
married and moved to Rapallo, the drawing was exhibited at the Leicester
Galleries and used with two other caricatures in a notice of the show in the
22 April 1911 *Daily Mirror* under the heading "Mr. Beerbohm Caricatures
Prominent Politicians." © Eva Reichmann; courtesy of the London *Daily Mail*.

assertion that he could not bear them: he could not talk with anyone whose eyes he could not see. Perhaps Alexander Woollcott or President Franklin Roosevelt in a fireside chat had approved the custom. He would never visit America again; he was too old. Greene, who had been on a tour of the East, presented Max with a netsuke from Japan. Max thought this an undeserved gift, but was assured that his writings justified it, as they had furnished the material leading to its donor's degree. Greene had sent a copy of his thesis to Max the year before and Max now complimented him on it, but the young American was not certain he remembered it. Still, the words were pleasant to hear, and when he left, Max urged him to come again, saying, "*Au revoir,* I hope."

In his conversation with Max, Greene told him that in American colleges the study of English literature was now carried up to at least 1900; this statement elicited a smile from Max, who said that seemed like the future to him, being spiritually of the Nineties. If he had stopped to think—and perhaps he did—he would have realized that he himself now belonged in American academic curricula.

During the Thirties Max had published little in America, or for that matter in England. A short poem, "Back to Town"—parodying John Drinkwater's poem on the Rothensteins' cottage at Far Oakridge—had been reprinted from the *Countryman* in the *Literary Digest* for 4 August 1932; "A Small Boy Seeing Giants," from his B.B.C. broadcast, had appeared in the *Living Age* for 7 October 1936; and "Going Out for a Walk" had come out in the *Reader's Digest* of September 1936. Yet in spite of this limited provender, Max was better known in America at the end of the Thirties than at their beginning. Increased recognition came in several ways, but mostly through the inclusion of his previous work in anthologies and collections. This reprinting, begun in the Twenties, increased year by year. Some of these books were intended for the general reader, some for the classroom; Max was entering the Groves of Academe.

In 1929 Professor Cornelius Weygandt of the University of Pennsylvania initiated a new course, English 108, "The Modern Essay," which he considered road-breaking with its treatment of such moderns as Max. Professor R. D. O'Leary of the University of Kansas read Max aloud to his classes, and discussed him in his textbook *The Essay* (1928). Annie Kimball Tuell, professor at Wellesley College, gave much attention to Max in her *Victorian at Bay* (1932). She had submitted this study to the *Atlantic Monthly,* which had rejected it on the rather unreasonable grounds that it was not written as Max would have done it. She was therefore gratified when Max sanctioned her effort and praised her writing. R. Clay

Bailey got his Master's degree from the University of Texas with a thesis on Max in 1932 and so did Mary Anne Reilly from the University of Pittsburgh in 1936 with a dissertation on "Max Beerbohm: Writer of Satire." Max was definitely a part of English Literature; when Carl and Mark Van Doren revised their *American and British Literature since 1890,* they gave four pages to Max under "Essayists." One of the *New Republic* writers, Robert Morse Lovett, and Helen Sard Hughes wrote *A History of the Novel in England* (1932), in which they spoke of the indelible mark Max had left on the age with his essays, burlesques, caricatures, and extravaganzas.

The name of Beerbohm appeared more often in the press. His picture was printed six times in the *New York Times* between 1931 and 1939. One of these portraits illustrated an article by Clair Price 28 August 1931 discussing his cartoons and displaying many of them. Two years before, Rebecca West in her London Letter to the *Bookman,* June 1929, had written rather spitefully of "Mr. Beerbohm and the Literary Ladies." His caricatures were often republished when any of their subjects made news.

Max was becoming known not only as a writer and caricaturist, but as a person, a human being. When Will Rothenstein's two volumes of *Men and Memories* were published in New York in 1931 and 1932, readers could piece together a surprisingly full account of Will's dearest friend—his character, his humor, his achievements, and the pattern of his life. Other memoirs, letters, biographies, and autobiographies written by Max's long list of acquaintances added information.

Thus through various agencies, Max, who had almost ceased to speak for himself, became an accepted figure in the American world of letters.

XVII

England and the Second War

THE ITALIAN SKY looking more and more ominous, Max and Florence reluctantly departed for England in 1938, and autumn found them at Inverness Terrace in Bayswater. After Prime Minister Chamberlain's meeting with Hitler, tensions were relieved and they could take part more freely in the social amenities of London. Miss G. B. Stern gave a dinner party at Quaglino's, attended by some fifty-four of the great and near-great, to welcome the Beerbohms home. Max enjoyed being the lion of the occasion. Miss Stern wondered why he had ceased to write, and Max explained that he could only write with a quill pen and there were no geese where he lived in Italy. In October they went to the Ellis Robertses' at Stroud in the Cotswolds, a happy reunion, but Ellis had suffered a heart attack and his activities were curtailed. In mid-November the death of Viola Tree Parsons brought sorrow to the family. Her husband had died in 1933 and she had edited his writings in *Alan Parsons' Book,* for which Max had written an Introductory Letter.

Reggie Turner's health was now a worry. In November Max had written him,

> We were so very glad to hear from you that you were feeling well. Of course the strain of the operation and the cure cannot *entirely* wear away in a short time, and you must take care of yourself and not get tired. When you were with us at Rap. you seemed so wonderfully better and stronger . . .

But on 7 December 1938 Reggie died. He was the earliest and dearest of Max's friends and would always remain the most treasured, Max said. By his will he had left Max £3,000, a not unappreciated item.

Violet and Sydney Schiff lent Max and Florence a cottage on Abinger Common in Surrey. Sydney wrote novels as Stephen Hudson, and Violet was a younger sister of Ada Leverson, who had died in 1936. Max gave the Abinger landscape his full approval—its Elizabethan rusticity had not been changed by the hideous hand of progress. In spite of its remoteness it sheltered a number of distinguished people who made the Beerbohms welcome: E. M. Forster, the Oliver Lodges, the Robert Trevelyans, Ralph Vaughan Williams, Wilson Harris, editor of the *Spectator,* Olive Heseltine, and Sylvia and Cecil Sprigge, who had founded the Abinger *Chronicle,* for which Max wrote on several occasions.

In June 1939 Max was notified that he was to receive a knighthood at Buckingham Palace. Although he had in the past been critical of those who coveted "the dingy Patent," he decided to accept it. Shortly after the notification he canceled an engagement, because he was "just off to the maw of London, where I have to submit to a final fitting of a morning-coat reluctantly ordered in honour of the King." After the ceremony he was pleased to report to Sydney Schiff that his costume was quite all right, "Indeed, I was (or so I thought as I looked around me) the best dressed of the knights, and quite on a level with the Grooms of the Chamber . . . I'm not sure that I wasn't as presentable as the King himself—very charming though he looked."

Sam wired his congratulations, adding, "England as usual thirty years late," but he continued to address his letters to "Mrs. Max Beerbohm," despite the fact that she reminded him this now was not her correct title. Florence had become a friend of the headmistress of the village school in Abinger, and after she returned from the ceremony in London she went in her "palace robes" to tell the enthralled children all the details.

In September Sir Max and Lady Beerbohm hovered over the wireless as the bleak news of the German invasion of Poland came from the B.B.C. Now the war became an ever-present undercurrent in their lives, and after the bombings started it was frequently overhead as well. Florence dreaded the night alarms and was appalled at the terrible air raids on London. The only way to endure the horror was to keep busy, and this she did. Her kindness to soldiers billeted in the neighborhood of Abinger was unending: she gave them teas, books to read, and, though the cottage was small, it furnished as many as six baths a week to a succession of fighting men. They came and went, and Florence knew she would not see them again.

Max invited his sister Aggie Knox to come and stay at the Cottage, but she refused; nor could Dora come unless her convent was evacuated. Dora loved Florence dearly, and when their sister Constance died in 1939 she wrote Florence:

> In moments like this, I feel I must say how I always pray and long for you to be a Christian by baptism as you already feel in heart and life . . . forgive me . . . Love makes me speak.

In the first year of the war Dora died as the result of a bad fall. Max had grieved when he took her to the gate of St. Saviour's Priory in 1893, feeling he had lost her forever; he was mistaken—he had not lost her until now. He wrote a tribute to her to be read at the services, now included in the Appendix of *Letters to Reggie Turner.*

Ike and Sam Kahn begged Florence and Max to come to America, but Florence brushed aside their proposal. Her hope was in America, but she and Max could not leave England. They had many problems: money was scarce and food was rationed; but before America was in the war, wonderful packages came from Memphis; English friends, too, were generous.

In October Max donated two manuscripts to a Red Cross sale in London and was gratified when they brought one hundred twenty pounds. Sylvia and Cecil Sprigge often came to the Beerbohms' cottage in the evening for conversation and games. Relations were pleasant with the Schiffs; though they lived on the same property, each family agreed not to infringe on the other's privacy, and such freedom led to harmonious give and take. Max found Sydney most congenial and the two often met in the garden to talk of the day's news. After they left Abinger Cottage Max wrote Sydney, "What horrible years to have lived through! And yet, for Florence and me, how vast an amount of happiness in the dear cottage."

During 1940 Max did rather more writing, perhaps urged by the hope of adding to the family exchequer. "From Bloomsbury to Bayswater" came out in the *World Review* and was reprinted in America in the *Living Age* for 6 October 1940. Two other essays, "The Top Hat" and "Then and Now," in the *Spectator* did not appear in the States. Two articles, just as carefully written, were given to the Sprigges' Abinger *Chronicle,* proceeds from which went to the war effort. In one of them, "Remembered Meals," Max recalled the halcyon days "before Paris in the goodness of her heart, built cocktail bars for the Americans."

In the summer of 1941 Sybil Colefax brought two Americans to lunch —Alexander Woollcott and Thornton Wilder, both of whom the Beerbohms had known before, Woollcott better than Wilder, for Woollcott had visited them in Rapallo. Shortly after the publication of Wilder's novel *The Bridge of San Luis Rey* (1928) he had gone to England and been warmly welcomed by English men of letters. Arnold Bennett recorded in his *Journal* on 25 August 1928 that he had dined with Lionel Fielding to meet Thornton Wilder and his sister Isabel, also a writer. Wilder, he said, was a nice, modest, dark young man. Later he wrote to his nephew, Richard, "Had a dinner party last night, the stars of which

Florence and Max at the Villino early in the 1930's. Courtesy of Morris Kahn.

were Max Beerbohm and Thornton Wilder." Max and Wilder had also lunched together at Bernard Shaw's with Gene Tunney as a special guest. Shaw, having written about a prizefighter, was interested in the literate American heavyweight, and Max admitted that he felt almost coarse in comparison with the champion's sensitive appreciation of the view over the Thames. He told Alan Dent that Tunney was a man of brains as well as brawn.

Now Thornton Wilder was again in England, having won two Pulitzer Prizes with his *Bridge* and the play *Our Town*. Alexander Woollcott, known to radio listeners in the States as "The Town Crier," had come to England, hoping through broadcasts on his return to hasten the United States into the conflict. He had traveled on an American battleship with a Santa Claus pack of gifts for his friends, but he had been so generous with his presents that all he had left for Shaw was razor blades and bacon, neither much prized by the bearded vegetarian.

Florence wrote her brothers about the Americans' visit to Abinger, saying "It was a happy little time in that they were all so nice and both Mr. Thornton Wilder and Mr. Alexander Woolcott are charming people." She had taken great pains with the lunch and the guests particularly admired her pudding; Woollcott talked about it in a broadcast the following October and Florence's family in Memphis decided it must have been a family delicacy, known as "Ambrosia." Woollcott pressed gifts upon his hostess; she must take her choice. Silk stockings? She never wore them, only black lisle. She had never heard a man offer silk stockings to a woman, and, old as she was, she could feel herself blush. At Woollcott's insistence she accepted a pair, very thin, very odd. Lipstick? Of no use to her, she hated make-up. But she took a jar of strawberry preserves, for she knew Lotte, the maid, would like them. Later Woollcott sent a gallon of maple syrup, rather a novelty to Max.

Max and Florence listened to Woollcott's broadcasts about his British trip and Max praised their "fullness, warmth, brilliancy, and cosiness." They hoped to see him again at Abinger, but Woollcott was not to come back; in January 1943 while broadcasting a discussion of "Is Germany Incurable?" he suffered a fatal heart attack.

Florence had written her brothers that "Mr. Wilder is a most sympathetic and appealing person." After the war when Max and Florence had returned to Rapallo, Wilder and his sister visited them several times, perhaps becoming their closest American friends in those last years. After Florence's death, Isabel Wilder carried back to the States the bequests Florence had left the Kahn family. Later she became a good friend to Elisabeth Jungmann.

One of Florence's pleasures in Abinger was visiting the village school. She organized a French class for some of the students and Max said they would doubtless soon be reading Proust. When the headmistress's only son, an R.A.F. pilot, was killed, Florence proved an understanding friend, going to sit with her in the evening and reading aloud to her. Once, at the suggestion of the vicar, Florence talked to the women at the parish church, telling them of her life in Memphis forty years earlier. Her audience listened enthralled, she told her brother Sam, not because what she said was so remarkable, but because it took their minds from the dreadful present.

And the present became increasingly dreadful. The loss of English youth was a constant grief to Florence, and after the United States entered the war she had Sam's soldier son to worry about. Their Italian friend Oscar Pio was now in England with the British forces and came often to stay at the cottage. Max had attested that Pio was not a Fascist and helped him enter the country.

Florence and Max listened regularly to the wireless, always grateful for American support, but a little impatient until America entered the struggle. On 21 November 1941 Max had written Will Rothenstein:

> The American strikes aren't charming, are they? Roosevelt, I think, has only himself to blame. In spite of his immensely powerful position . . . and his intense sympathy for England, he failed to do the obvious thing; he didn't raise the moral issue, merely the material one. . . . Had he said, "Are we to allow England to do all the fighting on behalf of civilization? What will posterity think of us . . ." Americans are immensely susceptible to anything in the way of Gospel. I am convinced that Roosevelt could have swept away all opposition, but now . . . who knows?

Max could never resist a chance to advise America.

On 22 January 1942 Orson Welles presented a broadcast in the States of *The Happy Hypocrite* under an arrangement with Dodd, Mead, but without Max's knowledge or consent. This seemed to Max an infringement of his rights. He deprecated his business ability—"I have in financial matters only a steadfast belief that I am an ignoramus"—but he had a firm faith in the acumen of Sam Kahn who took up the matter for him and effected a settlement of $98.16. Several of Max's stories were used by the B.B.C., but with proper recognition and recompense. In January Max made another much-praised broadcast on "Music Halls of My Youth."

His youth was slipping further and further away, for 1942 would see him seventy years old. The Maximilian Society, a group of distinguished men of letters gathered around a nucleus organized by Alan Dent, invited Max to dinner at the Players' Club in London on 24 August, his birthday. Appropriate festivities had been arranged and he was promised "no flash-light photography or other vulgarity." Max told Sydney Schiff:

> Really festal it was and very much did I enjoy it, despite the neces-sity of holding forth for a few minutes. I was surprised at the number of men who had been able and willing to turn up. I suppose some forty or fifty . . . were there.

He was given a present of wine, which he said he looked forward to drinking, always with Florence's very slight aid.

Among those present was Logan Pearsall Smith, whose encomium of Max had appeared in the *Observer* the day before. Max thought it was charming, though he had not realized Logan liked his work so much. But Smith said the editor had mutilated it and he was sending Max a clean copy. (This tribute appeared in the States in the November *Atlantic*.) Smith thought he and Max had lived too long, but he had an idea for a book of scenes from Shakespeare's garden which Max could illustrate divinely. Was he tempted? Apparently not. Smith was also present at Max's seventy-first birthday, which he called a "most horrible performance in his dishonour." Smith died in 1946.

Two Americans had been included among the Maximilians, George Jean Nathan and Frank Morley, brother of novelist and essayist Christopher Morley; neither of them was present at the London festivity in 1942, but the day did not go unnoticed in the States. Tributes to Max were numerous; Christopher Morley's "Letter to a Publisher" in the *Saturday Review of Literature* for 24 October 1942 was memorable. The publisher in the title was W. S. Hall, whom Morley described as probably Max's first collector in the United States. Speaking of the London celebration, Morley said, "I wish there might have been an American at the meeting, to take up some of Max's hilarious taunts at the U.S.A. But the particular sense of artistry in which he reared himself, that delicious and tempera-mental and acid-etched sense of comic form hardly exists in the United States and maybe never will."

Another honor came to Max that November when he was awarded an honorary degree from Oxford. America was not to be left out in this distribution of honors and on 19 January 1943 Arthur Train informed him he had been elected an Honorary Associate of the National Institute of Arts and Letters.

In May 1943 Max delivered the Rede Lecture at Cambridge University on Lytton Strachey, whom he had long admired. He wrote Violet Schiff that "it was written in the Cottage [Abinger] with awful difficulty bordering on despair, for I have always found anything in the way of eulogy hard to do without being dull—whereas it is easy to be bright if one is being rude"—a sentiment expressed by Max on many occasions. But "Lytton Strachey" was not dull.

In December Knopf brought out the American edition of the lecture, bound in boards, unlike the English one, which was in pamphlet form. Christopher Sykes in the *World Review* thought Strachey was the pretext for the lecture rather than the subject, and that Henry Wallace, Vice President of the United States, might claim some of the responsibility since he had recently lauded the Century of the Common Man, which Max derogated so thoroughly while extolling the creed of beauty. Christopher Lazare in the *New York Times* for 16 January thought Max used Strachey as an opportunity to voice his own particular antipathies and dogmas, "but perhaps Mr. Beerbohm's tribute to Strachey is his personal revenge on oblivion." Harry Hansen in the *World Telegram* for 1 December 1943 conceded that Max's light sparkling essays were out of tune "with the crack of guns, but when the world again cherishes Sèvres vases, Venetian lace, inlay cabinets and subtle art, the Beerbohms will make their own valuable contribution to aesthetic expression."

Late in the summer of 1943 Wilson Harris brought Edward Weeks, editor of the *Atlantic Monthly* to call. Harris told Florence that Weeks was a great admirer of Max. The tea was both pleasant and profitable, for the *Atlantic* purchased a number of essays—"Fenestralia" for April 1944; "Letter to James Bone" published in February 1949; "Nat Goodwin" in August 1949; "George Moore" for December 1950; and, after Max's death, "First Meeting with Yeats" in September 1957, and "Hethway Speaking," November 1957.

From 16 March to 16 April 1944, at the Grolier Club in New York, A. E. Gallatin staged a comprehensive exhibit of Max's books, caricatures, and manuscripts, mostly from Gallatin's own collection. At the opening Sir Harley Granville-Barker gave his recollections of Max. From 6 May to 6 June the exhibit was shown at the Houghton Library at Harvard. Later that year the Harvard University Press published Gallatin's *Sir Max Beerbohm: Bibliographical Notes*. So was Max honored in the "loathsome land."

The stay at Abinger was nearly over. In August 1944 the Germans scored a direct hit on the church, and the roof of the cottage was pierced by fragments of the bomb. E. M. Forster was the first to reach their side, and he found Max and Florence, who had been sleeping on a mattress under the kitchen table, unharmed, but badly shaken.

Their next refuge was Flint Cottage at Box Hill, Dorking, Surrey, once the home of George Meredith, whom Max had visited there forty years earlier. It pleased him now to find shelter in the great man's home. Collie Knox, Agnes's stepson, observed drily that Max "is the type of man to whom cottages, cosy, neat, and out of the way, are always being lent." At Flint Cottage Florence continued her wartime hospitality and a Polish soldier described her as "exquisitely petite and simply charming."

Sydney Schiff's death in November saddened them both. Max wrote an unsigned obituary in the *New Statesman,* being identified only as "a distinguished contemporary of the late Stephen Hudson." It was a feeling and appreciative tribute to this "very lovable and remarkable man" who would be long mourned. "He himself, dear man, was his sole detractor," concluded Max.

On 6 March 1945 Max undertook another sad task, delivering the Memorial Address for Sir William Rothenstein. He dreaded to do it, but felt he could not refuse. "His spirit will remain," said Max, "but that fine brain of his and that fine heart of his, have ceased to work."

May brought the end of the European war, and Florence hoped that the Japanese would soon see the futility of going on. It was a great blessing to have peace in England. Also, Florence felt they could accept invitations without pangs of conscience, and they went to London for dinners and lunches. At Sir Michael Sadler's they met a young Virginian, Raymond Murphy, a graduate of Yale. Florence wrote Sam about him, "such a nice young man." Murphy was writing a book on Lord Mountbatten, and he was a great admirer of Max; he owned three of Max's manuscripts and wanted to secure another for Yale. He was "nicely persistent" about it, said Florence, but with no success. An earlier attempt had also been ineffective: to an intermediary Max wrote—

> Many thanks for your letter. But I am sorry to say (for I don't like to seem avaricious) that the sum offered by Mr. Murphy isn't such as would at all tempt me to part with the MS.

Summer 1945 found them back at Abinger, this time at the Inn. Max was now perpetually committed to the alteration of photographs of the famous—whether cabinet portraits, frontispieces, or book illustrations. The lifting of an eyebrow, the flattening of a nose, or the jutting of a jaw could change the most beneficent countenance into an ogre's mask. An Oxford friend observed the process with amusement. Just before lunch Max would go out for the newspapers and weeklies, then sit down to read them, pencil in hand. After lunch he would leave them carelessly on the table while he composed himself for a nap. Then Florence, quietly pre-empting them, would run a surreptitious eraser over the illustrations while Max watched from under lowered lids.

In the late summer they moved once more to the Ellis Robertses' house at Stroud, the owners being in America. In the autumn Max did˙ another broadcast, "Playgoing." In September and October, Max the caricaturist was again before the public when Mrs. Philip Guedalla showed her late husband's collection at the Leicester Galleries. Guedalla had been one of the most faithful buyers at Max's exhibits and Max had been amazed when he visited the Guedalla home to come under the gaze of so many of his creations. He wrote a Foreword for the catalogue and the show was so popular that the catalogue went to a second printing.

The first Christmas of the peace found them still at Stroud with Elisabeth Jungmann staying only a few miles away and often walking over to see them. Having left Gerhart Hauptmann, whose secretary she had been when she met the Beerbohms at Rapallo in 1925, Elisabeth had lived in England since the onset of war. She had now become a British subject and Florence and Max were pleased by that. They liked to have Elisabeth near them, coming in every day to talk and laugh with them. That Christmas brought wonderful gifts from Florence's cousin Herbert Rossett of Cleveland: a great bunch of chrysanthemums, chocolates, and cigars for Max. Max said Florence deserved such kindness, he didn't; but to show Herbert his appreciation he sent him a small caricature of himself smoking a cigar, drawn on a page of the Guedalla catalogue.

In August 1946 Max wrote Violet Schiff, "A very little book of mine (too little to strain the 'shortage') will be appearing toward the end of this month," and in early September *Mainly on the Air* was published. In the States, Alfred Knopf honored Max by including it.among his distinguished Borzoi books. It consisted of. twelve essays, six of them broadcasts made between 1935 and 1945, and the others, which Max termed "narrowcasts," drawn from periodicals. One on the Charterhouse School had been written twenty-five years earlier. This book attracted more critical attention than had previously been accorded him in the American press. Max had come into his own; but there was little left on which to nourish this regard. He had virtually ceased to write for publication.

The world was at peace, but living was still difficult in England. The Beerbohms' unspoken thoughts were always of the Villino but they made no effort to return there. Then they heard from Oscar Pio that the Villino and Casetta were all right, barring the absence of copper utensils which had been requisitioned by the Italian government. Florence made a preliminary trip to investigate and on 24 September 1947 *The Times* of London carried the announcement, "Sir Max and Lady Beerbohm have returned to their Villa at Rapallo."

XVIII

Home to the Villino

THEY ALIGHTED FIRST at the Pensione Fernande, kept by their ex-servant Bertha, while the Villino was being made ready. Although the two houses had survived wonderfully well, painting and repairs were necessary. Florence went every day to superintend the work. At first she feared that the hall mural was ruined—the mural of Zuleika, the Duke of Dorset and Katie, the servant-girl who loved the Duke. The outlines were still good, but the color in them was smoked and blotched and the background had come off in patches. Max thought it had better be painted out as he could not stand on a ladder long enough to do it over; but Florence, who had once questioned the desirability of these figures, was now reluctant to part with them. She chose the best painter working on the house, and under her instructions he restored the color in the faces and figures and repainted the background. The operation was a success, and so, thanks to Florence and an Italian housepainter, Zuleika smiled once more from the oval medallion—Zuleika, and Katie, and the Duke.

At last they were back in the Villino and at first it seemed just the same —but it wasn't. Too many years had gone by. Neither was in robust health: Florence's heart was not strong and Max was particularly susceptible to colds and influenza. Florence did most of the cooking, tempting Max's appetite with his favorite delicacies, and felt repaid for her trouble as his health improved.

Gradually their contacts were resumed with dwellers in Rapallo and friends on the Riviera, but some like Ezra Pound and Gordon Craig were missing. Pound was in custody at St. Elizabeth's Hospital in the States and the Craig household had broken up; Gordon was living with his secretary, Daphne Woodward, in France. There were new friends, how-ever—the Selwyn Jepsons, sympathetic and helpful, and Siegfried Sassoon made frequent visits. As Max grew stronger their social contacts widened. With the tourist season, admirers from the States came to call: editors and publishers, college professors and visitors with letters of introduction from Florence's brothers. Visitors often found Max on the terrace and Florence before the downstairs fire. She welcomed them all, and Max, perhaps remembering his stricture of British hospitality, would descend to play the host.

When two pretty young ladies from Memphis arrived for tea with their current Italian escorts, Florence politely conversed with the young gentlemen in fluent Italian, though she was eager to hear the news from home. But she had been away too long; the young ladies knew few of the people she asked about. As she grew older, Florence's memory went more often back to the city on the muddy river and the exhilarating life with her brothers. Forgetting how hard she had struggled to get away, she wished they could somehow have stayed together.

Harriet Roberts has said that when Florence married, she expected she would have children. She told Harriet she thought she would have been a good mother and brought them up well. But there had been none, and Max became her child on whom she lavished her care and devotion. He was the center of her universe.

In his "William and Mary" (1920), Max wrote, "Had Mary been a mother, William's wonderfulness would have been less greatly important. But he was her child as well as her lover. And I think, though I do not know, she believed herself content that this should always be, if it were so destined."

It was not easy to be the wife of the idol of the Maximilians, and it grew harder as Florence grew older. She had to school herself to be part of the background, rather than a leading figure. She must be unobtrusive, yet alert to protect Max from too much strain. If visitors overstayed their welcome, she must extricate him; if he grew bored at a dinner party, tactfully she must get him away. Some friends objected to her firmness; others realized that she understood Max's limitations. She tried to curtail her conversation, to let Max do the talking, but at times she felt forced to correct a name or a fact or to add an observation of her own. This propensity was also criticized—she wanted to talk about herself when the eager listener wanted to hear from Max. Florence would not have been the woman she was, married to the man Max was, if she had not occasionally rebelled at always playing the lesser rôle, but that was the part to which many of Max's friends consigned her. By no means all, however, as a sheaf of poems and verses in her honor preserved in the Merton College collection bears witness. That she was reserved, aloof, and difficult to know was sometimes true; yet when barriers were removed no one could be more gracious and enchanting than she. To be fair to Max, he regarded her as an equal if not a superior. He was careful to bring "my wife" into the conversation, to ask her judgment or opinion, to acknowledge his indebtedness to her. He was as proud of her as she was of him—which is to say a great deal. No criticism of each other is reflected in their letters, though Florence once came close to it in a letter to Alice Rothenstein:

> Max has been into Rapallo three times in the year and eight months we have been home. We were to have gone to friends in Lombardy, but after Agnes's death, we didn't feel like going, so we have been here all the time. I sometimes think he might be better away from the sea now and then, but he is so reluctant to go away.

When Florence and Max returned to Rapallo, Florence had a little more than three years to live, Max four more than she. They were not eventful years. Max had virtually stopped drawing, except for his own amusement; as he wrote Florence's cousin, Herbert Rossett, he had lost the impulse for caricature. He did some reviews and refused to do others; he wrote Prefatory Notes to new editions of *Zuleika* (1947), *A Christmas Garland* (1950), and *Seven Men and Two Others* (1950). He worked on his broadcasts, most of which were drawn from previous writings, polished and emended for the occasion. His first broadcast from Italy was "Nat Goodwin," and he wrote Violet Schiff that he felt rather grand doing it there for English hearers. Although he produced no new work, he was continually faced with problems about the work he had already done—the sale of his manuscripts; film and broadcasting rights for *Zuleika Dobson* and *The Happy Hypocrite;* television versions of his essays—so the years were not free of perplexities. His correspondence was not inconsiderable, though he often failed to maintain his side of it. In 1948 it was announced that the *New Yorker* critic Wolcott Gibbs had gone to Florida to work on a musical comedy based on *Zuleika*. Gibbs was pleased to have Max's approval of this venture, for he had long admired the English critic, been influenced by his writings, and felt that the highest tribute paid to his criticism was to have it compared to Max's.

Max now spent more time with books, reading them as well as decorating them. He found much to interest him and stimulate his memory in Martin Secker's anthology *The Eighteen-Nineties,* which he reviewed for the *Observer* in October 1948. About a year later his review of Henry James's *A Little Tour in France* appeared in the same paper.

With the exception of James Gibbons Huneker and some of the early playwrights, Henry James is the only American author Max considered in print. It is therefore difficult to assess accurately his opinion of the world of American letters, but in a few instances he expressed himself

Sir Max in the XX Century, drawn in 1943. © Eva Reichmann.

decisively in letters or in conversation with friends. He, subscribed to no American newspapers, but he was familiar with the American comic papers; he thought their origin could be traced back to the Elgin marbles. In preparing a typescript of *The Happy Hypocrite* for an Italian translation he used the phrase, "Hello, there, Jenny Mere," explaining, "That's American slang." He received copies of American periodicals containing his own work and was critical of their advertising methods.

> I have seen American weekly and monthly magazines in which at first glance it isn't easy to find anything but advertisements. All the rest is printed in disjected fragments. An essay or story begins briefly, say, on page 20, and then you must turn to page 33, and thence to page 47, amidst the glare and blare of things for sale.

When Stephen Greene visited him in 1938 they talked of American magazines, and Max displayed an acquaintance with the *New Yorker,* praising the work of the staff: *Punch* used to have that individuality, he said. He delighted in the work of *New Yorker* cartoonists Helen Hokinson and William Steig, deducing from the former's that a good deal must still be done in the States for women's uplift. David Cecil says that Max liked Gertrude Stein's *Autobiography of Alice B. Toklas,* and the writings and drawings of James Thurber, saying, "His people are ugly, but not in an unpleasant way." Max's essays reveal a knowledge of Hawthorne, Emerson, Poe, and Whitman; he divided authors into two classes, lovable and unlovable—Whitman was lovable. He recognized America's absorption in psychology and the zest for self-improvement. When he was writing his "Meditations of a Refugee" for the Book of the Queen's Doll's House, the project that had intrigued Dody Kahn in 1921, he said he tried to reduce himself to a size appropriate for a contributor to the tiny volume: "I steeped myself in the latest American books about Auto-psycho-pseudo-metamorphosis." That he was aware of Prohibition in the Twenties is shown in a quip about Rabindranath Tagore who was having some difficulty being admitted to the States. Max said it was because of his Christ-like phase that Tagore was feared: he might turn water into wine.

He was scornful of much American magazine fiction. In 1904, writing of Frank Norris's short stories, he felt "their power seemed the power of melodrama, not of life." They did not rise above the level of magazine fiction—"A man who can create really good magazine fiction is not a man who could achieve great or sincere feeling; there were more to be hoped for from a bungler."

Max had a real enthusiasm for two very dissimilar American women writers, Anita Loos and Elinor Wylie. In 1927 he had written Reggie:

> Had *Gentlemen Prefer Blondes* already been published when you
> were here? If so . . . I must have raved to you about it. Anyway,
> of course, you've read it since at somebody's recommendation. If
> you inconceivably haven't, tell me, and I'll send it . . .

Did he send it, and did Reggie fail to return it? At any rate, Max's copy
now forms part of the Stephen Greene collection, with this note from Max
on the title page:

> This book explains itself perfectly and delightfully. It needs no
> illustrations. And its realism is contradicted and bedeviled by the
> dreadful little would-be funny pictures foisted in . . .

Max had gone through the book and blacked out all the illustrations
but one.

He did not part with Elinor Wylie's books, for at least two of them,
Mr. Hodge and Mr. Hazard and *The Orphan Angel,* were included in the
Sotheby sale of his books and papers after his death. In January 1950
Max wrote to a friend:

> You say that you think Mr. William Benét would like to have a
> greeting from me. On the chance that he would, you might tell him
> of my lasting admiration for the work of Elinor Wylie [the late
> Mrs. William Rose Benét]. My two favorite books of hers are,
> perhaps, "Jennifer Lorn" and "The Venetian Glass Nephew." They
> are for me as a lovely series of soap-bubbles blown in a garden
> on a sunny day and prismatically floating hither and thither—and
> not breaking. They float still, and will always do so.

This was written twenty-five years after Miss Wylie's death. Even more
tragic in the annals of "it might have been" is the eight-page letter he
wrote her about *The Venetian Glass Nephew,* and apparently never sent,
now in Robert Taylor's possession. Beginning, "I don't often read a book
which I feel I should have liked to have written," he proceeded to analyze
the book carefully, idea by idea, phrase by phrase, admiring her technique,
but occasionally taking issue with some assumption she had made, or
criticizing an infelicity of wording, such as the close conjunction of two
adverbs ending in "ly." In the strength of his appproval, Max could over-
look her sex, even admit it—"Here is a woman who can write (sacred
word and sacred function in which your sex so rarely partakes to advantage) and is a born and made ironist." How sad that this sensitive
writer never knew Max's verdict on her work. Or perhaps she did:
Burton Rascoe, writing in *Arts and Decoration* for September 1926, said
that Max Beerbohm was so taken with Miss Wylie's *Jennifer Lorn* and
Venetian Glass Nephew that he had asked her to visit him at Rapallo,

and her biographer said that Elinor was sorry she couldn't go to see Max Beerbohm on the Italian Riviera. So in some way Max must have made known his esteem.

Sam Kahn sometimes sent books to Rapallo about which Max found it hard to be tactful. Such a one was *Adventures Among the Immortals* by Percy Burton, done with the aid of Lowell Thomas. One of the Immortals was Beerbohm Tree, with whom Burton had acted in America; he said Tree was proud of his half-brother, but was a little jealous too, and hadn't read *Zuleika Dobson*. Florence wrote Sam that Max had enjoyed the book; then Max took the pen from her:

> I don't agree with all Mr. Burton's estimates of people—but what are estimates *for* if not to be disagreed with? And who cares two cents whether I agree or not. The point is that Burton is young and very alive and very genial and clever. And I freely forgive him for letting Mr. Lowell Thomas make him assure us that "Sarah Bernhardt . . . had died, literally in harness." Literally. A strange and dreadful picture. I turn that picture to the wall.

Max had ambivalent feelings about another gift sent by Sam—Shaw's essay on William Morris. He had great pleasure in reading it, but "pleasure mingled with pain—such as anything of G.B.S.'s always gives me." He admired Shaw's brilliance and cogency, he told Sam, but Shaw's style affected him unpleasantly; it was rather like "hearing the squeaking of a slate-pencil on a slate." The book was therefore "a mitigated joy—but certainly a joy."

Edmund Wilson has said that he agreed with the judgment on Joseph Hergesheimer he had heard attributed to Max—"Poor Mr. Hergesheimer —he wants so much to be an artist." About two more recent American writers of note, T. S. Eliot and Ernest Hemingway, Max held divergent opinions.

In the Birthday Book presented to Max on his eightieth birthday, now at Merton, T. S. Eliot had written that he was not one entitled to refer to him as "Max." "To me, he is Sir Max Beerbohm whom I once visited (though he will have forgotten) at Rapallo, and whom I once met (though he will not remember it) at a dinner table in London." Whether or not Max recalled these encounters with the poet, he apparently had not met his poetry until early in his stay in England during the war. On 10 February 1939 he wrote Sydney Schiff:

> . . . you did read "Prufrock" aloud to me; but I didn't recall this to you, because then you might have said you wouldn't read it to me again. Which is just what you have said now! Please re-

consider this saying: for I would like to renew the delight I had in that reading. I well remember that during it I was all aglow with admiration for T.S.E.—and continued to be so in retrospect, until I came (eagerly) in contact with another volume of his work, and —and—and—realized that the glow had been due entirely to your vivacious and calorific flow of interpretation—or rather of creation. I want to renew in my breast that illusion of great merits. So do please . . . thrill me again.

Schiff must have hoped to persuade Max himself to read Eliot, for he gave him Eliot's *Collected Poems.* The book was included in the Sotheby sale of Max's books, along with The *Cultivation of Christmas Trees,* sent by T.S.E. and inscribed for Elisabeth Jungmann, Christmas 1954 "(and for submission to Max B. if he will)."

Max's reaction to Hemingway was more favorable than his reaction to Eliot. When the critic Cyril Ray visited him in 1954, Max told him that he was not reading much any more, but Elisabeth interrupted to say that she hadn't been able to drag him away from *The Old Man and the Sea*; he couldn't put it down. "Ah," said Max, "that wasn't a novel; that was a poem. It's the first book of his I've read, and I think I must read more of—Old Man Hem."

Max must have received many books from American authors, respectfully inscribed: they turn up every now and then in book catalogues. Louis Untermeyer sent him *Heavens,* inscribed "For the incomparable Max from the too-unfortunately-comparable Louis Untermeyer, March, 1922." In Louis Kronenberger's *Anthology of Lively Writing* Max had penciled a note, "Good writing should never be hurried. Let twaddle be streamlined by all means." (But in "Lytton Strachey" in 1943 he had said, "Genius is, by the nature of it, always in a hurry.") Among the American imports listed after Max's death in the catalogue of the Sotheby sale were three books by S. N. Behrman; E. B. White's *Second Tree from the Corner;* Paul Gauguin's *Journals,* translated by Van Wyck Brooks; Ferris Greenslet's *Pater* (1903); Thornton Wilder's *The Bridge of San Luis Rey;* and Archibald Henderson's *George Bernard Shaw,* altered, annotated, and emblazoned by Max.

In 1954 Wilmarth S. Lewis of Farmington, Connecticut, a collector of Horace Walpole and a friend of Thornton Wilder's, visited Rapallo with his wife and gave Max a copy of his *Collector's Progress.* Max wrote Lewis what Geoffrey Hellman, in the *New Yorker* of 31 October 1959, called a "discriminating and enthusiastic letter" about it. Hellman would have liked to use the letter in his article, but its recipient carefully reserved it to include in his own *One Man's Education* (1967).

XIX

The Days Shorten

Now came the last year Florence and Max were to have together—1950. It was much like the year before. Max published one book review—of Bertita Harding's biography of Eleanora Duse—did a Prefatory Letter for *The Female Approach, with Masculine Sidelights* by his friend the British caricaturist Ronald Searle, and made a broadcast on George Moore. Florence busied herself about the house and garden; she had a good maid, the daughter of the first one she had had at the Villino. She made guests as welcome as ever, though invitations to tea were more frequent than those for luncheon. They went out very little; one of their favorite diversions was doing the crossword puzzle in *The Times*. Evenings they often played chess. Max had several bouts with influenza, but their good Italian doctor could always effect a cure by keeping him in bed. Max rather enjoyed that.

In August a young writer from the States named Kaye Webb asked for an interview and to take pictures. Florence usually refused such ordeals, but the young lady was so politely persuasive that she yielded and invited her to lunch. Florence's savory food was augmented by wine from the Maximilians ("I don't know why they should bother," said Max, "but it's extremely kind of them"). Kaye Webb seemed able to draw Max out on many subjects—his scorn of modern educational methods, his dislike of airplanes, and his fondness for the Italian sun and sea and people. They lived secluded lives, he said, and were strictly limited in the amount of money they could take out of England. The home was run comfortably, but carefully; Florence saw to that. Kaye Webb looked appreciatively about the Villino, at the murals in the hall and the many drawings in Max's upstairs desk.

When the photographs were taken, Florence asked to have proofs sent before they were printed. She told Sam Kahn she hoped the pictures would not shock her brothers. After all, she was more than seventy, she had lived through two world wars, and she was tired. The article and pictures came out in *Go,* a short-lived travel magazine, three months after Florence's death.

She was tired; she was very thin and had to spend more time resting, "to regain her strength." Masie Murray, a friend who had once lived next door to the Villino and had introduced Phyllis Bottome to them in the Thirties came often to see her. She would find Florence in bed, her face a beautiful triangle even though the flesh had shrunk, wearing a becoming Juliet cap which her brother Mannie had bought from a French peasant during World War I. Florence spoke lightly of her illness. "She had a unique gift of drollery," said Miss Murray, "which made her conversation enticing."

Everyone worried about what would become of Max if Florence were no longer there. Florence worried too; she knew her heart was weak—a doctor in England had told her so. She realized better than anyone else her frailty, but she minimized it that she might do more for Max. She had made her will in 1939, adding a codicil in 1949. One thing more she could do: she told Max that if anything happened to her, he must send for Elisabeth Jungmann, their long-time friend now living in England; and she made Elisabeth promise that she would come and look after the house and take care of Max. Elisabeth's last visit to Rapallo was in October 1950. She thought Florence seemed as well as usual, but she re-iterated her promise to come if Max should need her. And when he did, she kept her word.

Florence died 13 January 1951. When the seriousness of her condition was realized Max had wired Violet Schiff, "Darling Florence rather seriously unwell. Please tell Elisabeth. Love, Max." Elisabeth arrived two hours too late for Florence to know she had come. Florence had slipped quietly away, her hand in Max's. He sent a cable to Memphis: "Terribly sad news. Darling Florence died today. Peacefully. Heart failure."

Elisabeth took charge. There was to be no church service: Florence wanted to be cremated and her ashes scattered over the fields or the sea. Two days after her death Max was stricken with influenza and could not go with Elisabeth to Genoa for the cremation. Later a young gardener rowed Elisabeth and Max and the urn with Florence's ashes out into the bay at Rapallo; and there she who had been the Titian-haired actress from Memphis, rested at last in the blue sea she had loved so long, within sight of one who stood on the terrace and looked westward.

Condolences came to Max from many sorrowing and sympathetic friends. Heartfelt appreciations of Florence appeared in *The Times* of London. The Huddersfield *Examiner* recalled her appearance there:

It is no small tribute to Mr. Wareing's work for what he called the "living theatre" that Huddersfield should have been one of the few places in the world to see a great actress who made only two or three appearances in public in the space of forty years.

Gradually life was resumed at the Villino. In early March Max wrote Sam Kahn that he was still not able to go out. How he missed Florence, always so vital and alive! But Elisabeth took over with selfless devotion, guarding Max as Florence would have wished, and acting as secretary and nurse. Elisabeth was younger and more vigorous than Florence; she could manage the correspondence with a firmer hand, and the loving admiration she had always felt for Max was now directed towards making him happy and comfortable for the years that were left to him. Max began to emerge from the shadow of his loss.

In July 1951 the contract was signed for Wolcott Gibbs's stage production of *Zuleika* (unfortunately doomed to failure), and Newman Levy was working on a libretto for *The Happy Hypocrite*. Florence had left the manuscript of *Zuleika* to her brother Ike in return for his many kindnesses to her, and that was sold in 1952 to Scribners. Max was pleased when the sale was finally completed through Sam Kahn's efforts.

Sam was trying to arrange a meeting between the American newspaper columnist Leonard Lyons and Max, who said he would be glad to see Lyons if he came to Rapallo. Lyons often made mention of Max in his gossip about famous people. He had recently reported the visit of M. L. Schuster, the New York publisher, to Max, whose daily schedule, Schuster said, was "not to put pen to paper." When he spoke of books, Max told him, "I've been printed, but not published." He had once received from an American publisher a six months' royalty statement on *Seven Men*—the sum due him was $3.75. "That comes to fifty three and a half cents a man," said Max. In spite of this lack of financial response, Max wrote to Sam:

> I never get any "clippings" from America, so I hadn't seen "Time" or Lyons on the subject of me. One likes to be liked in America: it gives one a sense of carrying power—of "putting it across" the rather broad Atlantic.

This carrying power produced celebrations of Max's eightieth birthday in New York as well as London and Rapallo. Max was present at only one of these, the dinner at Montallegro, a hilltop between Rapallo and nearby Zoagli. Winston Churchill sent greetings and among the guests at dinner was Sir S. C. Roberts of Cambridge, who had in 1941 become a stepfather of *Zuleika* by publishing *Zuleika in Cambridge,* to which Max had given his approbation and, to its author, his friendship.

In London the birthday celebration had begun in May with an exhibit at the Leicester Galleries called "Max in Retrospect," the catalogue for which bore a note from the artist. The gamut of subjects ranged over the past fifty years, from personages of the Nineties to Winston Churchill. The London press took flattering note of the day, and the B.B.C. presented "The Seventh Man," made up of tributes from old friends, later gathered in a leather-bound book for Max. This homage to Max was also planned to include his portrait, painted by Grahame Sutherland, who had recently performed a similar service for Somerset Maugham. Max vetoed the idea, saying "I, with my pencil have been, in my time, a ruthless monstrifier of men. And the bully is, proverbially, a coward." He was not willing to sit.

In the States encomiums appeared in papers across the country, the most notable perhaps by Bertrand Russell in the *New York Times* of 29 August 1952. Russell praised the writing and pictures of "the most faultless of my contemporaries" who always secured the effect at which he aimed, and was "wholly delightful." In New York a post-birthday exhibit was held at the Academy of Arts and Letters with loans from the New York Public Library, from Harvard University, and from private collectors.

Just before his birthday Max had made the acquaintance of an American who became a treasured friend of his last years and his unofficial biographer, the playwright S. N. Behrman. Sent by the *New Yorker* to do a "Profile" of Max, Behrman feared he had come too late—Max seemed so fragile—but he soon learned that Max's mind was as sharp and keen as ever, and he persisted in his purpose. Max warmed to this new admirer, this man of the theatre; Elisabeth thought his visit did Max good, and she hoped he would come again. He did, three times more, bringing gifts and messages from the outside world, and stimulating Max to talk about himself and his memories, with all the old sly wit and sparkle. Behrman's *Portrait of Max* (1960) was the result.

In 1953 Simon and Schuster arranged to issue *Around Theatres* in a one-volume edition for which Max wrote only the briefest Preface, declaring that "I have nothing left to be said—by me—about myself as a dramatic critic." Its publication the following year brought more plaudits from American reviewers; said Harold Clurman in the *New Republic* 12 June 1954.

> What explains the durability of these pieces? . . . It is not enough to say they are exquisitely written and enchantingly witty. The important point is—they make sense.

Max explained their durability to an American visitor at the Villino that spring. He said that since the reviews were done for a weekly and the dailies had already divulged the plot of the play, he was often forced to resort to other material to fill his column. Perhaps it was these added observations, these "flowers picked by the wayside," that gave the reviews more interest today—the padding, as it were. The American objected to this ignoble word. "Would you accept 'divagations'?" asked Max. One would, though preferring "flowers picked by the wayside."

In June 1954 Behrman took the American critic Edmund Wilson to call on Max. Wilson had already analyzed the artist and essayist for *New Yorker* readers on 2 May 1948, an essay later included in his *Classics and Commercials*. He and Max tangled on the interpretation of Henry James's "Turn of the Screw," Max frankly denigrating the suggestion that the whole affair was a delusion of the psychotic governess, a theory, he said, advanced by "some morbid pedant, prig and fool." When Wilson acknowledged he was that person, Max passed off the incident with studied politeness. But later, having inquired who Wilson was and being told that one of Wilson's studies had been concerned with the social philosphies of Vico, Michelet and Marx, Max replied: "Ah, I see, the henchman of the unreadable." Seven years after Max's death, Wilson recorded his afternoon at the Villino in *Encounter*.

Another friend whom Behrman introduced to Max was Stanley Marcus, of Dallas, Texas. Marcus, a collector of rare books, had brought with him some sample pages for a projected limited edition of *The Happy Hypocrite*—an edition whose format and typography were by Bruce Rogers, dean of American book designers—and he hoped that Max would sign them. Max refused, saying that he had not slept well the night before and was too tired; but perhaps Mr. Marcus would leave them, and they could be returned to him later?

"I had no choice," Marcus recounted afterwards, "but to leave my book, precious as it was, not knowing whether I would ever see it again, because of Sir Max's fragility." But six months later in 1955 it did come back to him in the States. And Max had painstakingly inserted impromptu text to bridge the disconnected pages, creating a plausible and deliciously amusing continuity. He had worked weeks to achieve the faked narrative, and Marcus knew it was eminently worth waiting for. Behrman, commenting on the emendations, said they were the last literary work that Max was to do.

In July word came from Memphis of the death of Isaac Kahn, Florence's beloved "Ike." Max was saddened at the news, but "glad he did not die before darling Florence." He assured Ike's widow, "I am not strong, but I am not ailing." It was an optimistic statement. Still, the guest book at the Villino recorded many visitors, Truman Capote among them. One such caller mentioned Max's neat and still dandyish attire, the glass of Bardolino he took at tea time, and the sharp Italian cigarettes he smoked one after another—Elisabeth was trying to cut down on the number. As his stamina lessened, his worries increased; he told a visitor that the human race had lived through the atomic age, but now it was entering the era "Anno Hydrogensis," and as a protest he signed a petition asking the great powers to ban the hydrogen bomb.

During these last years he did at least one broadcast a year. In 1952 he paid tribute to the memory of Desmond MacCarthy, but refused to accept any stipend for honoring a friend. In 1954 he recalled W. B. Yeats for his listeners, in January 1955 he talked of Henry Irving, and the following December he did "Hethway Speaking." "Hethway" originally had been christened "Herringham," and in 1916 he was to have figured in a series Max had projected and planned to call "Mirror of the Past"—a series somewhat akin to the collection that became *Seven Men*. Max submitted the idea to the *Century:* a mirror left in his keeping by Herringham, a contemporary of Rossetti, would reveal scenes which had been enacted before it in years gone by, and Max had an elaborate scheme for working out the chronology in reverse of the events described. But the *Century* people were not interested, and so the work was never completed.

In December an article in the *Tatler* reported that Max, living in Rapallo, was short of money, to which Max replied succinctly, "Let me assure you that I live, now as heretofore, in very great comfort and with no anxiety, and that the winter in Rapallo is always a very mild affair." If he had been entirely truthful he might have admitted that the Villino was inadequately heated, and though Elisabeth Jungmann made every effort to keep him warm, he suffered from the cold. And without heat, the flame of life burned low.

In March 1956 he became seriously ill and was taken to the hospital for treatment by his Italian doctor. Daily bulletins of his condition were printed in papers on both sides of the Atlantic, but one piece of news was excluded. When Behrman paid his last visit to Max, Elisabeth had just become the second Lady Beerbohm. It could hardly be termed a happy event, occurring under the shadow of death, yet it brought a great relief to Max that Elisabeth could legally inherit his estate, and to Elisabeth a blessed satisfaction in now being irrevocably linked to one she had so long loved and cherished. They were married one day less than a month—Max died 19 May 1956.

After a short service in Rapallo Max's ashes were taken to London, and the new Lady Beerbohm attended the service held for him at St. Paul's, with an address by the Dean on 29 June. John Mason Brown of the *Saturday Review of Literature* represented the United States.

After the announcement of Max's death, eulogies appeared in journals in England and America. The *New York Times* gave him a two-column obituary, quoting from Bertrand Russell's tribute on his eightieth birthday, but *Newsweek* passed him quickly by as "one of the last of the great professional esthetes."

On 2 April 1962 a stone plaque, simply inscribed MAX BEERBOHM, CARICATURIST AND WRITER, 1872–1956 was placed over the crypt, with a memorial address by the late Sir Sydney Roberts, who thought Max would have been astonished, but also gratified, to know of his commemoration at St. Paul's, for he took pride in being a Londoner.

At the time of this unveiling, the second Lady Beerbohm had been dead three years. After Max's burial at St. Paul's, Elisabeth had returned to the Villino and begun the arduous task of putting Max's affairs in order, sorting books and papers, deciding what should go to Merton College. She found the undertaking more and more exhausting; she who had been so tireless in her care of Max was weary to death now that he was gone. No one quite realized her nearness to collapse till too late. On 9 January 1959 she was found dead in the Villino, having suffered a heart attack.

Her funeral was held at Golders Green, London, 24 February, and the unselfishness of her life was recalled, particularly her work in Geneva at the end of the war in restoring cultural relations between Germany and England. Later her sister, Eva Reichmann, and a cousin went to Rapallo and dismantled and sold the Villino.

The noisy stream of traffic continued up and down the coast road but the house on the edge of the hill stood quiet and empty, its windows shuttered against the sound; camellias withered in the old oil jars, and no one stood against the balustrade of the terrace to look out at the deep blue sea. All who belonged at the Villino Chiaro had gone.

Appendix I: American Collectors

ALTHOUGH MAX was a favorite with American editors and publishers, the general reading public has never accepted him unreservedly. As Wolcott Gibbs summed up this situation in the *New Yorker* for 3 October 1953:

> The members of the Beerbohm cult in this country have always been uncommonly vocal and possessed of memories nearly as tenacious as those of the followers of Sherlock Holmes, but the number of people who actually bought his books has never been really impressive and his success has seldom been anything but one of esteem.

However, these cult members have vied with their English counterparts in the zeal with which they collected Beerbohm drawings and writings. First editions of his books, his manuscripts, his original cartoons, and his letters are becoming exceedingly scarce, and many of these items have found their way into the rare book collections of American libraries. At the two-day sale of his books and papers in 1960, the leading bidders were largely from the States, for Merton College at Oxford had already received its impressive bequest. Among the successful bidders were the Berg Collection at the New York Public Library, the Houghton Library at Harvard, and the University of California at Los Angeles. Other universities with important holdings are Yale, Virginia, Columbia, Indiana, and Texas. These collections are available to students wishing to do research on Max, a desire he would undoubtedly have deprecated.

Despite the fact that the librarians responsible for these acquisitions have been aware of their duty to preserve Max for posterity, private collectors are the most ardent and devoted Maximilians.

One of the most dedicated was A. E. Gallatin, the abstract painter, noted for his "Black Tablecoth," and a great grandson of the Secretary of the Treasury, Albert Gallatin. He put his collection to good use in the preparation of his *Bibliographical Notes* on Sir Max, published by Harvard University in 1944. The book listed Max's separate and collected editions, data on his plays, introductions he had written for the books of others, and selected writings about him. Eight years later L. M. Oliver of Harvard collaborated in producing a second volume, a *Bibliography of the Works of Max Beerbohm,* intended as a supplement to the first, not a substitute. It was confined to the listing of Max's various editions, other materials being omitted, and a catalogue of the holdings of Harvard University. Most of this collection was the gift of Mr. Gallatin. In his Preface to the first volume, Mr. Gallatin had said that his first editions in each instance were acquired at the time of publication, an excellent method, it seemed to him: such a contemporary collection "possesses a certain flavor not to be found . . . in one made after the author has become a classic, for when that time arrives the sporting element and any question of intellectual acumen scarcely enter into the picture." Mr. Gallatin's acquisitions are proof of his prescience.

Another early Beerbohm collector, Robert H. Taylor of Princeton, New Jersey, reviewed the *Bibliography* in the *Book Collector,* for Winter 1952, regretting the omitted material, which would necessitate the study of both volumes—one of them now out-of-print—finding some minor errors, but praising the scholarship, and hoping for a third, enlarged, and complete edition. Mr. Taylor's collection, one of the finest in the States, is now in the keeping of Princeton University. Unlike Mr. Gallatin, he did not begin with a first edition of *The Works,* but came to Beerbohm through the chance purchase of *And Even Now* from a bookstall in Paris. It was not a first edition, but, his fancy captivated by the contents, he made haste to correct that error. In addition to books, he gathered a number of caricatures, manuscripts, and letters. Among the most interesting are the two manuscripts of *Zuleika Dobson,* one a nearly indecipherable scribble with drawings in the margins, and the other a fair copy for the printer. In 1956 Max gladly gave him permission to reproduce a page of the manuscript to accompany his *Authors at Work,* published by the Grolier Club of New York.

Raymond L. Murphy, who died some years ago, began as a young man to collect Max and was fortunate enough to meet his hero face to face at a dinner party mentioned in an earlier chapter, but he was not fortunate enough to secure the manuscript he wanted, *Zuleika Dobson.* Max said he would have to have more than £200 for it, but as he didn't mention how much more, Mr. Murphy gave up the quest. The results of his more successful endeavors were bequeathed to Yale.

Another collection which went to the same University was that of Professor Chauncey Brewster Tinker. Indeed, the territory around New Haven has nourished many Beerbohm collectors. Proof is to be found in the list of lenders to the 1952 Exhibit at the Academy of Arts and Letters: Donald Wing, Van Wyck Brooks, Thornton Wilder, and Chauncey Brewster Tinker. Others who lent memorabilia to that exhibit were John Mason Brown, Philip Hofer, R. C. James, A. A. Knopf, Robert Montgomery, Ray L. Murphy, and Robert H. Taylor.

Wilmarth S. Lewis, who is editing the Yale Edition of Horace Walpole's Correspondence, has, on occasion, turned his attention from the Duke of Oxford to Sir Max, and, in addition to many first editions, owns the manuscript of "Quia Imperfectum" and several books from Max's library. Another inhabitant of the Nutmeg State, Herbert S. Stone of Guilford, Connecticut, inherited his father's interesting *Chap-Book* collection of some two thousand items including letters from Max and four drawings, now acquired by the Newberry Library of Chicago.

Perhaps no American collector profited more from the Sotheby Sale than Robert Lang of Rye, New York, for he now possesses some of its most desirable offerings, among them Max's copy of *Twenty-Five Gentlemen,* with the caricatures lightly colored and some comments added, the *Souvenir of the Charing Cross Hospital Bazaar* (1899), in which the portraits of some forty-nine contributing celebrities had been altered by Max, and Queen Victoria's *More Leaves from the Journal* with its faked inscription—"For Mr. Beerbohm —the never sufficiently to be studied writer whom Albert looks down on affectionately I am sure."

The early enthusiasm which prompted Stephen Greene to visit Max in Rapallo in 1938 led him on to the serious collecting of Maximiliana year after year. His most unusual item is a colossal scrapbook containing clippings about Max from all over the world. Every serious writer on Max applies, as a matter of course, to Mr. Greene for a look at this repository, a request which is generously granted, even if it means sending the book across the continent or the Atlantic. This is only part of the Greene collection, which is rich in manuscripts, first editions, presentation copies, books, letters, and caricatures.

Not all Beerbohm enthusiasts live in the East. Mr. Alfred E. Perrin of Cincinnati, Ohio, held an impressive showing of his Beerbohm books, caricatures, letters, and manuscripts at the Cincinnati Public Library in April 1965. Among the items shown were autograph manuscripts of well-known essays, including both the pencil and revised pen draft of "A Relic," and the five drawings for *Bitter Sweet,* among many fine caricatures. The caricatures are now in the Lilly Library at Indiana University. In Chicago, Mrs. Theophile Steiffel owns most of the letters and drawings formerly belonging to the late Herbert Rossett, Florence's cousin.

California does not lack Beerbohm collectors. The late Professor Maj Ewing, former chairman of the English Department at the University of California at Los Angeles, owned many important Beerbohms which he left to the UCLA Library, whose original holdings he had been instrumental in building up. At an exhibit of Max's watercolors and drawings, held by the Achenbach Foundation for the Graphic Arts of San Francisco in the spring of 1964, most of the Ewing items were on display. Mr. Eric Ambler of Los Angeles also showed a watercolor of Edward VII deciding to abandon his neckwear. Mr. and Mrs. Joseph Branston and Mr. and Mrs. William von Metz lent a number of caricatures from their interesting collections. Since the Achenbach exhibit, the Branston holdings have been augmented by "Two Glimpses of Andrew Lang" in manuscript and a signed drawing of Frank Harris, inscribed, "For Antonio Cippico—this portrait of a man whom he was fortunate in not knowing and perhaps a little unfortunate too." In the von Metz collection are two unusual items, a profile bust of Florence Beerbohm in a roundel done by Will Rothenstein and an amusing caricature of the Rothenstein family by Max. At the Achenbach exhibit Dr. and Mrs. James D. Hart of Berkeley showed a preliminary sketch of Mr. Morley introducing John Stuart Mill to Rossetti, which Max had discarded as "spoilt." G. W. Patterson, also of the San Francisco area, held a commemorative exhibition at the San Francisco Public Library in 1972 in which he featured the signed manuscript for the Preface to the Collected Works and Max's copy of *Zulieka Dobson* containing lightly penciled sketches of the characters.

When the Grolier Club of New York and the Zamorana Club of Los Angeles visited the William M. Clary Collection at the Honnold Library of the Claremont Colleges in 1961, they received a "Keepsake," *Max Beerbohm and the Oxford Chancellor,* written by Mr. Clary and illustrated by Max's sonnet to Lord Curzon and the caricature of Curzon's "Young and Old Self."

Stanley Marcus of Dallas, Texas, prizes, in addition to the projected copy of Bruce Roger's edition of *The Happy Hypocrite* mentioned in the final chapter, some thirty or forty books from the Sotheby sale including Rothenstein's *Twenty-Four Portraits,* and his *Twelve Portraits,* both with Max's commentaries about the subjects; in the former is a diminutive watercolor of Rothenstein on the title page.

Among early collectors was A. Edward Newton, whose books were sold in 1941. Prices at that sale, such as $17.50 for *Yet Again,* would bring groans from modern buyers. Florence's brother Mannie tried to interest the noted bibliophile A. S. W. Rosenbach in the manuscript of *Zuleika,* but Dr. Rosenbach refused to be tempted. However, the published catalogue of Dr. Rosenbach's collection shows he had not always been so adamant, for it contains a number of Beerbohm items, among them the copy of *The Guerdon* and the "Sonnet to Henry James" with the autograph letter presenting them to Mrs. Hunter, priced at $675. Where are they now?

When the books of John Quinn, one of America's best-known collectors, were sold in 1923 a number of Beerbohm firsts went in the auction. Other early collectors included Christopher Morley and his friend W. S. Hall, Dr. Logan Glendenning, the caricaturist William H. Cotton, and Carl Van Vechten, the novelist. Earl E. Fiske of Green Bay, Wisconsin, must be mentioned for his 1926 Christmas card, bearing a self-caricature of Max, a letter from him, and a note of explanation from Mr. Fiske. Vincent Starrett was responsible for the printing of Max's account of Sherlock Holmes from his *Saturday Review* article (6 May 1905) as *Sherlockiana, A Reminiscence of Sherlock Holmes,* done by Edwin B. Hill at Tempe, Arizona, in 1948. In 1966 the *Mercury Press* of San Francisco reprinted, For Private Distribution Only, the Introduction which Max wrote for Dixon Scott's *Men of Letters* (1916). This was done at the instigation of Edgar Newton Kierveff.

The present writer treasures two colored drawings by Max, several autograph letters, most first editions, and a copy of *The Spirit Lamp,* containing his first signed essay, "The Incomparable Beauty of Modern Dress." Beyond a doubt many other Maximilians cherish memorabilia in letter files, in book-cases, or framed on study walls. These relics give them that sense of nearness to the originator which Max once suggested was the reason for collecting. Max himself was aware of the value of manuscript. When his brother-in-law Sam Kahn was negotiating a sale for him, Max wrote, "My own idea is that I should receive not less than 5 million gold dollars, tax free." Even the Max of the Nineties recognized the importance of the written word when he cautioned Reggie Turner, "Keep my letters," and "you will be known . . . as 'the friend of Henry Beerbohm' and 'the receiver of those confessions which have come down to us . . . and form one of the most luminous and fascinating pieces of self-exposition ever given to the world.' "

Max told his friend Sir Sydney Roberts of Cambridge, "It is only the good opinion of the few that keeps a book alive." Now these few, these happy American few, hold dear the possessions bequeathed to them by Sir Max Beerbohm, born in Palace Gardens, Kensington, in 1872.

Appendix II: Source Notes

The letters of Max to Reggie Turner are taken from Max Beerbohm, *Letters to Reggie Turner,* edited by Rupert Hart-Davis, London, 1964; unless otherwise stated the letters from Max to Mrs. Ada Leverson are in the Research Center, University of Texas at Austin; the letters of Florence and Max to Alice and Will Rothenstein are in the Harvard College Library; the letters of Reggie Turner to Max are in the same collection; the letters of Max to Florence belong to Mrs. Eva Reichmann of London; the letters of Max to Violet and Sydney Schiff are in the Merton College Library at Oxford; and the letters of Florence and Max to Samuel and Isaac Kahn are in the possession of Mrs. Constance Kahn Starr of Memphis, Tennessee. When these letters are mentioned in the text, the source is not repeated in the Notes unless the letter is in a different location.

The following abbreviations have been used: Max Beerbohm, MB; Saturday Review, *SR;* Florence Kahn, FK; and Merton College Library, Oxford, MCL.

I. MAX DISCOVERS AMERICA

Page 4—**MB on Wilde's American visit:** MB, *A Peep into the Past,* collected and introduced by Rupert Hart-Davis (Brattleboro, Vt., Stephen Greene Press, 1973), p. 6.

Page 6—**MB on Statue of Liberty:** David Cecil, *Max Beerbohm, A Biography* (London, Constable, 1964), p. 114.

Page 7—**MB on Harrigan:** S. N. Behrman, *Portrait of Max* (New York, Random House, 1960), p. 59.

Page 8—**MB letter to Stone:** *Chap-Book* collection of H. S. Stone in Newberry Library, Chicago.
—— **"clever young man":** *Musical Courier,* 20 Jan. 1895.
—— **"yellow nuisance":** *New York Times,* 10 Feb. 1895.

—— **"jig-saw, blue-light school":** New York *Tribune,* 3 Feb. 1895.

—— **"vulgar indecencies":** *Critic,* 16 Feb. 1895.

Page 9—**Criticism of "Vanity":** *New York Times,* 9 Feb. 1895.

—— **"A Dish of Prunes":** *Chicago Tribune,* 28 Feb. 1895.

Page 10—**MB on Chicago's corruptness:** Boston *Evening Transcript,* 30 March 1895.

—— **MB on an American Shakespeare enthusiast:** W. W. Whitelock in *Bookbuyer,* Jan. 1903.

—— **"The Infamous Brigade":** in MB, *More* (London, Heinemann, 1899), pp. 57–62.

—— **Ernest Beerbohm's marriage:** Chicago *Tribune,* 1 March 1895.

Page 11—**Philadelphia's reception of Beerbohm Tree:** Philadelphia *Public Ledger,* 25 March 1895.

Page 12—**Interview with MB:** Boston *Herald,* 30 March 1895.

Page 13—**Reaction to interview:** *Ibid.,* 31 March 1895.

—— **Interview with MB:** Boston *Evening Transcript,* 30 March 1895.

Page 14—**Maud Beerbohm Tree on American youth:** "Herbert and I," in MB, *Herbert Beerbohm Tree* (New York, Dutton, 1920), p. 95.

Page 16—**"tiresome melodrama":** Washington *Post,* 2 April 1895.

—— **"small, select spread":** *Ibid.*

—— **MB meets Kipling:** Behrman, p. 61.

—— **Beerbohm Tree on Wilde-Queensberry case:** Washington *Post,* 4 April 1895.

Page 17—**Lane in New York:** J. Lewis May, *John Lane and the 90's* (London, Lane, 1936), pp. 89 ff; and Katherine Lyon Mix, *A Study in Yellow* (Lawrence, Kansas, University of Kansas Press; and London, Constable, 1960), pp. 143 ff.

—— **Lane "in full bloom":** *Vanity,* 20 April 1895.

—— **MB on his caricaturing methods:** MB letter to Gosse, 16 March 1908, in British Museum.

—— **MB avoids Niagara Falls:** MB interview with K.L.M., 8 April 1954, at Rapallo.

II. MAX AND THE EXPATRIATES

Page 20—**Review of "More":** *Bookbuyer,* July 1899.

—— **Stone on MB's parodies:** Stone letter in Newberry Library.

Page 21—**MB letter to Stone:** in Newberry Library.

—— **Title of "The Works":** Arthur Waugh in *Critic,* 18 July 1896. Verified by MB letter to Gosse, June 1896, in British Museum.

—— **Lane's biography and bibliography of MB:** in MB, *The Works of Max Beerbohm* (London, Lane, 1896), pp. 163 ff.

Page 22—**Review of "The Works":** *Nation,* 10 Sept. 1896.

Page 23—**MB letter to Ross:** *Robert Ross Friend of Friends,* Margery Ross, ed. (London, Jonathan Cape, 1952), p. 43.

—— **MB praises Harland:** MB letter to K.L.M., 29 June 1930, in K.L.M.'s collection.

—— **Harland on "Happy Hypocrite":** Harland letter to MB, in MCL.

—— **Aline Harland letter to MB:** in MCL.

—— **MB self-description as "best dressed man":** in Beerbohm Collection, University of California, Los Angeles.

Page 24—**Harris in MB letter to Ross:** Ross, p. 45.

—— **MB parodies Harris:** "Christmas and Shakespeare," in MB, *A Christmas Garland* (London, Heinemann, 1912), pp. 69–73.

Page 26—**Whistler's reply to MB's criticism:** *SR,* 27 Nov. 1897.

Page 27—**Whistler on Wilde:** *Max Beerbohm, Letters to Reggie Turner,* Rupert Hart-Davis, ed. (London, Hart-Davis, 1964), p. 38.

—— **Whistler in the "SR case":** Hesketh Pearson, *The Man Whistler* (London, Methuen, 1952), pp. 168–169.

—— **MB's "Whistler's Writing":** later included with some changes in MB, *Yet Again* (London, Heinemann, 1909), pp. 103–110.

Page 28—**Influence of Whistler on MB:** J. G. Riewald, *Sir Max Beerbohm Man and Writer* (The Hague, Martinus Nijhoff, 1953; and Brattleboro, Vt., Stephen Greene Press, 1963), p. 176.

—— **MB's Whistlerian affectations:** *Nation,* 24 May 1894.

—— **Whistler and Swinburne in "No. 2 The Pines":** in MB, *And Even Now* (London, Heinemann, 1922), pp. 57–80.

—— **Whistler in "Enoch Soames":** in MB, *Seven Men* (London, Heinemann, 1919), p. 10.

—— **Carlyle's story of Whistler:** "Hethway Speaking," in MB, *Mainly on the Air* (London, Heinemann, 1957), pp. 111–112.

Page 29—**Mrs. Pennell's "evenings":** Elizabeth Pennell, *Nights* (Philadelphia, Lippincott, 1929), p. 154.

—— **MB on Pennell's illustrations of James:** in Sotheby *Catalogue* of the library and literary manuscripts of the late Sir Max Beerbohm (London, 1960), p. 36.

—— **MB on Sargent's art:** *SR,* 19 June 1909.

—— **Sargent in MB's caricature "31 Tite Street":** in MB, *A Book of Caricatures* (London, Methuen, 1907), frontispiece. Evan Charteris in his life of Sargent says that Lady Fendel Phillips and the Duchess of Sutherland are recognizable in the line.

—— **Edward VII's praise of Sargent:** *SR,* 14 Dec. 1901.

Page 31—**Sargent's invitation to MB:** Sargent letter to MB, May 1909, in MCL.
—— **MB's "Mr. Sargent at Work":** MB Letter to FK c. 1907, in Reichmann collection.
—— **MB's treatment of Sargent:** MB letter to Harris, in Robert H. Taylor Collection, Princeton University.
—— **MB on Sargent's landscapes:** MB letter to FK, in Reichmann collection.
—— **MB on Sargent's presentation of Jehovah:** MB letter to FK, in Reichmann collection.
—— **MB's idea for cartoon of Sargent and James:** *Letters to Reggie Turner*, p. 222.

Page 32—**MB on Sargent's later work:** MB, Introduction to "Portrait Drawings of Will Rothenstein," in *A Peep into the Past*, p. 59.
—— **MB's and Crane's admiration for Ouida:** MB and Crane wrote appreciations of Ouida, MB in *SR*, 3 July 1897, and Crane in *Bookbuyer*, Jan. 1897; both admitted her limitations but admired her spirit.

III. THE IMPORTANCE OF BEING HENRY JAMES

Page 33—**Failure of James's "Guy Domville":** *New York Times*, 24 Jan. 1895.
—— **James jeered by audience:** Boston *Evening Transcript*, 30 March 1895.
—— **James says "I am mortally unwell":** quoted in Lewis Hind, *Naphtali* (London, Lane, 1926), p. 89.

Page 34—**MB's comparison of James and Shaw:** *SR*, 24 Nov. 1906.

Page 35—**James's reaction to MB's parody:** Gosse letter to BM, quoted in Evan Charteris's *Life and Letters of Edmund Gosse* (New York, Harper & Bros., 1931), p. 350.
—— **MB letter to Gosse:** in British Museum.
—— **James deplores MB's cruelty:** Diary of Sir Sydney Waterlow, quoted in Leon Edel, *Henry James*, Vol. V. (New York, Lippincott, 1953–1972), p. 387.
—— **MB's favorite saying of James's:** Behrman, p. 300.
—— **MB on "Portrait of a Lady":** MB letter to FK in Reichmann collection.
—— **James and Trollope in MB letter to Fisher:** Fisher collection in Bodleian Library, Oxford.

Page 36—**MB on James's "terrible grey eye":** MB letter to FK, in Reichmann collection.
—— **MB on "The Golden Bowl," etc.:** *SR*, 27 Feb. 1909.

Page 37—**James letter to MB,** 19 Dec. 1908: in MCL.
—— **MB on Spencer Boyden:** in Berg Collection, New York Public Library.
—— **MB on dramatization of James story:** MB letter to Balderston, 27 March 1929, in Taylor Collection.

Page 38—**MB's parody of James:** "The Guerdon." Privately printed (New York, 1925), 210 copies on crown and scepter paper. No publisher named, but known to be G. A. Baker and Co. Later included in MB, *A Variety of Things* (New York, Knopf, 1928), p. 193.

—— **MB and Gosse's sonnet to James:** in *Max in Verse*, J. G. Riewald, ed. (Brattleboro, Vt., Stephen Greene Press, 1963), p. 19.

—— **MB's "sincere reverence" for James:** MB letter to L. Kahn, in Brotherton Library, Leeds University.

—— **MB's expanded version of the "Mote":** and MB letter to Gosse, in Princeton University Collection.

—— **MB's illustrated version of "A Christmas Garland":** MB letter to Gosse, in MCL.

—— **MB's caricature of James at keyhole:** Edel, Vol. IV, p. 353.

Page 39—**MB on James's "Italian Hours":** Sotheby *Catalogue*, p. 36.

—— **MB on James's love of Italy:** MB review of *A Little Tour of France* in *Observer*, 13 Nov. 1949.

—— **James's mind "typically American":** MB note in Berg Collection.

—— **James's Notebooks published first in America:** Sotheby *Catalogue*, p. 38.

—— **James's editing "Notes of a Son and Brother":** *loc. cit.*

—— **MB's "Half Hours with the Dialects of England":** in Riewald, *Max in Verse*, pp. 21–25.

Page 42—**MB meets James in Piccadilly:** MB, "An Incident," in *Mainly on the Air* (1957), pp. 119–120.

IV. Some Transatlantic Visitors

Page 43—**MB's "Hosts and Guests":** in *And Even Now*, p. 39.

—— **Stone on MB's "Beardsley stuff":** Stone letters in Newberry Library.

Page 44—**Fitch's visits to London:** MB's notebook, in Berg Collection.

—— **MB mentioned in Fitch's postcards:** Montrose J. Moses and Virginia Gerson, *Clyde Fitch and His Letters* (Boston, Little, Brown, 1924), pp. 50, 151.

Page 45—**Shaw calls MB "Incomparable":** G. B. Shaw in *SR*, 21 May 1898.

—— **Fitch "lunched, dined and supped" with MB:** Fitch letter, 15 July 1901, in Moses and Gerson, p. 299.

—— **Fitch letter to MB:** in MCL.

Page 46—**Tree letter to Fitch:** Hesketh Pearson, *Beerbohm Tree* (New York, Harper's, 1956), p. 138.

—— **MB on Fitch's "The Truth":** *SR*, 17 August 1907.

—— **MB on Fitch's reaction to Moore's plagiarism:** MB, "George Moore," in *Mainly on the Air* (1957), p. 85.

—— **MB books inscribed to Fitch:** and MB letter to Fitch, in Fitch Collection, Amherst College.

Page 47—**MB's exchange with Fitch ("Have you never stopped?"):** Fitch letter to MB, in MCL.

—— **Fitch and MB's visit to Rye:** MB's notebook, in Berg Collection.

—— **MB, Fitch's "uncrowned king":** Fitch letter to MB, in MCL.

—— **MB's dog hit by hansom:** *Bookbuyer,* Jan. 1903.

—— **MB's rhyme for A. Leverson's daughter:** Violet Wyndham, *The Sphinx and Her Circle* (London, Andre Deutsch, 1963), p. 71. Ada Leverson was called "the Sphinx" by Oscar Wilde. Violet Wyndham was her daughter.

Page 48—**MB has no faith in Goodwin's horse:** MB, "Nat Goodwin and Another" in *Mainly on the Air* (1957), p. 63.

—— **Goodwin's account of his story-telling:** Nat Goodwin, *Nat Goodwin's Book* (Boston, Badger, 1914), pp. 254–268.

—— **MB on Goodwin's story-telling:** "Nat Goodwin and Another" in *Mainly on the Air* (1957), p. 68.

Page 49—**MB review of Goodwin in "American Citizen":** *SR,* 24 June 1899.

—— **MB review of Goodwin in "When We Were 21":** *Ibid.,* 21 Sept. 1901.

—— **"Acting is a matter of geography":** Goodwin, p. 273.

—— **MB on American women in "1880":** first published in the *Yellow Book,* IV, pp. 275–283; then included with some changes in *The Works,* p. 52.

—— **MB and Mrs. Keppel:** Rothenstein letter to Ross, in Ross, p. 69.

Page 50—**MB review of Mrs. Craigie's "The Ambassador":** *SR,* 11 June 1898.

Page 51—**MB review of Mrs. Craigie's "Wisdom of the Wise":** *Ibid.,* 1 Dec. 1900.

—— **MB review of Mrs. Craigie's "The Bishop's Wife":** *Ibid.,* 4 June 1902.

—— **Mrs. Craigie thanks MB:** P. Craigie letter to MB, 4 May 1899, in MCL.

—— **MB on Mrs. Craigie:** in MB letter to Gosse, 30 June 1914, in British Museum.

Page 52—**MB's inscription in biography of Mrs. Craigie:** Sotheby *Catalogue,* p. 49.

Page 53—**Mrs. Atherton's review of "Happy Hypocrite":** *Vanity Fair* (London), 29 April 1897.

—— **Mrs. Atherton on Reggie Turner:** Gertrude Atherton, *Adventures of a Novelist* (New York, Liveright, 1932), pp. 276–279.

Page 54—**Mrs. Atherton letter to MB:** in MCL.

—— **Mrs. Wharton recalls MB's "lapidary comment":** Edith Wharton, *A Backward Glance* (New York, Scribner's, 1934), p. 220.

—— **MB writes Mrs. Wharton:** MB letter to Mrs. Wharton, 11 Aug. 1915, in Beinecke Library, Yale University.

Page 55—**Mrs. Wharton letter to MB:** in MCL.

—— **MB refuses to draw Kipling:** in MB letter to Mrs. Wharton, 25 August 1915, in Beinecke Library.

—— **MB's caricature of Curzon and Cammaerts:** in *Book of the Homeless*, Edith Wharton, ed. (New York and Paris, 1916).

—— **Cross on Mrs. Wharton's denunciation of MB:** Wilbur Cross, *A Connecticut Yankee* (New Haven, Yale University Press, 1943), p. 195.

Page 57—**MB has "carpet slippers in his soul":** Constance Collier quoted in *Saturday Review of Literature*, 3 July 1948.

V. MAX AROUND THEATRES

Page 58—**Review of "More":** *Critic*, August 1899; *Dial*, 10 June 1899.

Page 59—**MB's "impromptus seem the work of years":** *Dramatic Mirror*, 3 Jan. 1901.

—— **MB's sketch of Sir George Hell:** *Critic*, Feb. 1901.

Page 62—**MB on Augustus Daly's farces:** MB, "Playgoing," in *Mainly on the Air* (1957), p. 55.

Page 63—**MB on American jokes:** Interview with MB in *Cassells*, Feb. 1903.

Page 64—**MB on Ethel Barrymore:** *SR*, 12 May 1904.

—— **MB on Billie Burke:** *Ibid.*, 15 May 1909.

Page 65—**MB on Knowles, a "peculiar American":** MB "Music Halls of My Youth" in *Mainly on the Air* (1957), p. 40.

—— **MB on Sothern and Marlowe:** MB letter to FK, in Reichmann collection.

—— **Reaction to MB review of Jerome play:** Boston *Herald*, 23 Nov. 1908.

VI. INTRODUCING MISS FLORENCE KAHN

Page 67—**MB review of FK:** *SR*, 15 Feb. 1908.

—— **FK's family and background:** data furnished by FK's niece, Constance Kahn Starr, friends in Memphis, and items in the Memphis *Commercial Appeal*.

Page 70—**FK in "L'Intérieur":** *New York Times*, 19 Feb. 1896.

—— **FK appears in Memphis:** *Commercial Appeal*, 24 Feb. 1898.

Page 71—**Independent Theatre dedicated to "improvement of taste . . . etc.":** *Course of Modern Plays* (Yadkin Press), p. 6.

—— **Review of FK in "El Gran Galeoto":** *Cosmopolitan*, March 1900, p. 513.

—— **Review of FK in "Osberne und Ursyne":** clipping from *World*, 29 Nov. 1899, in Theatre Collection, New York Public Library.

—— **Dithmar's praise of FK:** *New York Times*, 3 Dec. 1899.

Page 72—**Review of FK in "Master Builder":** *Ibid.*, 24 Dec. 1899.

—— **FK to join Mansfield:** *Ibid.*, 18 Jan. 1900.

—— **Dithmar review of FK in "The Storm":** *Ibid.,* 4 March 1900.
—— **FK in New Orleans:** H. G. Rogers letter to Kester, 2 April 1900, in Kester Collection, New York Public Library.

Page 73—**Hapgood praises FK:** *Bookman,* Nov. 1900, p. 268.
—— **Trouble between FK and Mansfield:** *Munsey's Magazine,* April 1900, p. 131.
—— **Kester letter to his mother:** in Kester Collection.

Page 75—**Dithmar criticizes FK:** *New York Times,* 29 March 1904.
—— **Hapgood praises FK:** Norman Hapgood, *The Changing Years* (New York, Farrar & Rhinehart, 1931), p. 136.

Page 76—**MB's early friendship with FK:** data from MB's letters in Reichmann collection.
—— **Dithmar review of FK in "When We Dead Awaken":** *New York Times,* 8 March 1905.
—— **"You have to develop a taste" for FK:** *Dramatic Mirror,* 18 March 1905.

Page 77—**Huneker on FK:** *Metropolitan,* May 1905.

VII. BEERBOHM *vs* HUNEKER

Page 78—**Huneker on MB:** "Raconteur" column in *Musical Courier,* 15 June 1898.
—— **Huneker expects MB to write a play:** *Ibid.,* 19 March 1902.
—— **Huneker on MB's "Contrast in Hospitality":** New York *Sun,* 7 Oct. 1903.

Page 79—**Peck's article on MB's critique of Huneker:** *Bookman,* Sept. 1905, p. 4.

Page 80—**Mencken on MB's critique of Huneker:** H. L. Mencken, *Prejudices, Third Series* (New York, Knopf, 1922), p. 77.
—— **Shaw and MB review "Iconoclasts: A Book of Dramatists":** Arnold T. Schwab, *James Gibbons Huneker* (Stanford, Calif., 1963), pp. 167–170.
—— **MB's review of "Iconoclasts":** *SR,* 27 April 1907.
—— **MB a character in Huneker's mock drama:** Huneker, "Blarney at the Box Office," in New York *Sun,* 6 Sept. 1908. Repeated in Huneker's *Unicorns* (New York, Scribner's, 1917), pp. 24–48.
—— **MB's review of Huneker's "Egoists":** *SR,* 3 July 1909.

Page 81—**Huneker calls MB "Mud-Victorian":** Huneker, *Steeplejack,* Vol. II. (New York, Scribner's, 1920), p. 250.
—— **MB on his exchange with Huneker:** MB letter to Schwab, 26 June 1952. Kindly made available by Prof. Schwab.

VIII. THE DEAR LITTLE FRIEND

Page 82—**FK with Daly:** New York *Morning Telegraph,* 10 Feb. 1906.

Page 83—**Morgan's purchase of Anne Hathaway's cottage (MB's jest):** *SR,* 26 April 1902.
—— **MB on Americans' lust for "antiquities":** *Ibid.,* 21 April 1906.
—— **MB on horses of St. Mark's:** MB, "A Stranger in Venice," in *A Variety of Things* (Knopf edition), p. 93. (Taken from London *Daily Mail,* Nov. 1906.)

Page 85—**FK arrives in New York:** *New York Times,* 16 Nov. 1906.
—— **FK letter to Kester,** 23 Feb. 1907: in Kester Collection.

Page 86—**"murky sea of Ibsenism":** William Winter, *The Wallet of Time* (New York, Moffat, Yard, 1913), p. 562.
—— **MB on illustrations of James:** MB letter to Gosse, in Berg Collection.

IX. THE ACTRESS AND THE CRITIC

Page 90—**MB on DeWolf Hopper and American humor:** *SR,* 15 July 1899.
—— **MB meets Twain:** MB letter to Cyril Clemens: *Hobbies,* Nov. 1958.
—— **MB has not read Twain:** MB letter in Newberry Library.
—— **MB as "Knight of Mark Twain":** *Hobbies, loc. cit.*

Page 91—**FK and Rothensteins:** Sir J. Rothenstein in conversation with K.L.M.
—— **M. Kahn letter to FK:** in MCL.

Page 92—**Stage manager's letter on MB:** in MCL.
—— **FK praised in MB letter to Shaw,** 11 Feb. 1908: reproduced in Sims Catalogue, in Stephen Greene collection, Brattleboro, Vt.

Page 93—**Reviews of FK in "Rosmersholm":** *SR,* 15 Feb. 1908; *Athenaeum,* 22 Feb. 1908; *Pall Mall Gazette,* 11 Feb. 1908.
—— **Swinnerton praises "Rosmersholm":** Frank Swinnerton, *Figures in the Foreground* (London, Hutchinson, 1956), p. 15.
—— **Sutro letter to FK:** in MCL.
—— **MB's review of FK in "Man on the Kerb":** *SR,* 28 March 1908.
—— **MB letter to Housman:** Laurence Housman Collection, Somerset County Library, Street, England.

X. "NOT AT ANY PRICE"

Page 96—**MB refuses American lecture tour:** MB letter to Hind, 21 July 1921; in Stephen Greene collection.
—— **MB refuses American tour:** MB letter to Reid, in MCL.

Page 97—**MB refuses American visit:** MB letter to S. Kahn, in Starr collection, Memphis, Tenn.

—— **MB refuses American broadcast:** Behrman, p. 265.

—— **Page letter to MB,** 25 June 1909: in MCL.

Page 98—**MB on American politics in "George the Fourth":** in *The Works of MB,* p. 124.

—— **MB exchange with Chesterton on democracy:** *SR,* 23 Oct. 1909.

Page 99—**MB on Americans' "struggle for wealth":** *Ibid.,* 11 July 1903.

—— **MB on American sale of Whistler's etchings:** *Ibid.,* 21 April 1906.

—— **MB on Americans' "sentiment for the past of Europe":** *Ibid.,* 29 May 1909.

—— **MB on Rhodes Scholarships:** *Ibid.,* 4 Oct. 1902.

Page 100—**MB's caricature of T. Roosevelt:** in Ashmolean Museum, Oxford.

—— **MB's caricature of Wilson:** in MB, *A Survey* (London, Heinemann, 1921).

—— **MB's caricature of Wilson, Clemenceau and Lloyd George:** *Ibid.*

—— **MB's verse for Le Gallienne:** in Richard Le Gallienne, *The Romantic '90's* (London, Putnam & Co., Ltd., 1926), p. 171.

—— **MB upbraids American critic Dale:** *SR,* 10 Jan. 1910.

XI. LIFE BEGINS AT RAPALLO

Page 102—**Review of "Yet Again":** *Nation,* 7 July 1910.

Page 103—**Review of "Yet Again":** *New York Times,* 9 April 1910.

—— **Egerton predicts MB's marriage:** George Egerton, *A Leaf from the Yellow Book,* T. deV. White, ed. (London, Richards Press, 1958), p. 137.

Page 104—**Account of MB and FK wedding:** *The People,* 3 May 1910; in Theatre Collection, New York Public Library.

—— **MB and FK letter to Reggie Turner:** in Research Center, University of California, Los Angeles.

—— **Report of MB-FK marriage:** *New York Times,* 2 May 1910.

Page 106—**News items on wedding:** New York *Review,* 21 May 1910; Memphis *Commercial Appeal,* 3 May 1910; New York *Telegraph,* 3 May 1910; *Academy,* 14 May 1910; *Daily Mirror,* 4 May 1910.

—— **Harris's version of the wedding:** Frank Harris, *Contemporary Portraits, Fourth Series* (New York, Brentano's, 1923), pp. 130–131.

—— **MB objects to Harris's version:** MB letter to *Times Literary Supplement,* 28 Feb. 1924.

—— **MB on Rostand and Fitch:** *Letters to Reggie Turner,* p. 187.

Page 107—**Viola Tree visits MB:** Viola Tree Parsons, *Castles in the Air* (London, Hogarth Press, 1926), p. 67.

Page 108—**FK letter to MB:** kindly supplied by J. Fletcher, London.

—— **Rothenstein and FK's brothers:** M. Kahn letter to MB, at MCL.

—— **Rothenstein on American intellectual standards:** Robert Speaight, *William Rothenstein* (London, Eyre & Spottiswood, 1962), p. 250.

XII. ABIMILECH V. OOVER

Page 110—**Zuleika in America ("There she was"):** MB, *Zuleika Dobson* (London, Heinemann, 1911), pp. 18–20.

Page 111—**Oover's speech:** *Ibid.,* p. 119.
—— **Dorset and Oover ("The president showed much deference"):** *Ibid.,* pp. 120–121.

Page 112—**Dorset's opinion of Rhodes Scholars:** *Ibid.,* p. 122.
—— **Oover's moral tone ("Duke, I hope I am not incognisant"):** *Ibid.,* p. 125.
—— **"certain that Oover went to heaven":** *Ibid.,* p. 126.
—— **"Mr. Oover, too, looked grave":** *Ibid.,* p. 130.

Page 113—**Oover's speech:** *Ibid.,* p. 132.
—— **Oover determined to die ("d'you take me for a skunk?"):** *Ibid.,* pp. 227–228.
—— **Morgan's bid for Dorset's verses:** *Ibid.,* p. 264.
—— **Scribner's refuses "Zuleika":** Roger Burlingame, *Of Making Many Books* (New York, Scribner's, 1943), p. 66.

Page 114—**Reviews of "Zuleika":** New York *Sun,* 2 March 1912; *Dial,* 16 April 1912.
—— **Mansbridge on "Steve," Oover's original:** Mansbridge letter to *Saturday Review of Literature,* 18 Oct. 1947.

Page 115—**Death of Oover's original:** *New York Times,* 12 August 1945.
—— **MB on Zuleika's original:** Behrman, p. 228.
—— **G. Conover as Zuleika's original:** G. Conover letter to MB, in MCL.
—— **C. Collier as Zuleika's original:** C. Collier in *Saturday Review of Literature,* 3 July 1948.
—— **L. McCarthy as Zuleika's original:** Lillah McCarthy, *Myself and Friends* (London, 1933), p. 258.

XIII. AMERICA DISCOVERS MAX

Page 116—**Reviews of "A Christmas Garland":** *Outlook,* 21 Dec. 1912; *Independent,* 26 Dec. 1912.
—— **MB's caricatures exhibited in New York:** *New York Times,* 26 Jan. 1913.

Page 117—**Mackenzie meets MB:** Compton Mackenzie, *My Life and Times* (London, Chatto & Windus, 1963), p. 95.
—— **FK letter to MB from America,** 10 Feb. 1914: in Reichmann collection.

Page 118—**MB and "comic muse":** MB letter to Sargent, 11 Aug. 1915, in Beinecke Library.

—— **MB on humor in wartime:** MB letter to Mrs. Wharton, 11 Aug. 1915, in Beinecke Library.

—— **MB's case of "Rossettitis":** MB letter to Ross, in Ross, p. 259.

—— **Agnes Beerbohm Neville's wedding:** The *Times* (London), 9 April 1917.

Page 120—**MB complains to American publisher:** MB letter to Century Co., in Taylor Collection.

Page 121—**Dowson not Enoch Soames's original:** MB letter to *Bookman,* October, 1923, p. 235.

—— **Gorman reviews MB's writing:** Herbert S. Gorman, *Procession of Masks* (Boston, Brimmer, 1923), p. 58.

Page 122—**Van Doren reviews MB's "Seven Men":** Carl Van Doren in *Nation,* 25 Feb. 1920.

—— **Littell reviews "Seven Men":** Phillip Littell in *New Republic,* 25 Feb. 1920.

—— **McFee reviews "Seven Men":** William McFee, *Swallowing the Anchor* (New York, Doubleday, Page, 1925), pp. 56–69.

—— **Mencken appreciates MB:** *Letters of H. L. Mencken,* G. S. Forgue, ed. (New York, Knopf, 1961), p. 30.

Page 123—**Wright on first American publication of MB:** Willard H. Wright, Introduction to *Smart Set Anthology,* Burton Rascoe, ed. (New York, Grayson, 1930), p. xxvi.

—— **Nathan on MB:** *World of George Jean Nathan,* Charles Angoff, ed. (New York, Knopf, 1952), pp. 48–49.

—— **Preparation for Collected Edition of MB ("That I was old I knew"):** Preface to Collected Edition of MB. (London, Heinemann, 1922), pp. ix–xv.

XIV. HAPPY DAYS ON THE COAST ROAD

Page 124—**MB and FK family diary:** in Berg Collection.

—— **Robertses visit MB:** Harriet Roberts letter, 17 Dec. 1931, remembering first evening at the Villino, in MCL.

Page 126—**Sitwells visit MB:** Osbert Sitwell, *Noble Essences* (Boston, Little, Brown, 1950), p. 125.

—— **M. Russell visits MB:** Leslie De Charms, *Elizabeth of the German Garden* (London, 1958), p. 125.

—— **Maugham invites MB:** Maugham letter to MB, in Berg Collection.

—— **Newton on MB:** A. Edward Newton, *The Greatest Book in the World* (Boston, Little, Brown, 1923), p. 214.

—— **Newton letters to MB,** 20 May 1923 and 19 Jan. 1926: in MCL.

Page 127—**Newton claims "Zuleika" among hundred best books:** Newton, *The Book Collecting Game* (Boston, Little, Brown, 1928), p. 383.

—— **MB caricature of Newton:** now at Harvard.

—— **Rascoe reviews MB's "And Even Now":** *Bookman*, May 1920, p. 74.

Page 128—**MB and FK's life at Rapallo:** from Alexandra ("Dody") Kahn's letters to her family, 1921–1922, now owned by Dody—Mrs. Alexandra Kahn Bagshawe, Wetherby, England.

Page 129—**MB letter to Dody Kahn:** through kindness of Dody, in possession of K.L.M.

Page 130—**Review of MB's writings:** *Dial,* Jan. 1922.

Page 131—**MB caricature of Wilde in America:** in MB, *Rossetti and His Circle* (London, Heinemann, 1922).

—— **Guedalla warns Nathan about Lewis:** Angoff, p. 32.

—— **Lewis outburst on MB:** Hall letter to *Saturday Review of Literature,* 19 Sept. 1931.

Page 132—**Woollcott on MB's verse:** Alexander Woollcott in *Ladies' Home Journal,* clipping, no date, in K.L.M.'s collection.

Page 133—**Review of MB's "Observations":** Helen McAfee, in *Yale Review,* July, 1926. MB, *Observations* (London, Heinemann, 1925).

Page 134—**Whitlow on FK's finger:** related by Mrs. Harriet Roberts.

Page 136—**Quote from MB's "Not That I Would Boast":** in *A Variety of Things* (Knopf edition), pp. 229–268.

Page 137—**Riewald on MB's "Dreadful Dragon of Hay Hill":** in Riewald, *Sir Max Beerbohm,* p. 107.

XV. AGAIN THE ACTRESS

Page 139—**Reviews of FK in play at Huddersfield:** Charles Morgan in The *Times* (London), 12 May 1931; W. A. Darlington, *Morning Telegraph,* 12 May 1931; Ellis Roberts, *New Statesman,* 16 May 1931.

Page 140—**Mrs. Thomas Hardy letter to FK:** in MCL.

—— **FK meets Yeats:** FK letter to MB, in Reichmann collection.

—— **FK in London:** George Freedley's account in interview with K.L.M.

—— **Agate's reference to FK's hurt finger:** in Harriet Robert's account; but not in James Agate's review as given in *Ego 2* (London, Hamish Hamilton, 1936), p. 247.

Page 141—**MB visits Oxford:** J. Espey letter to K.L.M.

Page 142—**FK on Vivian Leigh:** FK letter, in Starr collection.

—— **MB sees FK in "Richard II":** *Spectator's Notebook,* 24 Feb. 1935.

—— **Gielgud and FK:** Espey letter to K.L.M.

XVI. AMERICANS AT RAPALLO

Page 143—**MB's early theory of caricature:** *Letters to Reggie Turner,* p. 301.
—— **MB draws Peggy Wood:** Wood letter to K.L.M.

Page 144—**Account of Dody Kahn's marriage:** kindly furnished by George Bagshawe.
—— **J. Barrymore at Dieppe with MB:** Cecil, p. 223.

Page 146—**Barrymore letter to MB, 25 April 1925:** in MCL.
—— **Barrymore and MB:** letter and cable, in MCL.
—— **Barrymore values MB's friendship:** Louis Sobel, "New York Cavalcade," Harrisburg (Pa.) *News,* 19 Sept. 1943, clipping in Stephen Greene collection.
—— **P. Bottome visits MB:** Phyllis Bottome, *From the Life* (London, Faber, 1946), pp. 35–46; and *The Goal* (London, Vanguard, 1962), pp. 237–240.

Page 147—**Pound subject for caricature:** Cecil, p. 329.
—— **Pound believes MB to be Jewish:** Ezra Pound, *Hugh Selwyn Mauberley,* John Espey, ed. (London, Faber & Faber, 1955), p. 124.

Page 148—**Pound's note to FK,** 18 Sept. 1933: in MCL.
—— **Pound gives FK "A. B. C. of Reading":** Sotheby *Catalogue,* p. 64.
—— **Pound out of place in Europe:** P. Bottome, *The Goal,* p. 240.
—— **Pounds visit MB:** D. Pound letter to J. Espey.
—— **Pound's projected "Life and Times of Max Beerbohm":** in *Letters of Ezra Pound,* D. D. Paige, ed. (New York, Harcourt, Brace, 1950), p. 381; and Riewald, *Sir Max Beerbohm,* p. 305.
—— **Pound in MB and FK letter to S. Kahn:** in Starr collection.

Page 149—**P. Bottome letter to MB ré Pound petition,** 12 Nov. 1945: in MCL.
—— **Berenson neighbor of MB:** Sylvia Sprigge, *Bernard Berenson* (London, 1960), p. 169.

Page 150—**Gosse warning to Smith:** quoted in The *Observer,* 23 August 1942.
—— **Arthur Bendix's copy of "Trivia":** in Stephen Greene collection.
—— **MB letter to Smith with Birrell contribution:** in MCL.
—— **Smith sees himself in "Seven Men":** Smith letter to MB, 31 Oct. 1919, in MCL.
—— **Greene visits MB:** Stephen Greene, *A Visit to Max* (Brattleboro, Vt., Stephen Greene Press, 1965). Also in conversation with K.L.M.

Page 152—**MB in college curriculum:** Cornelius Weygandt, *On the Edge of Evening* (New York, G. P. Putnam's Sons, 1946), p. 102.
—— **A. Tuell writes on MB:** Annie Kimball Tuell, letter to MB, 1 Dec. 1932, in MCL.

Page 153—**M.A. theses on MB:** R. Clay Bailey and Mary Ann Reilly, letters to K.L.M.

XVII. ENGLAND AND THE SECOND WORLD WAR

Page 154—**MB and FK welcomed in London:** G. B. Stern, *And Did He Stop and Speak to You?* (London, 1958), p. 46.

Page 155—**MB on his knighthood ceremony:** MB letter to S. Schiff, in MCL.
—— **FK tells children of ceremony:** in M. Carpenter letter to K.L.M.
—— **Data on life at Abinger:** drawn from FK's letters to her brothers, in Starr collection.
—— **D. Beerbohm letter to FK,** 3 Sept. 1939: in Reichmann collection.

Page 156—**MB's "Remembered Meals":** in Abinger *Chronicle,* Sept.–Oct. 1942, pp. 35–38.
—— **MB and Wilder at Bennett's dinner party:** Arnold Bennett, *Letters to His Nephew* (New York, Harper's, 1935), p. 268.

Page 158—**MB meets Tunney:** Alan Dent, *Saturday Review of Literature,* 30 Aug. 1952.
—— **MB praises Woollcott's broadcasts:** MB letter to Woollcott, in MCL.
—— **S. Kahn effects settlement for MB on Welles broadcast:** MB letter to S. Kahn, in Starr collection.

Page 160—**Smith's tribute to MB:** Smith letter to MB, in MCL.
—— **MB elected to National Institute of Arts and Letters (U.S.):** Arthur Train letter to MB, 19 Jan. 1943, in MCL.

Page 161—**Review of MB's "Lytton Strachey":** *World Review* August 1943, in Stephen Greene collection. MB, *Lytton Strachey* (Cambridge, 1943).
—— **Exhibit of MB's papers at Grolier Club, N.Y.:** New York *Tribune,* 26 March 1944.

Page 162—**Knox's comment on MB's new cottage:** Collie Knox, *People of Quality* (London, MacDonald, 1947), p. 163.
—— **FK at Flint Cottage ("exquisitely petite"):** *New Statesman,* 2 June 1945.
—— **MB's tribute to Schiff:** *Ibid.,* 18 Nov. 1944.
—— **MB's memorial address for Rothenstein:** Curiven Press, 6 March 1945.
—— **MB letter on sale of MS,** 26 August 1942: in Beinecke Library.

Page 163—**MB's self-caricature for Rossett:** now in possession of Mrs. T. Steifel, Chicago.

XVIII. HOME TO THE VILLINO

Page 164—**Restoration of "Zuleika" mural:** FK letter to S. Kahn, in Starr collection.
—— **Pound in custody:** Charles Norman, *Ezra Pound* (New York, Macmillan, 1960), p. 424.
—— **Craig gone from Rapallo:** Edward Craig, *Gordon Craig, Story of His Life* (New York, Knopf, 1968), p. 340.

Page 165—**MB's "William and Mary":** in *And Even Now,* p. 277.

Page 168—**MB's use of American slang:** Sims Catalogue, in Stephen Greene collection.

—— **MB on American advertising:** in *Mainly on the Air* (1957), p. 49.

—— **MB appreciates Stein and Thurber:** Cecil, p. 484.

—— **MB calls Whitman "lovable":** *SR,* 26 May 1906.

—— **MB's preparation for writing for the "Book of the Queen's Doll's House":** in E. V. Lucas, *Post Bag Diversions* (New York, Harper's), p. 166.

—— **MB on Tagore in America:** MB letter to Rothenstein, in Harvard College Collection.

—— **MB on Norris's stories:** *SR,* 23 April 1904.

Page 169—**MB's note in "Gentlemen Prefer Blondes":** copy of book in Stephen Greene collection.

—— **MB on E. Wylie in letter with greeting to Benét,** Jan. 1950: in Beinecke Library.

Page 170—**MB invites E. Wylie:** Nancy Hoyt, *Portrait of an Unknown Lady* (Indianapolis, Bobbs-Merrill, 1935), p. 106.

—— **MB on Burton's "Adventures Among the Immortals":** MB letter to S. Kahn, in Starr collection.

—— **MB on Hergesheimer:** Edmund Wilson, *Shores of Night* (New York, Farrar, Strauss, Giroux, 1952), p. 231.

Page 171—**MB on Hemingway:** Cyril Ray in *Sunday Times* (London), 4 Oct. 1954.

—— **MB's copies of Untermeyer and Kronenberger:** in Stephen Greene collection.

—— **MB's remark "genius is . . . always in a hurry":** in *Lytton Strachey,* p. 7.

—— **MB writes to W. Lewis:** Geoffrey Hellman in *New Yorker,* 31 Oct. 1959.

XIX. The Days Shorten

Page 172—**MB's review of "Life of Eleanora Duse":** *Sunday Times* (London), 5 Feb. 1950.

—— **Webb article on MB:** in *Go,* May–June 1951.

Page 173—**FK's failing health:** Account of Masie Murray, in MCL.

Page 174—**Lyons column on MB:** clippings in Starr collection.

—— **MB letter to S. Kahn:** in Starr collection.

Page 175—**MB declines to have his portrait painted:** recorded in Christopher Hassall, *Edward Marsh* (New York, Harcourt Brace Jovanovich, 1958), p. 669.

Page 176—**MB on E. Wilson ("henchman of the unreadable"):** in *The Listener,* 31 May 1956.

—— **E. Wilson on MB:** "Meetings with Max Beerbohm," in *Encounter,* Dec. 1963, pp. 16–22.

—— **Account of S. Marcus visit:** Behrman, pp. 297–298, 304; and S. Marcus letter to K.L.M.

Page 177—**MB on "Anno Hydrogensis":** in conversation with K.L.M.

—— **MB's prospectus for "Mirror of the Past":** in Taylor Collection.

Page 178—**MB's obituaries:** *New York Times,* 20 May 1956; *Newsweek,* 28 May 1956.

—— **Sir Sydney Roberts Address on MB:** delivered at Unveiling and Dedication (Printed as a booklet at Cambridge), p. 1.

—— **Death of second Lady Beerbohm:** *The Times* (London), 12 Jan. and 25 Feb. 1959.

Acknowledgments

For HER KINDNESS in permitting the use of published and unpublished material from the writings and drawings of the late Sir Max Beerbohm, the author is grateful to Mrs. Eva Reichmann, London, holder of the copyrights. The author is also indebted to the following publishers and authors for permission to quote from published material: The Bodley Head, London, for excerpts from *The Works of Max Beerbohm* and *More*, by Max Beerbohm. Dodd, Mead & Co., Inc., New York, for excerpts from *The Works of Max Beerbohm; More;* and *Zuleika Dobson,* all by Max Beerbohm. Copyright 1911, 1938 by Max Beerbohm. E. P. Dutton & Co., Inc., New York, for excerpts from *A Christmas Garland,* by Max Beerbohm; and from *And Even Now* by Max Beerbohm. Copyright 1921 by E. P. Dutton & Co. Renewal, 1948 by Max Beerbohm. Both published by E. P. Dutton & Co., Inc. and used with their permission. Faber & Faber Ltd., London, for "Brennbaum," from Ezra Pound, *Collected Shorter Poems.* Stephen Greene Press, Brattleboro, Vt., for excerpts from *Max in Verse,* J. G. Riewald, ed. and *A Peep into the Past,* Rupert Hart-Davis, ed. Rupert Hart-Davis, Ltd., for excerpts from *Max Beerbohm, Letters to Reggie Turner,* Rupert Hart-Davis, ed. William Heinemann, Ltd., London, and the estate of the late Max Beerbohm, for excerpts from *Seven Men, Zuleika Dobson, A Variety of Things* and *Mainly on the Air,* by Max Beerbohm. Alfred A. Knopf, Inc., New York, for excerpts from *A Variety of Things, Mainly on the Air,* and *Lytton Strachey,* by Max Beerbohm. New Directions Publishing Corp., New York for "Brennbaum" from "Hugh Selwyn Mauberly" in Ezra Pound, *Personae.* Copyright 1926 by Ezra Pound. Reproduced by permission of New Directions Publishing Corporation.

For their courtesy in making available original and hitherto unpublished Beerbohm material, the following sources are gratefully acknowledged: The Trustees of Amherst College. Beinecke Rare Book and Manuscript Library, Yale University. Department of Western Manuscripts, Bodleian Library, Oxford. The British Library Board and Department of Manuscripts, British Museum, London. Brotherton Collection, Brotherton Library, University of Leeds, England. Department of Special Collections, Research Library, University of California at Los Angeles. Literary Executors of Mrs. Roger Clark, and the

Housman Collection, Somerset County Library, Street, England. Harvard College Library. The Warden and Fellows of Merton College, Oxford. The New York Public Library, Manuscripts and Archives Division, for use of material in the Paul Kester Papers; Theatre Collection at Lincoln Center; and the Henry W. and Albert A. Berg Collection; all collections maintained under the auspices of the Astor, Lenox and Tilden Foundations. Herbert S. Stone, Jr., and the Newberry Library of Chicago. Melville E. Stone for the autograph sonnet and the caricature of Henry James on pages 40 and 41. Robert H. Taylor Collection, Princeton University Library. Humanities Research Center, University of Texas at Austin. Mrs. Alexandra Kahn Bagshawe, Wetherby, England. Mrs. Constance Starr Kahn, Memphis, Tenn. Mr. M. F. Kahn, Fairfax, Va. Mr. Louis Kronenberger.

Books About Max

Beerbohm, Max, *Letters to Reggie Turner*, Rupert Hart-Davis, editor. London, Rupert Hart-Davis Ltd., 1964; Philadelphia and New York, J. B. Lippincott Company, 1965. Max speaks most delightfully for himself in letters written from 1891 to 1938. Carefully footnoted. Appendix with four hitherto unpublished pieces by Max. Illustrated.

Behrman, S. N., *Portrait of Max*. New York, Random House [*Conversations with Max*. London, Hamish Hamilton Ltd.], 1960. An informal memoir of Sir Max drawn from conversations between author and subject, warmly and sympathetically written. The eighty-year-old Max looks at the past. Illustrated.

Cecil, David, *Max, A Biography*. London, Constable and Company, Ltd., 1964; Boston, Houghton Mifflin Company, 1965. The authorized biography. Comprehensive account of Max's life, based on letters, manuscripts, and personal recollections. An illuminating portrayal of Max as a person, with lesser attention to his work. Illustrated.

Felstiner, John, *The Lies of Art*. New York, Alfred A. Knopf, Inc., 1972; London, Victor Gollancz, Ltd., 1973. An enigmatically titled study of Max as a caricaturist and satirist. From his extensive research, reading, and examination of Max's drawings, the author arrives at his own theories of the motives behind Max's work. Illustrated.

Gallatin, A. E., *Sir Max Beerbohm: Bibliographical Notes*. Cambridge, Massachusetts, Harvard University Press, 1944.

——— and Oliver, L. M., *A Biography of the Works of Max Beerbohm*. Harvard University Press [London, Rupert Hart-Davis, Ltd.], 1952.

Hart-Davis, Rupert, *A Catalogue of the Caricatures of Max Beerbohm*. Macmillan London Ltd [Harvard University Press], 1972. An alphabetically arranged catalogue of Max's caricatures and cartoons from his Charterhouse days to his final work. Original place of publication and present owners (if known) are given. A monumental memorial for Max's centenary. Lavishly illustrated. The *Catalogue* has been of special help in dating and presenting history of any prior publication of drawings used as illustrations in this book.

Lawrence, Jerome and Lee, Robert E., *The Incomparable Max*. New York, Hill & Wang, 1972. A two-act play in which the stories of "Enoch Soames" and "A. V. Laider" are presented with Max as interlocutor.

Lynch, Bohun, *Max Beerbohm in Perspective*. London, William Heinemann, Ltd. [New York, Alfred A. Knopf, Inc.], 1921. Earliest study of Max. No biography and more explicit attention to caricatures than to writing. Interesting illustrations.

McElderry, Bruce J., *Max Beerbohm*. New York, Twayne Company, 1972. An abbreviated but adequate account of Max's life and work, drawn from secondary sources. Good for the average reader or the undergraduate.

Riewald, J. G., *Sir Max Beerbohm, Man and Writer*. The Hague, Martinus Nijhoff, 1953, and Brattleboro, Vermont, The Stephen Greene Press, 1963. The most informative book on Max's writing with a brief account of his life. Invaluable for its scholarly accuracy. Bibliographical listings up to 1950.

The Harvard University Press has in preparation at this writing the correspondence of Max Beerbohm and William Rothenstein, edited by Mary Lago and Karl Beckson.

Index